The Morning After:
a Study of Independence

BRIAN CROZIER

The Morning After

A Study of Independence

LONDON

METHUEN & CO LTD

36 ESSEX STREET · WC2

This book is dedicated
to the peoples of
the newly independent countries

AUTHOR'S NOTE

Some western liberals have probably done a disservice to the peoples of the newly independent countries by identifying themselves uncritically with the protracted anti-colonialism of their leaders. I am a western liberal, but I believe an unsentimental look at things as they really are is overdue. It may hurt feelings, but can do nothing but good in the long run.

This book was written, in the midst of many other commitments, in a few scattered weeks, some of which were a gift from the Editor of *The Economist*, Mr Donald Tyerman, whom I thank for his patience and generosity. My thanks are also due to the Editors of *Encounter*, who kindly allowed me to dip into material which first appeared in their pages.

CONTENTS

Part I The Myth of Independence

1 · THE MYTH EXAMINED   *page* 15

2 · THE NEW LEADERS   25
   1   THE FATHER-FIGURES   25
   2   THE MILITANTS   27
   3   THE MODERATES   44
   4   THE SOLDIERS   61

3 · THE NEW COUNTRIES   77
   1   THE BEST AND THE WORST   77
   2   BURMESE WORST   78
   3   THE POLITICS OF INSECURITY   86
   4   MALI'S BEST   113
   5   HOPEFULLY ALONE   118

4 · THE ASSERTION OF INDEPENDENCE   129
   1   IDEAS AND CONFERENCES   129
   2   ACTS OF DEFIANCE   138

Part II The Frailty of Independence

1 · THE COLD WAR   173

2 · THE COMMUNIST THREAT   177

3 · CLIENT STATES AND SATELLITES   192

CONTENTS

Part III Happy though Independent?

1 · TOWARDS VIABILITY   213

2 · RIVAL EXAMPLES   230
  1   THE SINO-INDIAN RACE   230
  2   THE MEN AT THE TOP   233
  3   CONTRASTS IN PLANNING   239
  4   TODAY AND TOMORROW   258

3 · THE PITFALLS OF PLANNING   262

4 · TOWARDS POLITICAL STABILITY   278

5 · TOWARDS INTERDEPENDENCE   284

   INDEX   291

ILLUSTRATIONS

A country divided: Ho Chi Minh of North Vietnam *and* Ngo Dinh Diem of South Vietnam
facing page 48

The assertion of independence: Indonesia expels its 'Dutch' population 48

Africa's new leaders: President Bourguiba of Tunisia, with Mme Bourguiba 49

Modibo Keita of Mali and Leopold Senghor of Senegal, before they quarrelled 49

The Army takes over: General Ne Win in Burma *and* Colonel Nasser in Egypt 64

Links with the Colonial past: The Queen as President Ayub Khan's guest in Pakistan 65

Independence at its worst: The mob and the soldiery between them made Leopoldville a hazardous capital in 1960 128

Malaysia's leaders: Lee Kuan-yew of Singapore *and* Tunku Abdul Rahman of Malaya 129

The violent morning after: *Les Paras* do their worst at Bizerta 144

Afro-Asians discover themselves: The Bandung Conference, 1955 145

Home for new nations: The UN General Assembly in session 145

ILLUSTRATIONS

between pages 232 and 233

War comes to a land of peace: Laotians prefer festivals to fighting

Princes dominate politics: Neutralist Premier Prince Souvanna Phouma and his deputy, 'red' Prince Souphannouvong, vow friendship while their factions fight it out

India's legacy of the past: Hinduism and sacred cows

China's 'leap' into the future: The backyard furnaces that fell flat

The search for maturity: African summit, Addis Ababa

New leaders meet: President Radhakrishnan of India greets Prince Sihanouk of Cambodia

Acknowledgments to photographers:

Associated Press Ltd: facing pages 48 (*top right*), 65, 144, 145 (*top*), 232 (*bottom*), 233 (*top*).

Paul Popper Ltd: facing pages 48 (*bottom*), 49, 64 (*top*), 145 (*bottom*), 233 (*bottom*). Between pages 232 and 233: 'India's Legacy to the Past'.

Planet News Agency: facing page 64 (*bottom*).

Keystone Press Agency: facing pages 48 (*top left*), 129 (*top*).

Camera Press Ltd: facing pages 128, 129.

E. H. S. Simmonds: facing page 232 (*top*).

Henri Cartier-Bresson: between pages 232 and 233: 'China's Leap into the Future'.

PART I

The Myth of
Independence

Chapter 1

THE MYTH EXAMINED

Independence is a magic word to those who are fighting for it. It sustains them through trials and imprisonment and reconciles them to the hardships of insurrection and guerrilla warfare in inhospitable mountains or jungles, and to the discouragements of political struggle. Some of the fighters for independence fought hard for it; others won it with hardly a struggle. Among the winners must be many who find the fruit of victory bitter in the tasting, though pride and self-control forbid them to grimace in public. Was it, in fact, worth fighting for? Are the peoples of independent countries better off for their independence?

In the minds of the new leaders – the Sukarnos and Nkrumahs, or even the Abdul Rahmans or Nyereres – there's no doubt whatever about the answer to the first question. In those minds 'independence' and 'freedom' are synonymous. The concepts of *Uhuru* or *Merdeka* or other emotive words merge into a thunderous 'Yes'. The answer to the second question is less simple, and usually more distressing.

We are better placed than ever before to look at the realities of independence. More than fifty countries of Africa and Asia have become independent since 1945. That independence has brought problems as well as joys, disenchantment as well as elation. It is not their fault, however, that their leaders have achieved independence – that status symbol of rebellion – at a moment in history when independence has lost a good deal of its meaning. Or to put it another way, it is not their fault that there are more sovereign States than ever before, at a time when the sovereign state shows signs of having outlived its usefulness.

It would be too much to expect the new leaders and the *élites* that follow them to agree with either of these propositions. A man finds it hard to concede that the thing he has been fighting for can be valueless or insignificant. And indeed in certain circumstances it may not be. I shall try to define these circumstances.

It will do no harm at this early stage to grope for a definition of independence itself, the condition we are examining. In an age of semantic confusions we are all, to a greater or lesser degree, victims. I suspect that what I mean by independence isn't at all what it means to, say, President Bourguiba of Tunisia or President Sékou Touré of Guinea. 'Democracy', for that matter, means different things in London and Peking, or Paris and Moscow.

I happen to take an absolute view of independence. I consider a country to be independent when it runs its own army and civil service, pays its way, and controls its own foreign policy. By this token, a country must be strong enough to *have* a foreign policy in the first place; whether it can then apply it will depend on whether it is stronger than the other countries at whose expense the policy might be applied. It may be objected that this is arguing as though we still lived in a world of unrestrained power politics – a world without the United Nations or the nuclear balance of terror. That is a fair objection, but it happens to prove the point that 'independence has lost its meaning'. In the absolute sense, very few nations indeed can claim to be truly independent. Perhaps only the two super-powers, the Soviet Union and the United States. And even they find their independence more and more circumscribed, both by the assertiveness or stubbornness of their allies and by one another's power. It has become very hard indeed for the Russians to tell the Chinese how to run their affairs, if it was ever possible. President Kennedy, on his side, has had time to find out how hard it is to persuade General de Gaulle to give up his ambition of making France a nuclear power in its own right. As for the super-powers, Mr Khrushchev would no more allow President Kennedy to march his men into Hungary than President Kennedy would allow Mr Khrushchev to land the Soviet Army in Cuba. A century ago, the probability of counter-action from one side or the other wouldn't have prevented either from trying this kind of thing. Now the fear that it would spark off a nuclear world war restrains both.

If Russia and America enjoy only limited freedom of action, what are we to think of Niger or Tchad, Ceylon or Cambodia? It is, in fact, clear enough that most of the newly independent nations are too weak to have a foreign policy of their own, too poor to pay their own way, too meanly provided with doctors and lawyers, civil servants and technicians, to be regarded as independent in any but a nominal sense. Such States – Laos or the Congo, Mali or Jordan, to name random examples – seem to face one of two alternatives: either to abandon their pretensions to modern statehood, reverting to traditional ways of living; or to become more or less permanently dependent on the assistance of richer States. Can such nations really claim to be independent?

There is, of course, a more cynical view of independence: that it really means a seat in the United Nations, chauffeur-driven Cadillacs for the boys, the desks and the offices and houses of the former colonial masters. (A widespread view of independence in the former Belgian Congo, before 30 June 1960 was that it meant the Belgian's house, car and wife – 'especially his wife', as a friend of mine, writing from Leopoldville in those expectant days, prophetically put it.) That this view *is* cynical and is often expressed by last-ditch colonialists fighting to delay their own departure does not mean that it is untrue. It is not, however, more than part of the truth. The humiliation of colonial days is a powerful factor in independence movements; the joy of becoming VIP, Tuan, or Baas in one's turn, by stepping into the white man's shoes, should not be underrated.

These are legitimate as well as humanly understandable aspirations. It was never a birthright of the white man to sit in a rickshaw and be drawn to his destination by brown or yellow men. Nor is there any reason why the black man, having acquired the right qualifications, shouldn't represent his country at international conferences or give orders to white men in government offices. Whether this constitutes independence is another matter. General de Gaulle, who has a feeling for the value of words, prefers to call it 'secession' if it is achieved

B

against the wishes of the colonial power, and 'sovereignty' when it comes by mutual consent.

There is, however, a limit to the value of definitions. They may clarify ideas, but they do not alter facts. I may choose to doubt the independence of Tchad, or even of Guinea, but ambassadors are accredited there, and both are represented in the United Nations. Yet membership of the UN alone is not a criterion of independence: the Chinese People's Republic, which governs the most populous country on earth, is not a member; nor is the German Federal Republic, which is the third largest steel producer in the world. Recognition by the great powers is no criterion either; once again, communist China would be excluded. Control of the greater part of a country's territory, which is, at least, in theory, the traditional British qualification for recognition, is again, a dubious criterion of independence. The Congo and Laos continued to be regarded as independent throughout 1961; yet during the whole of that year Laos had two rival governments, neither of which was in undisputed control of the country; and for most of that time the Congo's central government governed only in the most nominal sense and in restricted areas.

There is really no need to go on. Just as it has proved impossible to define a nation to everybody's satisfaction, so it may be impossible to define independence in a way that stands up to critical examination. Let us say, for the time being, that few nations are independent in anything approaching an absolute sense. We can then go on to ask two more practical questions. Can anything be done to make the 'emerging' countries more independent? Is this, in any case, a desirable goal?

Having made the limitations of independence clear, as I see them, I shall, from this point forward, use the terms 'new', 'emerging', and 'newly independent' indiscriminately to describe the former colonies of the West. It will do them no disservice to point out that even the limited degree of independence they now have is exceedingly frail, and beset by threats and problems of many kinds. Some of the problems are inherent, others are inherited. It has long been the fashion of militant nationalist leaders, both before and after independence, to blame all their country's problems on the 'colonialists' or 'imperialists'. Sometimes, but not always, such accusations are well founded. The French ought to have trained more than one or two doctors or lawyers in Cambodia, and the Dutch could have produced some higher Indonesian administrators; the Belgians might have had the foresight to see the dangers of universal primary education in the Congo without an outlet to the universities. These are inherited problems.

The inherent problems are harder to get over. Some of the French-speaking States of West Africa are desperately poor in natural resources, as far as anybody knows. Independence is not going to make them any richer. The Tunisian hinterland is arid; should this be laid at the door of the 'imperialists'? But next to these problems, which in the last resort are problems of viability, there is another class of problems that could be called either inherent or inherited, for they concern human nature, climate, and national disposition. Indonesia is potentially a country of enormous wealth, certainly among the half-dozen richest in natural endowments. Its people are highly intelligent and quick to learn. Yet within a decade of independence, Indonesia was on the verge of bankruptcy in its international payments and had become one of the most chaotically ill-managed countries in the world. How much of this can be blamed on the Dutch for failing to train enough natives for the technical and administrative jobs that make a going concern of a country, however rich or poor? And how much on the vanity of Indonesia's President and the irrelevance of his ideas to the country's real needs? How much again, on the corruptibility of its politicians?

The outside threats, as distinct from the economic and administrative problems, are few but formidable. Much against their will, the new countries find themselves caught in the race for power or influence between the two super-powers and their respective allies. A few of them – Pakistan, Siam, and the Philippines are the best examples – chose to ally themselves with the western powers. The great majority of them followed Pandit Nehru's lead and declared themselves 'uncommitted'. The derogatory western term 'neutralist' was coined to fit them, and

President Nasser of Egypt turned it to advantage by speaking of
'positive neutralism'. To what extent did this course increase
their freedom of action, their 'independence'?

Only, I think, to a limited degree. Nationalism was a powerful
force in East Asia when Pandit Nehru started preaching the
need to be uncommitted. To favour neither of the military
blocs seemed a natural expression of this nationalism. The
leaders of the new countries, having struggled for independence,
wished to assert it by demonstrating their freedom from their
former colonial masters. One way of demonstrating this freedom, at least symbolically,—was to keep out of western military
alliances. The late Mr John Foster Dulles and the government
which he represented found this attitude hard to stomach, on
two grounds. One was the proud memory of America's own
struggle for independence; it was painful to discover that
Americans, no less than British or French, were regarded as
'imperialists'. The other ground for Mr Dulles's distaste was the
belief that 'freedom' was absolute good and 'communism' absolute evil. It was hard for anyone holding such a belief to con-
ceive that any responsible statesman should not unhesitatingly
align his country on the side of the United States. So hard that
the former Secretary of State poured his bitterness into a long-
remembered phrase: 'Neutralism is immoral.'

What Mr Dulles and the American officials of the McCarthy
era overlooked was that the new leaders had no desire to exchange one form of colonial rule for another. They asserted their
new freedom by travelling to Moscow or Peking, but the Warsaw Pact was no more attractive to them than Nato or Seato
(the south-east Asia treaty organization). Moreover, neutralism,
positive or not, brought certain impressive advantages. The new
leaders could hold one hand out for the Russians to fill it and
the other for the attention of the Americans. Although for the
greater part of President Eisenhower's term of office, it was considered desirable to recompense Asian allies for having stood up
to be counted on the side of the 'free world', the neutrals could
not be neglected altogether. To do so, it was reckoned, would
send them into the arms of the Russians or Chinese. Much of the
aid that went to allies of the United States was, however, of a

military character. It contributed to the prestige of national armies, but neither filled bellies nor built factories. And in time, even at the beginning of 1959, shortly before Mr Dulles died, the US Administration had begun to recognize that some countries, notably India, deserved to be helped even if they persisted in being neutral. There were even some officials in Washington willing to admit that neutralism might be good in itself, as an expression of nationalism and therefore a barrier to communism.

By and large, though, economic assistance, whether from the Sino-Soviet block or from the western one, continued to be, to a disproportionate degree, directed towards political ends connected with the cold war. In Laos, for instance, the Americans spent some $50 million a year, mainly with the object of paying and training an army and civil service that would keep Laos in the western camp. The attempt was a disastrous failure. Similarly, the Russians rushed aid, largely of an inappropriate kind, to Guinea when President Sékou Touré broke with the French, with the object of encouraging the Guineans to develop their country on Marxist lines. That attempt, too, showed every sign of dismal unsuccess, at the time of writing, four years later.

Given the facts of the cold war, what can be done to set the emerging countries on the road to economic and political viability? It will be noticed that I am really asking two questions, not one. And indeed there are two problems. One is a human one, which appeals to humanitarian instincts. Too many babies are being born and there is too little to feed them with. (More precisely, there is still, in the mid-'sixties, plenty of food for everybody, but a few of the people get too much to eat, and the great majority don't get enough.) The other question concerns political viability, and it deserves a close and unemotional look.

Political stability is, of course, one of the conditions of economic progress. This is an axiom, but anybody who doubts it need only look at Burma or Indonesia. Political stability, however, is not the same as political viability. The second implies the ability to stand on one's own feet, that is independence. But stability can be perfectly well achieved, without independence,

indeed better, until such time as nationalist demands have run
the gamut of riots, terrorism, and insurrection. There is indeed
a case for the proposition that the more an underdeveloped
country tries to assert its independence, the less likely it is to
make economic progress. It is not, of course, a watertight case.
It seems to be true of Guinea, Cuba, and even China (to the
extent that by trying to assert their ideological independence
of Moscow, the Chinese leaders deprived themselves of Soviet
economic assistance). Malaya, on the other hand, continued to
be a going concern even while it was retiring British advisers
and officials in large numbers under the Malayanization programme. Then again, the tiny sheikhdom of Kuwait is well able
to stand on its own feet economically, now that it is independent
(but Kuwait, which rests on the richest oilfield in the world, is
a freak case; and when Iraq threatened to swallow it in 1961
only prompt British military action saved it).

The real point is whether it is more important to feed people
adequately and give a rising standard of living than to say 'We
are independent' and set out to prove it in ways that may do
economic damage. For economic loss is too often the consequence of intemperately expressed nationalism. When Sékou
Touré said 'No' in 1958 to France's offer of autonomy within
the French Community, he may have earned the right to hold
his head higher than, say, President Houphouet-Boigny of the
Ivory Coast (though that is debatable); but he condemned his
people to an immediate drop in their already low standard of
living. In Cuba the effect of Fidel Castro's cocking a snook at
the Americans was delayed but similar.

Anybody who looks at the problem of the poor countries as it
really is must take account of the fact that the donor countries
are few, that they, too, have their susceptibilities and that the
provision of aid is unlikely to be entirely disinterested. Each
time an African or Asian makes an anti-western speech in the
UN he harms his own country's interests in two ways. He builds
up opposition to the UN as a body among the richer nations,
such as the US, Britain, or France, without whose contributions
the UN would soon cease to exist. And he strengthens the determination of right-wing American Congressmen to resist the

Administration's economic aid programmes, except where they
concern allies of the United States. In the same way, Sékou
Touré deprived his government of French assistance because of
the manner of Guinea's advent to independence. And should
Mr Senghor of Senegal or Mr Fulbert Youlou of the ex-French
Congo start making militant anti-colonialist speeches, he would
fan the resentment of the already numerous Frenchmen who
feel that the enormous sums their government pours into Africa
could be better spent at home.

In that sense, independence really is incompatible with
economic development. That is, indeed, part of the Soviet
dilemma in its relations with the uncommitted world. Guinea,
and later Cuba, provide spectacular examples of the fact that –
in the present stage of communist development – Communist
aid and trade are no substitute for the links established in
colonial or semi-colonial times. This awkward fact makes it
difficult for Mr Khrushchev and his team to make their charges
against 'neo-colonialism' attractive to those who are supposed
to listen to them. What the Communists say, in effect, is that a
country is not truly independent until it has thrown off *all* links
with the colonial power: economic and cultural as well as
political. That is, they must kick out western companies and
turn down western aid and advice, and even education, before
they can be considered truly independent.

The Communists are, as it happens, right, but for the wrong
reasons. For there is a corollary to the communist argument.
The Communists go on to say that communist aid being
'Marxist', and therefore disinterested, does not reduce a
country's independence. It is true enough that a country that is
unviable and dependent on outside aid cannot be considered
truly independent. But that is true whether the aid comes from
the 'socialist' camp or from the West.

In an ideal world aid would come from a disinterested international organization, and its origin would be merged in the
general anonymity. In the world as it is, this can mean only the
United Nations, which is maddeningly far from perfection but
is the best world body we have. Here again, however, unpleasant facts have to be faced. One of these is that the political

leaders of the richer countries, being no less human than those of the poorer, are reluctant to funnel their aid into an anonymous world fund. To do that would be to lose what most of them may regard as the justification of giving: the thought that the gift will make the donor popular in the eyes of the receiver.

As it happens, this is very often untrue. The Americans, to their great mortification, were highly unpopular among the ungrateful French after the war when US aid had helped to put France on its feet. The Russians are finding out, in their turn, that giving to Egyptians or Cubans or Guineans has been a short cut to unpopularity. Ex-colonies, on the other hand, don't seem to resent the money they get from their former masters. The French are more popular in South Vietnam than they were during the Indochina war, and the British get on better with the Indians now than when Gandhi was fasting for freedom. This fact is unpalatable both to the Russians, who find it unMarxist, and to the Americans, whose ex-colonial sense of justice it offends.

Such facts, however, are persistent. If the twelve French-speaking African states known as the Brazzaville group jointly asked the French to channel their economic aid through the UN it is quite certain, however unfortunate, that they would all become more or less destitute within a very short time. 'Inter-dependence', which is one way of describing France's relations with its ex-colonies, is a more profitable condition than plain independence.

There is, of course, no easy answer to the human problems of poverty and overpopulation; nor to that of political instability in countries that lack the apparatus of a modern State. This need not deter us from considering them in greater detail in the chapters that follow.

Chapter 2

THE NEW LEADERS

I. THE FATHER-FIGURES

In the dangerous but simpler times between world wars the activities of a Nehru, a Sukarno, or a Ho Chi Minh were domestic preoccupations of the British, Dutch, or French. Since the war nations have proliferated, and national leaders – several to each nation – even more. The three I have mentioned are heads of State or Government. In their company are several dozen others, whose advent has greatly complicated the lives of those whose job is to inform the public, while adding to the bewilderment of newspaper readers.

The only common strand linking the new leaders is the fact that their countries were, until lately, colonies of the West. Some, but not all, were formed in revolutionary struggles of greater or lesser violence. But independence having become a fashion, a contagion or an irresistible movement of history, many others hardly had to exert themselves for the fruit that fell into their laps; others had shaken the tree. Now, as one looks at them, waiting their turn to speak in the UN General Assembly, or gathering for one of their rather frequent summits, one sees that they divide fairly satisfactorily into two main categories: those who want to assert their independence of the West at almost any price, and those who realize that their best hope of an economic future for their peoples lies in some kind of association with the West (while not necessarily ruling out useful relations with the communist world).

In Africa especially, the leaders in the first group tend to be known as 'militants' and those in the second as 'moderates'. There are other labels, however. The 'militants' are often called 'extremists', 'revolutionaries' (even after their revolutions have brought independence) or 'radicals'; and the 'moderates' are sometimes known as 'conservatives'.

Such labels, of course, often tell more about those who use them than those they are supposed to describe. They are a convenience and no more. I happen to prefer the terms 'militant' and 'moderate', because they are politically neutral (as 'radical' and 'conservative' are not). The militants are often violent in speech, and sometimes in deed; the moderates are more careful not to offend. But sometimes the lines are blurred: a militant – such as President Nasser of the United Arab Republic – may make a moderate speech, or a moderate – like President Bourguiba – may find his oratory spilling over into immoderation.

The distinction between the groups is, however, by and large valid. It first became apparent on a world-wide scale at the Afro-Asian conference held at Bandung, in Indonesia, in the spring of 1955. In Africa, at least, it hardened in 1960 and 1961 into the creation of two rival blocs known as the Casablanca and Brazzaville groups, the first being militant and the second moderate.

One would expect the leaders who had to fight for independence to be among the militants and those who received it without a fight to associate with moderates, but this is not always the case. Faced with the problems of office, ex-militants like Nehru or Bourguiba sometimes turn to moderation; conversely, since the militants speak louder than the rest and make the running at international gatherings, moderates sometimes feel they have to keep up with them for fear of insulting epithets like 'collaborator', 'stooge', or as the Communists quaintly put it, 'lackey of the imperialists'. At such times even men of moderate disposition make militant speeches.

In the relatively simple societies which many of the new leaders have come to rule the top man is boss in a way he rarely is in more complex countries. It is scarcely possible to understand the problems of independence unless some attempt is made to see them through the eyes of these new men who are the bosses or father-figures of the underdeveloped world. For the stuff of politics is what goes on in the minds of politicians: not objective truth, but what they believe to be the truth.

2. THE MILITANTS

One cannot meet men like Gamal Abdel Nasser, Sékou Touré, or Ho Chi Minh without being struck by the deep wound of bitterness they keep alive. Eyes and voices harden at some hidden memory of earlier injury, and the smile of welcome vanishes in a scowl, habitually followed by a tirade.

Indeed, national or personal humiliations make militants of potential leaders. The boss or father-figure readily identifies himself with his people; in turn, the people, more or less prompted by minor militants, sees itself personified in heroic form in the leader's physical presence. The potential leader often discovers his vocation by the identification of a personal slight with a more general degradation in which the sufferers are his fellow-countrymen. Having made this discovery, he fights for recognition of the right to hold his head high, and does so in the name of his people.

Gamal Abdel Nasser, writing his little book *The Philosophy of the Revolution* during the discouraging Palestine campaign in 1948, had twin fires of humiliation to spur him on. One was the British, the last of Egypt's long line of masters and, as he saw it, the authors of the decadence he had known as schoolboy and student. The other was the flaccid monarchy that could send Egyptian soldiers, ill-equipped and often armed with munitions that wouldn't fire, into battle against a twentieth-century enemy. He had his revenge on both: on the monarchy in July 1952 by the *coup d'état* that brought the Free Officers to power and drove King Farouk into exile; and on the British in November 1956, when combined pressures forced them and the French to abandon their joint attempt to bring Nasser's régime to heel.

I met Nasser in his home in Cairo in May 1956, about five weeks before he nationalized the Suez Canal company. It was a modest home, for Nasser is a man of simple tastes and puritanical behaviour. As I waited in an unpretentious room, furnished with chairs and little else, with Tom Little of the

Arab News Agency, sipping a sweet lemon drink, a small brown head with a white smile would peep at us now and then from behind a curtain: one of the President's children.

Nasser's face must be one of the most familiar in the world, and it is no more classical in the flesh than in effigy. But he cannot be denied a certain charm, which indeed he shares with all, or nearly all, the new leaders. His mouth seems small, almost delicate in contrast with the massive jaw and the untidy beak of a nose; yet it curls readily enough in a strong-toothed smile beneath the black moustache. Though over six feet tall and powerfully built, he is not a giant like General de Gaulle or Modibo Keita of Mali. I noted what I took to be a dictator's trait: a crushing handshake on arrival and departure, with his arm fully extended from the shoulder while looking, not at me, but at the wall beyond me, or perhaps, in imagination, at a muster of his followers in the middle distance.

Just as Nasser seemed in Sir Anthony Eden's eyes to be a kind of Arab reincarnation of Hitler, so Eden seemed, in Nasser's eyes – even then, before the Suez crisis – to incarnate the people who had brought humiliation to modern Egypt. Perhaps I, too, having come from London, was tarred with Eden's brush. At any rate, Nasser made several derogatory references to 'your Mr Eden', thereby depriving Lord Avon of his former title and giving me proprietary rights to which I laid no claim. It was 'my' Mr Eden who had attempted to get Russia to agree to UN manoeuvres to limit arms in the Middle East. And indeed that was why the Egyptian Government had recognized communist China that very week, for the Chinese Communists, not being members of the UN, were not bound by that body's resolutions on Israel, as Russia might have been. This meant that he could get Chinese arms if Russia stopped sending them.

At that time the United Nations had not yet become the universal free platform of anti-colonial leaders. Clearly, Nasser saw it mainly as a device for 'imperialists' like my Mr Eden to further the designs of the Israelis on the Arab nation, for he added in his high, rather light voice: 'I don't like the Security Council. I don't like the United Nations.' Not long afterwards,

however, he found himself, probably much against the grain,
leaning heavily on the UN for protection against the British and
French aggressors.

A few months after my talk with Nasser I found myself in
Hanoi, the capital of the Democratic Republic of Vietnam, a
minor communist State better known simply as North Vietnam.
Hanoi was always, for my taste, a gloomy city, even in French
times, but it has become a place of bottomless depression which
even the flowers in the neatly kept public places seem unable to
relieve. East Berlin produces much the same feeling of stifled
longings, but even East Berlin does not, to my knowledge, rouse
its citizens by martial music through a public-address system at
5.30 a.m.

On my last morning, however, I saw the occasional value of
matutinal loud-speakers. The previous evening, I had found a
message scrawled in pencil in my pigeon-hole at the clean but
austere Hotel Metropole. 'M. le Président,' it said, 'will receive
you tomorrow at 6.30 a.m. A car will call for you at 6.' I had
despaired of seeing Ho Chi Minh, but I had already heard of
this new form of torture he had devised for visiting Western
correspondents. No capitalist airlines connected Hanoi with the
non-communist world. There was only one way in and the same
way out: in the overloaded aircraft run on behalf of the International Control Commission set up after the Geneva conference of 1954 to supervise the truce in the countries that used
to form French Indochina. From Hanoi, the plane flew to
Vientiane (Laos), thence to Pnom Penh (Cambodia) and
Saigon, capital of President Ngo Dinh Diem's anti-communist
Republic of (South) Vietnam. It being unthinkable to fly from
South Vietnam to North, the plane went back to Hanoi the way
it had come.

The plane I was supposed to take that morning was due to
leave Gia Lam airport at seven-thirty, and half an hour had to
be allowed for the journey from the Presidential palace. There
was thus a mischievous advantage, from Ho Chi Minh's point
of view, in summoning me for six-thirty, for circumstances
limited the interview to half an hour, and the onus for ending it

was neatly placed on the visitor, who wouldn't wish the plane to leave without him.

Ho Chi Minh is a legend and I had looked at him, several times larger than life, on the public building opposite the hotel, for the past few days. He has a face that lends itself to sublimation. An El Greco face built vertically but hanging from prominent cheekbones, surmounted by the luminous eyes of a prophet and brought to a close by the long, straggly beard of the traditional Vietnamese scholar. The real man, shrunk to natural dimensions, was illogically disappointing for a few moments. The Vietnamese are among the tiniest of civilized peoples, and Ho Chi Minh is no taller than most. In his shapeless, colourless communist battledress, shuffling in his sandals, he seemed no greater than a village notable from that prolific Red River Delta which I had first known when it grew rice by day and became a battlefield by night. His eye was hard and tough, except when he broke into a smile of permeating charm.

The young official who accompanied me was of sullen, impenetrable purity. He stayed out of our conversation, which was predictably disagreeable, for I had come determined to raise as many controversial issues as I could within the half-hour. There were, however, warmer moments, when my host, at his most avuncular, pressed me to accept another cup of jasmin tea, or when, in reply to some particularly disagreeable question about the victims of certain official excesses, he had said, with an impish smile: 'England is a very liberal country, isn't it – a very liberal country. But where would you be without your good London policemen?'

Ho knew his London bobbies. It must have been thirty years earlier that he had spent some months in London as a youthful assistant to the great chef Escoffier. This was during the formative years, the years when he was stockpiling his bitterness. Against the French, first, for having conquered his country and denied its people the dignity of equality; and perhaps, as a subsidiary outlet, against the capitalist system which, Lenin wrote, bred imperialism by iron laws, historically determined.

I have no wish to oversimplify a personality of great complexity, in which even those who have known him best have found it hard to untangle the actor from the real man. Was it the real man who, when offered an apple at a critical stage of his negotiations with the French in 1946, went outside to offer it to a little girl? Without passing judgement, it is fair to note that the incident brought him a good press in France. Is this man of subtle intelligence an uncritical believer in Marxism, for all that he was a founder-member of the French Communist Party, and that he belonged to the Soviet and Chinese parties before founding the Communist Party of Indochina in 1930? Is he even anti-French, this fighter for independence, who greeted Jean Sainteny, his former negotiating partner of 1946, on his return to Hanoi as French delegate-general after the Indochina war, with the accolade reserved for long-lost friends?

It would be presumptuous to answer such questions. All I can do is to record that the bitterest moment in my half-hour of unpleasant exchanges with Ho Chi Minh came not when I asked him about the land-reform programme in which thousands of innocent people had lost their lives, or about press freedom, which had been effectively snuffed out after a period of breezy independence, but when I broached the subject of the Geneva agreements that had brought the Indochina war to an end. I had provoked him with the suggestion that the Vietnamese Communists had been sold down the river at the 1954 conference by their bigger brothers from China and Russia. He flared instantly, exclaiming in a passion of dissent: 'No, no, not the Russians, not the Chinese! Only the French have sold us. An agreement is an agreement, and the French have violated it.'

Though I was not, at that moment, in a mood to placate my host, there was some point in his exclamation. For though the Chinese and the Russians had forced the Vietnamese Communists to settle for a smaller share of Vietnam (about half, in area) than their military prowess might have justified, Ho Chi Minh had some reason for thinking that the French had deprived him of the fruit of victory by withdrawing their expeditionary corps from South Vietnam. This made it possible for President Diem, with American support, to ignore the provision in the agreements for nation-wide elections aimed at

reunifying Vietnam, which Ho Chi Minh would have had a
good chance of winning.

In fact, American influence had already superseded French
power by the time I met Ho Chi Minh, and after his anti-
French outburst he had added: 'Look what the Americans are
doing in South Vietnam.' One felt a new acid of frustration and
bitterness was at work within him. By 1960 its burning had
become intolerable and he had laid plans for taking by force
what he felt was his due. Now (in 1963) his guerrillas, in tens of
thousands, have brought terror, havoc, and insecurity to large
areas of South Vietnam, and 12,000 or more American troops
are getting themselves ever more deeply involved in an unre-
warding war against them.

From 1958 on I had many contacts with the Algerian FLN or
Front of National Liberation, in London, Montreux, Tunis, and
Geneva. No revolutionary struggle in modern times has been
more mercilessly contested on either side, and no set of new
leaders had been more deeply seared by it. As these words were
being written, the leadership of the FLN was rent by rivalries
and dissensions, but at the time of my contacts with it, it presented a monolithic front, aptly labelled 'collegiate leadership'.
Berbers and Arabs, moderates and extremists, all were united,
or appeared to be united, in their concentration on the single
objective of acquiring mastery over Algeria.

French official propaganda during those years naturally
enough made great play of supposed rivalries between the
groups – racial or ideological – I have mentioned. Doubtless
they existed. Nevertheless, however acrid the debate or hot
tempered the clashes of temperament may have been behind
closed doors, they were never allowed to emerge into public
view. To each member of the FLN, every other member was a
'brother'. That was the term they invariably used, and of
brothers admitted to the innermost councils of the revolution,
none was more equal than the others.

For this reason, I find it more satisfactory to speak of them as
a group, rather than single out an individual. As a group, then,
they were extremists, as are all men who have once made a

decision to stop short at nothing to achieve their objectives. The labels of 'moderate' and 'extremist' were therefore misleading; but they were not pointless if one remembered that they referred to the past rather than the present. The 'moderates' were those who had once believed in the possibility of winning independence, or at any rate equality with the Europeans of Algeria, by political means, and who were reluctant to abandon this belief even after the rebellion had begun. The 'extremists' were those who had decided, as soon as they became interested in politics, that only violence would bring them success. By that definition, the moderates were those, like Ferhat Abbas, the first Prime Minister of the Algerian Provisional Government, who did not join the FLN until a year or two after the rebellion had been launched. And the militants or extremists were those, like Benbella and Belkacem Krim, who killed for political ends years before launching it.

Perhaps, in fact, the bitterness of the moderates was even deeper, for they had had to travel farther along the road that leads to violence. Nobody had travelled farther than Ferhat Abbas, who during the Second World War had proclaimed in a report to Marshal Pétain that France had 'never been dearer' to the hearts of the Moslems. All he wanted in 1943, when he published his famous Manifesto of the Algerian People after the allied landings in North Africa, was an Algerian constitution guaranteeing the equality of all inhabitants regardless of race or religion, and the usual freedoms. Had the French Algerian administration not faked the elections of 1947 and 1951, Ferhat Abbas's faith in evolutionary progress might have remained unshaken. And it was not till the spring of 1956, after the Mollet government in France had embarked on a policy of pure repression in Algeria, that he gave up all hope and went to Cairo to join the FLN.

I went to Montreux to see him early in February 1958. He was recuperating after a serious car accident in Morocco, and had rented a flat with his French wife and his children, on the heights overlooking the great arc of the bay. He is a compact man of middle height, and this surprised me, for pictures of him seated around some negotiating or administrative table suggest

a much taller man. This, I now realized, was due to his facial
formation, which is vertical and bony, the curving nose reaching down like a scimitar over the Arab moustache that over-
shadows a full and mobile mouth.

I thought it would improve my chances of a frank discussion
if I made it clear that, though French-speaking, I was not a
Frenchman, but I needn't have bothered. In his fluent North
African French, assisted by gesticulation and a characteristic
rolling of Rs, he said: 'Oh, you know, it would be just the same
if you were a Frenchman.' This, I discovered much later, was
true enough. Jean Lacouture, of *Le Monde*, records, in his
interesting study *Cinq Hommes et la France*, a conversation with
Ferhat Abbas, which must have taken place in the same room
a few days later. Abbas seems to have told him, as well as me,
of the plans the FLN were even then making for the formation
of a Provisional Government (which was announced in September seven months later).

In one other respect, too, he showed that his anti-French
feelings were far from indiscriminate. I had asked him what
would happen to the French of Algeria after independence, and
he replied with much waving of arms: 'Of course they wouldn't
all have to go! But all the ultras would have to get out. Say,
6,000 people. The others could stay on perfectly well. We can
get on together, once the ultras have gone.'

His bitterness was less anti-French than anti-western and
anti-Christian, but always with the proviso that if only we, the
westerners, the Christians, would be reasonable, reconciliation
would be possible. He saw the Suez expedition as a Christian
expedition against Islam and the Algerian war as a Christian
aggression. 'We are nearer to you than the Jews are,' he said.
'The expansion of Islam belongs to the past. We went as far as
Poitiers, but all that is over. The time has come for reconciliation.'

Among the western and Christian nations, he seemed perhaps
to be more bitter against Britain – perhaps because he was
talking to me – than against France or the United States. 'You
were doubly in a position to put pressure on the French,' he
exclaimed, 'first because you stood alone in the war when

France was defeated, and second, because you gave independence to *your* colonies. Yet you've done nothing to stop the French.'

Suez came in for reproaches. He thought it utterly indefensible for the British and French to drop bombs and kill thousands of ordinary people. 'Yet I would have been implacably opposed to closing the Canal and denying you the petrol you need,' he added.

Ferhat Abbas is, or was, a decent man with a conscience. I put the matter to the test by asking why he had associated himself with a terrorist movement, and was disappointed when he took the easy way out. 'The French make a lot of fuss when a little bomb explodes in Algiers. But not a word is said when French planes kill Algerian women and children in the villages.'

But I insisted, how could he support terrorism against his own compatriots, for instance the elimination of his rival Messali Hadj's followers, members of the MNA or National Algerian Movement? He looked at the wall behind me as he said, with a Gallic shrug of the shoulders: 'You know, Monsieur, these so-called clashes with the MNA, they aren't always genuine. The French police often kill MNA people, then put the blame on the FLN. Incidentally, Messali created the MNA after November 1954 (when the FLN's rebellion began) because he wanted to substantiate his claim to be the only national leader.'

Further argument would have been sterile, and I took my leave. I travelled on to Tunis, and there I saw the FLN for the first time as it liked to be seen, working together as a group, in semi-clandestinity. It was, in some respects, a stirring sight, and in others, a disturbing one. My Algerian contact in London, who had put me in touch with Abbas, had given me a friend's name, and the friend showed me to the dingy, anonymous door in the mean back street in Tunis that led to the FLN's working headquarters. The door was open and I mounted two flights of littered stairs to another door. But the uncompromising young revolutionary who barred my passage was unwilling to trust my explanations until a formidable shape loomed in the background.

It belonged to Maître Boumendjel, who ushered me into a

kind of waiting-room. A table with FLN pamphlets in several languages, three or four rickety chairs, a couch with its stuffing missing. Boumendjel left me to go to an adjoining room where a typewriter was clattering, and I heard him reading a text that was handed to him, ordering the substitution of a conditional for an indicative before giving it back to the younger man at the typewriter. Boumendjel ran the FLN's press service, and the copy that was being typed was for inclusion in *El Moudjahid* ('The Fighter'), organ of the Algerian revolution.

A few days later, in Algiers, lost in the enormity of the French administrative building, I thought back to the proletarian miseries of the FLN's headquarters and wondered whether the spirit of fanaticism would be sufficient to overcome the wealth and power of the French Republic. But massive though it was, the Algiers administrative centre was fragile at the core. Three months later, it was captured by a group of students, led by the men who later created the OAS or Organization of the Secret Army. Files were scattered to the winds, and as the crowds gathered in euphoria in the Forum below, General Salan appeared at the window and defied the crumbling Fourth Republic.

But this was in the future. I found Boumendjel, by definition another moderate since he had rallied to the FLN only in 1956, far more bitter even, and more specifically anti-French, than Ferhat Abbas. In his case the turning-point may have been his elder brother's death, hurtling to the ground from the top story of a building where he was being tortured by French interrogators. Built like a wrestler, with the fair, crinkly hair and grey eyes of a family that must have Kabyle blood in its veins, Boumendjel speaks the polished French of a Paris barrister (which he was). By disposition genial, he was overflowing with the kind of rancour that can never find relief. Multiplying his erudite examples of French injustice, he reached his climax when I interrupted him to remind him that there were Frenchmen still, as there had always been, who denounced injustice and argued in favour of colonial emancipation.

I cannot forget his answer. 'Do you really believe this?' he asked. 'This has always been the way the French work. When they sense defeat they start denouncing injustice to make sure in advance of preserving the image of a France devoted to liberty. No, Monsieur, we cannot be taken in so easily. The world always falls for the arguments of French intellectuals. But we, we know the true face of France.'

Boumendjel wore a shabby blue suit that was too narrow for his bulging bulk, and it was Sunday: revolutionaries work seven days a week. Next time I saw him, however, he was smartly dressed and the FLN had lost its proletarian look. It was in February 1960 and the revolutionaries had promoted themselves from FLN to GPRA or Provisional Government of the Algerian Republic. This rise in status had brought a first touch of *embourgeoisement*, recognition by the Arab countries, villas put at their disposal by the Tunisian Government and clean, though utilitarian offices. Boumendjel again, and he took me to see Mohammed Yazid, the Information Minister, who learned his English in New York and likes to use it. Indeed, it has been useful to him since that day in November 1958 when he wrote to the *New York Times* to say:

In 1948, fifty-nine of us nationalists were candidates for election to the Algerian Assembly. We hoped to reach our goal by way of French constitutional means. What was the result? Some thirty of us were arrested during the election campaign and imprisoned for years. The list of detained candidates is about the same as that of the present leaders of the Algerian revolution.

He, too, was bitter.

. . . Then there were the Geneva days in the summer of 1961, when those of us who were admitted to the villa lent to the GPRA by a minor Arab potentate could have access to the entire Algerian team then negotiating with the French at Evian. Dogs, barbed wire and armed Swiss guards were discouragements, but the experience was rewarding. Saad Dahlab, later Foreign Minister, with his warm smile and his reasonable words; the more reserved Dr Ahmed Francis, Ferhat Abbas's brother-in-law, whose job was to find finances for the revolution; Ben Yahia, pale, young, intense, and intelligent; Boumendjel again; and in the background the round but sturdy figure of Belkacem Krim, at that time the real master of the movement.

African nationalism is different in kind from the national aspirations of Arabs or Asians. So different that it needs a few words to itself. The very term 'African nationalism' is a *non sequitur*, since there were no nations, as the West understands the term, in Africa when the white man took possession of its soil and drew the artificial boundaries corresponding to those of the African States now admitted to the United Nations. Lacking the cultural unity of the scattered Arabs or the long national histories of the States of South-East Asia, Africans express their 'nationalism' in the vague and perhaps indefinable concept of an 'African personality'.

The difficulty of finding a definition of the 'African personality' should not, however, blind us to its power. Elspeth Huxley, in a perceptive study written for *Encounter* (June 1961), came as close to a definition as anybody is likely to come, when she wrote:

> After years of being made to feel inferior, Africans are beginning to think that, after all, they had something of value (in the pre-colonial past).
> They want to revive it: that is their meaning when they speak of the African personality.

Since the white man had established more or less viable administrative units, the only way in which the African personality (that is, African nationalism) could reassert itself was by first gaining control of these units. All Africans, however (and by Africans, I mean Negro Africans South of the Sahara), are aware of the artificiality of colonial boundaries. The concept of an African personality is supplemented by other incantatory words such as 'pan-Africanism' (a favourite expression of Dr Nkrumah's) and 'négritude' (which is frequently on the lips of Leopold Senghor of Senegal). Hence there is much talk of the need to surrender national sovereignty, or to merge one country with another, or to form a 'United States of Africa'.

Such talk is sincerely meant, and may even, in time, come to something; but for the time being, any attempt to merge sovereignties is stopped short by hard realities. The most frustrating of these, from the point of view of pan-Africanists, are linguistic and administrative barriers, and the force and ambition of the individual personalities that have emerged as the new leaders of Africa.

The first of these obstacles is real enough. The main linguistic division in post-colonial Africa is between the States that use French and those that use English. Moreover, it is more than just a matter of language. Along with French, the French-speaking African States have inherited Napoleonic justice, the metric system and Gallic turns of thought, while the English-speaking ones know about common law and traditional English weights and measures. As for individuals, that, too, is a major obstacle which is a matter of politics, not administration. Each African State has thrown up its boss or father-figure. Each has got used to power within his own realm, and none is likely to move over to make room for, say, Dr Nkrumah.

For all the talk of African unity, then, its realization is not even within sight. Even to move towards it is not easy, for where should the African leaders begin? Teaching French-speaking Africans English and vice versa is an obvious first step, but it is a retrograde one from the point of view of African purists, for it means borrowing, yet again, from the white man. But there is no consolation in suggesting a return to African languages, for most of them are unwritten, and their multiplicity would set unity still farther back. History is little help, either. That there were once great and cohesive empires in Africa, including those whose names were borrowed by present-day Mali and Ghana, is interesting on any count, but not a guide for future action, except as an inspiration for conquest. Indeed, conquest is one of the possible ways in which the pan-African idea may spread. Other ways are through federalism or confederalism of one kind or another.

This is not the place to discuss these ideas in detail, and the point of these generalizations is to make it clear that the nationalism of African leaders, whether it takes a militant form like Sékou Touré's or a moderate one like Senghor's, springs in the deepest sense from sources that are peculiar to Africa.

Having said this, the fact that a given leader is impassioned or temperate in his behaviour is a matter of individual disposition and personal history; and the form taken by African nationalism in various countries is determined in the great majority of cases by the influence of western ideas upon individual leaders. How could it be otherwise, since there is no written inheritance of African political philosophy? Climate and the termites have destroyed most of the remains of past empires, and the texts – if there were any – along with the walls. When the African turns to tribal traditions for inspiration, as Jomo Kenyatta did in *Facing Mount Kenya*, the political outcome (Mau Mau) is in danger of being a form of atavism, rather than the re-creation of a lost golden age. In time, the new leaders of Africa may – indeed, probably will – produce an acceptable synthesis of western technology and the ancestral philosophies of Africa. But for one Kenyatta there are a dozen younger men whose idea of an African future is not a return to the past but a one-way ticket to the twentieth century.

Certainly when one meets men like Modibo Keita of Mali or Sékou Touré of Guinea what impresses one is not their Africanness but the fact that they express Marxist concepts in the logical French of Descartes. It is only after deeper acquaintance that one realizes how profoundly they are transforming such western influences as Marxism and Cartesianism, in the process of adapting them to the needs, as they see them, of their own countries.

Both are impressive figures, especially Modibo Keita, who stands six and a half feet and whose presence is correspondingly majestic. When I first met him in November 1960, in his air-conditioned office on the hill outside Bamako, he was wearing an open-necked slate-coloured bush jacket, with trousers to match, and to see him at his best I had to wait until his state visit to London in June 1961, when he appeared to greater advantage in his flowing white bou-bou. In Bamako his greeting, though polite, was gravely dignified. When away from the platform he is a man of few words. I found him reasonable enough, even when roused by importunate questions, and indeed in some respects his militancy is the result of an accident.

True, this ex-schoolteacher turned trade unionist and politician had long been receptive to Marxist ideas, but that was not what made a 'militant' of him, in the sense that the other characters of this chapter are militants. Indeed, in September 1958, when France's colonies voted for or against General de Gaulle's offer of association with France, Modibo Keita's people were among the overwhelming majority that opted in favour of it, even though it fell, at that time, well short of full independence. In those days Mali was called Soudan, and not long afterwards the Soudanese and Senegalese decided to merge their sovereignties under the name of 'Federation of Mali'. The present Mali is all that is left of this hopeful name, for the Federation exploded in the faces of its founders only two months after it had achieved independence and international recognition.

In its current phase, at least, Modibo Keita's militancy can be traced back to that still mysterious night of 19 August 1960, when a short but sharp struggle for power between Senegalese and Soudanese ended with Keita in a Senegalese jail in Dakar. The rights and wrongs of the dispute need not concern us. The point is that Modibo Keita blamed the break on the French. He was soon back in Bamako, but the experience must have been traumatic, and several consequences flowed from it. The frontier between Mali (that is, Soudan) and Senegal was closed, and rail traffic between the two countries ceased. Mali went neutralist and its representatives made extravagantly anti-western speeches in the UN. Moreover, when the other French-speaking African States started conferring together the Malians, like the Guineans, stayed away.

By the time Modibo Keita came to London he seemed firmly set on an anti-western course (though the break with France was never complete and he was accepting American aid). I heard him give a lecture, at which he denounced western colonialism in Algeria, Angola, and South Africa, and I could not refrain from asking him why he didn't denounce Communist colonialism in Soviet Central Asia and Tibet. His reply was instructive: 'Parce que nous ne pouvons dénoncer que le colonialisme que nous avons nous-mêmes subi' – *because we can only denounce the colonialism we ourselves have suffered.*

By temperament, Sékou Touré is, I think, even more militant than Modibo Keita, but in his case, too, the fact that he belongs to the militant Casablanca group is partly the result of accidental circumstances. There are several versions of these circumstances, but the one I believe to be authentic is that given in *Cinq Hommes et la France* by Jean Lacouture, who was in Conakry at the time. It is clear enough that General de Gaulle, who was touring the French-speaking African countries in the summer of 1958, seeking support for his new Constitution, decided on the spot that if Guinea wanted independence it would be cut off without a penny. And it is equally clear that he reached this decision at least partly as a result of a misunderstanding, and that Sékou Touré, at the time of his visit, didn't really wish to push matters to the point of actual rupture.

True, the Guinean leader, in his aggressive, bitter manner, had long been saying he wanted independence, but he meant independence in some kind of association with France, and the draft of the speech he proposed to read in the presence of General de Gaulle that fateful 20 August contained a passage to that effect. Moreover, General de Gaulle had publicly offered independence to any French colony that wanted it. But whereas to Sékou Touré independence need not rule out a partnership of 'equals' with France, to General de Gaulle it meant that any country that chose it would be left entirely to its own devices. Given the will, this is the kind of difference that can be discussed honestly within silent walls, but that was not the way things happened.

Sékou Touré had shown the draft of his speech to the officials accompanying the General, who saw nothing much wrong with it, although one pointed out that there was no need to ask for the right to independence, since General de Gaulle had already conceded it, and another persuaded Sékou Touré to write in a favourable reference to the General. Later the text was shown to de Gaulle, who, however, put it in his pocket without reading it.

When Sékou Touré actually delivered his speech before the Guinean crowd, fiercely loyal to him and obedient to a man, it was the tone and manner of his delivery rather than the well-known matter that shocked the General. When he in turn rose to speak it was clear that in the midst of all the saving phrases, only one had really caught his attention: 'We prefer poverty in freedom to riches in slavery.'

And poverty in freedom was exactly what Guinea got from General de Gaulle, who packed his bags and cut his visit short, leaving Conakry by air the following morning. One need look no further for the origins of Sékou Touré's bitterness.

For this descendant of the great chief Almany Samoury, who fought on when the French thought they had conquered Guinea, is a proud and intractable man. Largely self-educated, he speaks with an intellectual eloquence that is served by a metallic power and harshness of voice. His smile, which comes readily enough, is that of the political boss bestowing conditional protection. His eyes remain hard and seem happiest in a scowl. The first time I met him was at a reception at 10 Downing Street, and one's major preoccupation was whether the decaying floors of the British Prime Minister's residence would stand the strain of the guests they had to bear. The second time was in an antechamber of the Presidential Palace at Conakry. It was his day for receiving petitions and grievances, and I had many competitors. Twice he came out to assure me he would soon be with me, and an hour after the first occasion I had my turn.

There was no measuring the depth of his resentment at French actions, and indeed they had made the break as painful as possible, taking with them archives and telephones, stripping the bank of currency and diverting a rice ship on its way to Conakry. These are things that must be remembered when one wonders why African or Asian politicians take up an anti-colonial stance. In Sékou Touré's case, of course, it is difficult to disentangle cause from effect, since most of his life had been spent in militancy of one kind or another from the time he was expelled from the French technical school at Conakry for leading a food strike to his trade-union days in 1953, when he led a general strike of Guinean workers and forced the then Governor-General of French West Africa to give in to their demands. His 'No' to de Gaulle in 1958 was in logical line of descent from such earlier actions.

But it is worth recording also that when I met him in Conakry he denounced Communism and hoped the West would help him strike a balance between the two world blocs. With most of our militants, indeed – except those, like Ho Chi Minh, on whom history played a bad turn – to strike a balance is all they seem to want. Only some go about it more quietly than others.

3. THE MODERATES

Some moderates are reformed militants. Others are mild by nature. Others still speak militantly but act moderately. The first, having learnt moderation the hard way, have the wisdom of acquired self-control and the advantage of knowing a militant and seeing through him when he comes into view. The mild ones are rare, if only because men who are mild by nature are rarely leaders; their rarity makes them all the more valuable. Those who speak militantly but act reasonably are the hardest to recognize. Uncomfortably often they feel more in harmony with their supporters when lashing at 'imperialists' or 'colonialists'; this is disconcerting for such imperialists and colonialists as may be listening in; and sometimes tempts them to stray, or appear to stray, from the path of moderation in deeds as well as words.

A Prince Sihanouk of Cambodia, his high, piping voice shrieking complaints against American plotters, understandably worries Senators who may feel that 'anti-American' must mean 'pro-communist'. A President Bourguiba of Tunisia, his voice hoarse with imprecations against the French, should not be surprised if this merely delays the settlement of differences with the former colonial power. A Tunku Abdul Rahman of Malaya, or a Sir Abubakar Tafawa Balewa of Nigeria, makes life easier for others as well as himself by simply behaving as an essentially courteous nature tells him he ought. But in the end perhaps an ex-Marxist and racialist (his own description) like President Leopold Sédar Senghor of Senegal, who reached moderation through poetry and philosophy, has distilled a more pervasive wisdom from his experience.

Senegal is the intellectual centre of French-speaking Africa, and the University of Dakar is the Mecca of aspiring officials, engineers, and teachers from surrounding countries as well. The Senegalese are the most articulate – indeed voluble – French speakers south of the Sahara, and the most Gallicized in their thinking processes. This is hardly surprising, since the French first came to Senegal in the seventeenth century, 200 years before the more determined colonizing wave which took them down to the great Congo river. The relative antiquity of the French presence has given the modern Senegalese *évolué* a dialectically supple mind and, perhaps, a slight feeling of superiority over slower-thinking neighbours. The Senegalese have ideas and use them to dazzle; which does not always make them popular with those who are being dazzled. Islam came to them in ripples of military and cultural conquest from the tenth century, but by some theistic alchemy was softened in the process, so that whereas the women of Algiers or of Kano are thickly veiled in public, those of Senegal, like those of distant Muslim Java, are bare-faced and full of laughter.

My first impression of Dakar, indeed, was of perhaps ten thousand Dakaroises in peals of laughter, or whistling and shrieking in tremolos of enthusiasm, their fantastic, many-hued head-dresses turning the scene into a festive riot of colour upon sound. When their frenzies disturbed the babies strapped to their backs a comforting black bosom would be produced at intervals. Every seat in Dakar's municipal stadium was taken, and the women outnumbered the men by two to one. I was on the dusty ground, standing within the energetic mass of those who had failed to find seats. Whenever my eyes needed a change of scene they could study the fascinating objects tied to the plaited wisps of hair on the head of a barely nubile girl in front of me; one of them was an English sixpence bearing a likeness of Queen Elizabeth II.

Politics, not sport, was the attraction, but the special flavour of the occasion lay in the appearance on the same platform of two men who were said to have been on opposite sides on that crowded and mysterious night of 19 August 1960, when the short-lived Federation of Mali exploded in the faces of its Senegalese and Soudanese creators. One of the speakers was the then Prime Minister of Senegal, Mr Mamadou Dia, a hard-working and unspectacular figure who lacked a popular following. He was listened to in silence and sat down to a round of dutiful applause. It was the other speaker, Mr Lamine Gueye, whom the crowd, especially the women, had come to hear, and when he rose, the serried ranks of women rose in their turn to greet him with a delirium of dancing, clapping, singing, leaping, and whistling. Mr Gueye was the Mayor of Dakar, and the women of his city, who have had the vote since the end of the Second World War and know how to use it, remember him as a man who has always had their interests at heart. As Mr Gueye was speaking in Woloff, the local dialect, with only an occasional sentence in French, I was unable to tell whether his words justified the feminine enthusiasm they were generating.

The political career of Lamine Gueye has long been intertwined with that of Leopold Senghor, sometimes in friendship and as often in enmity, but always in rivalry. In the end Senghor emerged as the undisputed master of Senegal, at once a grassroots politician who has tramped his country from end to end building up a popular following and a statesman with a vision of co-operation with neighbouring countries and with France and its European partners as purveyors of capital, trade, and education. Above all else, however, he is the philosopher of a special brand of Africanism, called Negritude, which might best be described as a self-conscious attempt to give Africans a cultural pride in being Negroes. Senghor is the high priest rather than the prophet of Negritude, whose authorship he freely attributes to Aimé Césaire, the Martiniquais poet. But if Césaire invented it, Senghor gave content to it and diffused it throughout French-speaking Africa.

If culture is one element in Negritude, another is race. When addressing the youth of Federated Mali in May 1960 Senghor declared: 'The natural environment is not the only determination that helps one to understand Negro-African civilization. There is also race.'

'Negro', indeed, means 'black', and Senghor's intellectual and emotional obsession is the rediscovery of 'Negro-African civilization'. The prophet, and poet, Césaire, had no such obsession and extolled the Negro-Africans as those who never invented anything, who never conquered anything, 'but who, in awe, give themselves up to the essence of things'. Senghor, the disciple and high priest, also a poet but a scholar too, told the youth of Mali, in that same lecture, about:

> . . . the surprise of the first European navigators disembarking in Africa at discovering well-organized States, each with its government, administration, justice, and army, with techniques – remarkable for the period – in wood, ivory, bronze, iron, basket-making, weaving, and terracotta, with medical and agricultural techniques worthy of Europe.

This, then, was the deepest preoccupation of the mild-mannered man who received me in his immense office on the top floor of le building, the towering administrative centre of Dakar. Windows all round gave a truer version of that selling point of automobile manufacturers – panoramic vision – across the bay. The President's desk also was panoramic: I have never seen so sweeping a curve of mahogany. The man who rose from behind it to greet me was of no more than medium height, compact in build, and the very purest black. Senghor's normal expression, compounded of slightly raised eyebrows above steel-rimmed glasses, is one of philosophical blandness. The mild eyes gently protest their innocence of such crimes as the visitor might be tempted to impute to him.

I had sat myself on one of the low leather chairs in front of his desk, but President Senghor invited me to use a higher seat and rest my notebook on my side of the desk. This, I thought, was the sign of a man who knows he is a master of words and hopes the listener will record them faithfully. Much of what he said to me was, however, determined by political immediacies and therefore ephemeral. There is no need to resurrect it here. But since we are concerned with the state of mind of a moderate it is worth outlining the rest – that is, the emotional and intellectual journey that made Senghor think the way he does.

The journey was not without its bumps and crevasses. Studious and intellectually curious, he did brilliantly, first at a Catholic school, then at the Lycée in Dakar, before going on to that highly competitive forcing ground of the French intellect, the Ecole Normale Supérieure. There, he became the first African ever to pass the toughest of intellectual hurdles, the *agrégation*. His immediate reward was a teaching job at a Lycée in Tours, where – it is said – the best French is spoken; twenty years later, in 1946, came a second and little known reward, when General de Gaulle engaged him to correct and improve the French in the draft Constitution of the Fourth Republic. In between, he had served in the French Army, been captured by the Germans, refused to turn against the French, and gathered other prisoners around him in a cell of resistance.

This bare recital of biographical highlights leaves unsaid the bitter inner struggle that seems to have tortured Senghor as a youth. That he was by far the most brilliant student black Africa had sent to Paris had brought him other things besides a legitimate pride – a torturing doubt, for instance, about the validity of his own culture. He was an African intellectual, certainly, but an African intellectual who had won his laurels in French – an alien culture. Doubtless this was why, on returning to Paris from his teaching job at Tours, he enrolled at the Ecole des Hautes Etudes to study African languages. The African past had to be rediscovered, and language was to be the key.

But there was another and more private struggle. The French are among the least colour-conscious of peoples, but racialism is far from unknown among French *bourgeois bien pensants*. In his student and teaching days Senghor was made to feel acutely conscious of the colour of his skin and discovered that his brilliant examination results did not necessarily constitute a passport into French homes. Moreover, if the French, or some of them, were colour-conscious, so was Senghor. 'I was a racialist to such a degree,' he told me, 'that at that time a white woman left me cold. . . . Yet I've married a Frenchwoman.'

Like so many African students made to feel inferior or worried by the heavy fact of colonialism, Senghor turned to Marxism; and for him as for many others, white or coloured, Marxism

A COUNTRY DIVIDED:

Ho Chi Minh of
North Vietnam

Ngo Dinh Diem of
South Vietnam

THE ASSERTION OF INDEPENDENCE:
Indonesia expels its 'Dutch' population

President Bourguiba of Tunisia, with Mme Bourguiba

Modibo Keita of Kali (*left*) and Leopold Senghor of Senegal,
before they quarrelled

AFRICA'S NEW LEADERS

turned out to be the god that failed. He had, in fact, turned to
Marxism in a search for universal brotherhood; and having
found only a form of universal servitude, he went beyond
Marxism. Now, looking back over the phases of that emotional
and intellectual journey, he finds three dominant ideas that
have become, as he says, the guiding principles of his Union
Progressiste Sénégalaise. Negritude was the first fundamental;
it led to nationalism and to humanism. Nationalism, in turn,
must lead beyond to internationalism. Then Marxism: 'We go
beyond Marxism,' said Senghor that day, 'to rediscover religion. Our socialism is therefore humanist.'

I cannot pretend that I swallow Senghor's philosophy without digestive pangs; nor can I repress an occasional feeling of
distaste or tedium when his erudition crosses the border into
pedantry. But I do not for a moment doubt that he did live
through the struggle of heart and mind he outlined for me. And
indeed it must be of great political value to him to be able to
claim a Marxist and anti-colonial past. In the terms of African
nationalism, this means Senghor has paid his dues and entrance
fee: he can hardly be denied admission to the club. But the long
years of co-operation with France, starting with the proven
loyalty of war-time, have made him suspect in the eyes of the
more vociferously anti-colonial militants.

Fortunately, this extraordinary man is a tough – and indeed
ruthless – politician as well as a poet, grammarian, and philosopher. I have already mentioned that mysterious night of
19 August 1960, when the Federation of Mali broke up and Keita
of Soudan found himself in jail. It was Senghor who put him
there. Such a man should clearly never be under-estimated.*

Rapid change is in the nature of African politics in their present state of flux, and it is by no means certain that the balance
of forces that prevailed in the continent in the autumn of 1962,
when these lines were written, will last. But at that time the tide
had been flowing strongly in favour of the moderates.† That this

---

* He came out on top again in December 1962, when his Prime Minister,
Mamadou Dia, tried to seize power.
† It was still flowing that way after the African summit conference at Addis
Ababa in May 1963.

was so was very largely the work of Leopold Sedar Senghor, together with that even more famous nationalist and moderate, Felix Houphouët-Boigny of the Ivory Coast. When I met Senghor the two men, together with ten other heads of state of French-speaking Africa, had lately gathered in conference at Abidjan, capital of the Ivory Coast, with the object of organizing a regrouping of the countries south of the Sahara. A few months later, in December of the same year, 1960, the twelve heads of state met again at Brazzaville in the former French Congo and reached general agreement on their relations with France, on the desirability of setting up a customs union, and on consulting each other on foreign affairs. Since then they have been known as the Brazzaville group. A month later the militants of Africa, headed by President Nasser of the United Arab Republic and President Nkrumah of Ghana, met at Casablanca, with the late King Mohammed V of Morocco as host, and formed the rival Casablanca group.

The militants had made more noise in their communiqué than the moderates in theirs, but the Brazzaville group has shown itself more durable than the Casablanca group. It has formed a permanent association, known as the Union Africaine et Malgache, met in conference with non-French-speaking African states at Monrovia and Lagos, and made progress with joint financial arrangements. When the group met at Libreville, in Gabon, in September 1962, observers from Somalia and the ex-Belgian Congo were knocking at the club's doors, hoping for admission,* and even the irreconcilable militant, Sékou Touré of Guinea, was letting it be known he would gladly come back to the fold if only General de Gaulle would forget the past. And Modibo Keita of Mali, having lately exchanged state visits with Houphouët-Boigny of the Ivory Coast, was trying to find a way of rejoining his French-speaking friends without actually shaking hands with Senghor. In contrast, the Casablanca group was in tatters. Syria had broken away from the UAR, leaving Nasser with Egypt and a diminished reputation; Morocco under the young King Hassan was losing much of its fugitive militancy;

* The ex-Belgian colonies of the Congo and Rwanda have since been admitted to the UAR.

Nkrumah was going his own way; and Modibo Keita and Sékou Touré, who had attended the Casablanca conference in January 1961, could no longer be called loyal members of the group. This left only the new Algerian Republic under Benbella, a disciple of Nasser's and suitably militant; and even he, shortly after, committed himself to co-operation with France.

If Senghor is quiet, grave, and knowing, Prince Sihanouk of Cambodia is vehement and excitable; but he, too, has wisdom. Both, in their strikingly contrasted ways, are moderates at heart. Sihanouk shares another quality with Senghor, and perhaps he has it to an even greater degree: political genius. But in his case the genius, though often bright to the point of incandescence, is sometimes wild, unpredictable, and even self-destructive. Though Sihanouk, like Senghor and many other remarkable new leaders, had the benefit of a French education and is capable of lucid analysis, his tempers verge on hysteria, and some of his most brilliant ideas have fallen victim to the mercury in him.

It is Sihanouk's constricting misfortune to be the head of a very small state; indeed, with a population of an indeterminate number over 4 millions, Cambodia has about as many people as the London *Daily Mirror* has paying readers. This must at times frustrate a man of such genuinely big ideas, as men in similar situations – such as Spaak of Belgium or Bourguiba of Tunisia – must at times have felt frustrated. What might a Sihanouk have done had history placed him in charge of, say, 90 million Indonesians, instead of 4 or 5 million Khmers? But, of course, if offered this hypothetical opportunity Prince Sihanouk would indignantly reject it. He is a Khmer through and through, the descendant of the fabulous Jayavarman VII, whose ruined temples fuse with the encroaching jungle at Angkor. Moreover, he – as single-handedly as any other new leader – wrested his country's independence from its colonial leaders. Sihanouk, in effect, *is* Cambodia.

Though far more than a mere demagogue, he does love the dramatic gesture. The way he won independence from the French, who had thought of him as just a playboy prince, was pure theatre. He did it in two stages. In January 1953 King Norodom Sihanouk, as he then was, dissolved the National Assembly. A month later he started on a foreign journey, the primary purposes of which were clearly to draw the world's attention to the fact that Cambodia existed and was still a dependent territory; and to embarrass the French – and perhaps shame them into giving him what he wanted – by the publicity he knew his statements would get.

First he went to Rome, then he moved into the 'enemy's' camp. Setting up headquarters in the south of France, he wrote twice to the President of the Republic, claiming that most of the people who mattered in Cambodia – the Buddhist clergy, the officials, the students – were on the side of the outlawed independence movement, Khmer Issarak. This, he argued, was because Cambodia, despite various concessions by France, was still not really independent. He was ready to discuss the matter.

Silence for a week or two; then the President invited the King to lunch at the Elysée Palace. There was a communiqué recording an agreement 'in principle' on the course of action that might give satisfaction to the Cambodians. The French term *en principe*, as King Norodom well knew, can mean anything from 'we are not against this' to 'an agreement is about to be concluded'. Embarrassingly, the Khmer King chose the second of these interpretations. He took quarters at Fontainebleau, the scene of French tussles with Ho Chi Minh of Vietnam seven years earlier, and announced that he was ready to negotiate. The French, however, had a more leisurely timetable in view, and Jean Letourneau, at that time Commissioner-General in Indochina, sent word that the King was embarrassing France by his presence.

King Norodom left, in silence but not in retreat. He went to Canada, officially to thank the Canadian Government for having recognized Cambodia diplomatically, but in reality to attack the 'enemy' from another vantage point. As soon as he reached Montreal he called in the Press to state that his government needed complete sovereignty to drive out the communist guerrillas who were fighting in the name of independence. The United States was next, and in New York the King told the *New*

York Times that he was afraid the Khmers would join forces with the Communists unless independence came within a few months.

Instead of coming home after these repeated manifestations of nationalism, King Norodom stopped in Tokyo and announced he would stay there until the outcome of the negotiations with the French was clear. For by then – it was at the beginning of May – the King's candid tactics were beginning to pay and the French had consented to talks of a kind. In mid-May, however, he surprised everybody yet again by agreeing to return to Cambodia, after French representations. Some French officials may have heaved a sigh of relief and allowed themselves to think that perhaps, after all, they had been right in rating Norodom no higher than a playboy. But the King was merely preparing his second *coup de théâtre*. It came shortly afterwards when he slipped across the Siamese border while on an inspection tour of northern Cambodia, and took refuge in Bangkok, among the hereditary enemies of his ancestors, the Khmer Kings. The Siamese Government seems indeed to have been just as embarrassed by his presence as the French had been when he was at Fontainebleau, and forbade him to do anything political. His followers, however, had already done what he wanted them to do, by issuing a press statement mentioning the disappointment and exasperation of the Cambodians and calling on the King to fight the French.

Uncomfortable in Bangkok, where undignified quarters had been put at his disposal, King Norodom went back to Pnom Penh, his own capital, on 22 June. Four days later the French, who had been going through a prolonged ministerial crisis, had a government again, under M. Joseph Laniel; and on 3 July the Laniel Government invited representatives of their three Indo-chinese possessions – Vietnam, Cambodia, and Laos – to final talks on independence.

The King had won, but final victory did not come until a year later, when the protracted international conference at Geneva ended the Indochina war and gave full independence to the three Indochinese states (though Vietnam, alone of the three, was partitioned into communist and nationalist zones).

Though I had been stationed in South-East Asia during most

of this period, I did not meet Norodom Sihanouk until 1 went
back to the Far East, for *The Economist*, in 1956. By that time
Cambodia had been independent again for more than two
years and he had startled his people and the world repeatedly,
first by abdicating in favour of his father (the Khmer throne is
not directly inherited, the King being chosen by a council of
the throne), by turning himself into a political leader and forming a party which won *every* seat in the National Assembly, by
exiling or executing his political enemies, and by ranging Cambodia firmly among the uncommitted nations. His method of
government was curious and disconcerting. He would form a
government, rule for a few months, working hard while it
lasted, tramping the country, rolling up his shirt sleeves and
doing physical work in the villages, calling the people into the
Palace grounds to hear their grievances and treating them to
Coca-Cola and ice-cream. Then he would resign abruptly and
leave it to some lesser-known personality to carry on, possibly
taking the blame for the promises or half-promises the Prince
(as he now was) might have made when Prime Minister. Soon
the country would sink into a gentle Cambodian chaos and
Sihanouk would emerge from his self-imposed rest and rescue
the people from their rulers. This happened so many times that
Cambodia, in effect, ran out of temporary Prime Ministers.
Indeed, life cannot be easy for *any* Cambodian politician, however loyal, for while in office Prince Sihanouk awed his sub-
ordinates and when out of office he overshadowed them from
afar.

These circumstances had caused me to write, before my
journey, that Prince Sihanouk was at once his country's greatest
asset and its greatest liability. The first thing he did when I
called on him in his Palace at Pnom Penh was to quote this
phrase back at me and ask me what I meant by it. I was in the
company of a young official from the British Embassy, who
looked slightly alarmed at this turn of events. And indeed the
chubby little Prince, whose smile of welcome had faded rather
fast, had put a potentially worrying note into his high, piping
voice. Thinking fast, I looked him in the eye and said depre-
catingly: 'Monseigneur, that is why I have come to Cambodia:

to find out what the truth really is!' He laughed and changed the subject.

The unspoken fact was that I had other things in mind besides the Prince's temperamental administrative technique when I had described him as an asset and a liability. I did mention these things to him, but not in the context of this description; and he reassured me. In retrospect, I now believe that he was right and I was wrong in the argument we had, and the points he made throw light both on the limitations of a small country's freedom of manoeuvre and on the rewards of intelligence and initiative.

At that time I was worried about the international consequences of neutralism, though I would never have gone as far as Mr John Foster Dulles in condemning it as 'immoral'. Whether it was moral or immoral was beside the point; what mattered was whether or not it was setting the stage for a communist take-over. In Cambodia's case there were certainly grounds for anxiety. Being friends with both sides meant that the country was soon swarming with Soviet and Chinese officials. There was a Chinese economic mission and a Chinese football team (football matches constituting 'cultural relations'). The one presentable hotel at that time, the Royal, was already permanently full of Indians, Poles, and Canadians belonging to the International Commission that was supervising the Geneva agreements on Indochina. When I left, thirty Russian families, plus servants (the Russians bring their own gardeners, chauffeurs, and cooks), were expected. I have no conception where they spent their first few nights. Accommodation, then, was a problem, quite apart from subversion.

I felt at the time that Cambodia was letting itself in for a weight of trouble in the future, and I said so to Prince Sihanouk. He pointed out that in the past Cambodia had suffered from the unseen presence of 'communism' – meaning agents of the Vietnamese communist leader, Ho Chi Minh – and commented: 'In those days, the Communists were there and they were a danger, but I had nobody to complain to. Now the danger that exists is in the open, and if I do want to complain, I have somebody to complain to. I can complain to the Russians or to the

Chinese, and they can tell their Vietnamese friends what to do.'

I heard these words with the deepest scepticism, but time has proved Prince Sihanouk right. He has performed, more successfully than Mr Nehru in India, the difficult feat of keeping on good terms with communist diplomats while treating domestic (including Vietnamese) Communists with the utmost severity. The Chinese Communists, by and large, have behaved 'correctly' in Cambodia, the Russians not always; and the Prince has not hesitated, when the occasion seemed to warrant it, to criticize the behaviour of the Russians, as well as of the Americans. By and large, he has succeeded in preserving Cambodia's neutral balance. True, he has had border troubles with the Siamese to the north-west and the Vietnamese to the south-east. But the great powers have left him reasonably alone while vying with each other and with the international bodies to provide economic aid for Cambodia. And relations with France are excellent. This seems to clinch the neutralist argument in Prince Sihanouk's favour.

Exuberantly Mediterranean, Habib Bourguiba of Tunisia can be as excitable as Prince Sihanouk. Geography has been almost as unkind to Tunisia as to Cambodia, and nature far more. Cambodia's trouble is to be condemned to sit on the doorstep of the Chinese giant with ill-disposed Siamese and Vietnamese neighbours at the windows. Tunisia's was to be an unwilling ringside spectator of the Algerian war, one of the most savage conflicts of modern times. Cambodia, on the other hand, has had bountiful favours from nature: there is plenty of land and of food. Tunisia, which sits on the edge of the great Sahara desert, is cruelly poor and many of its 4 million people go hungry.

These circumstances help to account for Bourguiba's political behaviour. They explain, for instance, why this fundamentally moderate and reasonable man finds it necessary from time to time to make incendiary speeches. While the Algerian war went on his dilemma was indeed insoluble. Though he valued France's friendship (and personally admired General de

Gaulle), it was more than his political power was worth to deny aid and comfort to his Algerian brothers while the war went on. Moreover, Tunisia was far too weak militarily for him to say 'No' to the Algerian insurgents, even if it had been politically possible for him to do so. So Tunisia harboured perhaps 100,000 Algerian refugees and – in the latter stages of the Algerian war – the bulk of the Algerian Army. This in turn earned Bourguiba permanently disturbed relations with France and two savage physical assaults, on the village of Sakiet in 1958 and on the town adjoining the Bizerta naval base in 1961. Yet he was still in power when the Algerian war ended in the spring of 1962. For he, too, like Sihanouk, is a political genius of high calibre.

President Bourguiba's heavily guarded palace is at La Marsa, some miles from Tunis and not far from the disappointing ruins of ancient Carthage. I had two talks with him there, in February 1958 and almost exactly two years later. On each occasion the weight of the Algerian war hung like a presence over our heads. The first time his dominant anxieties were to prevent the Algerian war from spreading, especially to Tunisia, to persuade the British and Americans to stop aiding or tacitly supporting the French (by implication, against the Algerian independence fighters), and to make sure the Algerians did not turn to the Communists for assistance.

In voicing these understandable fears or objectives, Bourguiba was served by exceptional histrionic gifts and a striking face, which together more than made up for an insignificant stature. The firm jaw and jutting chin are those of a fighter; the startling blue-grey eyes in the deeply tanned skin are a reminder that the modern Tunisian is the product of many races and diverse histories; the greying hair and the deep furrows advertise the experience of the man of action. It is an extraordinarily mobile and expressive face, and every feature has its carefully allotted role. The eyebrows lift in astonishment or horror; the eyes roll with the frenzy Shakespeare found in his imaginary poet; the mouth smiles, laughs, or hardens into a mask of political will or defiance. When Bourguiba speaks, however, he uses his hands, shoulders, and spine as well as his face. His oratory is kinetic and emotional. And persuasive.

When I first met him he turned on every resource of Bourguiba the orator, although it was for an audience of one; and he needed them, for unhappily he had made too many speeches of late and his voice was reduced to a raucous whisper. Besides the major recurring fears he had described, there was another, more immediate and specific one: that the Algerian National Liberation Front (FLN) would transfer its headquarters back to Cairo from Tunis. To have persuaded the Algerians to come to Tunis in the first place had been one of the Tunisian President's personal triumphs. While they had been in Cairo, he had felt they were out of his control, under the expansionist, interfering influence of President Nasser, whom Bourguiba deeply mistrusted because he had given asylum to Bourguiba's bitterest enemy, the exiled Salah benYoussef (since assassinated, though that is another story). And now the Algerians, said Bourguiba, had felt the pull of Cairo once more. A dangerous pull, he thought, because Nasser was too mixed up with the communist powers. 'What I am afraid of,' he said, 'is that the FLN will go to the Communists by way of Nasserism' and he curled his tongue with sinister emphasis around that word 'Nasserism'.

He need not have feared on the score of Cairo and Nasser, for the FLN, in the event, stayed on in Tunis. But one of his major fears – involvement in the Algerian war – was dreadfully realized on 8 February, the day after our conversation, when French bombers from Algeria attacked the frontier village of Sakiet Sidi Youssef. It was market day, and the streets were thronged. A school was destroyed and children were among the eighty dead.

Why had the French done it? The High Command in Algiers claimed that Algerian guerrilla fighters had taken refuge there. Certainly there had been fighting in this region and Algerian fire had forced a French military plane down. On the other hand, Tom Brady of the *New York Times*, who was in Sakiet a few hours after the raid, told me when I telephoned him from Algiers that he had found no evidence that Sakiet harboured either FLN soldiers or their weapons; and a western diplomat who had visited the place a few days earlier said the same. But whether the attack was made with military intent or to vent the rage of frustrated French commanders, it did prove that Bourguiba's fears were more than mere histrionics.

Understandably, when I next met President Bourguiba, he exclaimed repeatedly: 'I'm sitting on a volcano.' This time, however, the volcano he had in mind was Bizerta, the French naval base in Tunisia. He did not seem to be afraid that the French would break out of their military area to attack the Tunisians (although that is exactly what they did, a few months later). His fear was more subtle and complex. The Algerian revolutionaries also had a major base on Tunisian soil. Whatever their strength in 1958, at the time of Sakiet, there is no doubt that by 1960 the bulk of the Algerian Army had been driven out of Algeria and most of it had taken refuge in the mountainous country on the Tunisian side of the border. The French, meantime, had erected a powerful – indeed almost impenetrable – line of forts and electrified barbed wire along the frontier, so that the Algerian fighters could not return to continue the war in their own country. Would their frustration explode as French frustration had, in some senseless or suicidal act, such as an attack on Bizerta or on the French residents of Tunis? This was evidently what Bourguiba had in mind.

In the event, what happened was that Bourguiba himself misguidedly ordered an attack on Bizerta and that the French took an unnecessarily savage revenge. The story of this bitter episode is told elsewhere in this book. What concerns us here is Bourguiba's state of mind. Why did this moderate, fundamentally pro-French politician, the master of gradualist tactics that had long been known as *Bourguibisme*, take this potentially suicidal course?

The answer lies tangled in the undergrowth of Maghrebin and Afro-Asian politics. So precarious and exposed was Bourguiba's position that he continually felt the need to demonstrate his nationalism afresh. After Sakiet, the ordinary people of Tunisia had started saying: 'Bourguiba is not our *habib* ("darling") any more.' This galling pun on Bourguiba's first name was potent. It meant that Bourguiba had gone too far to appease the French, and all he was doing was to bring French bombs down on helpless Tunisians. Truc, he had once broken off diplomatic relations with France, but once General de Gaulle had returned to power, he had again begun talking wistfully of his favourite vision of a united Maghreb – Morocco, Algeria, and Tunisia – living together in harmony and reaching for prosperity with French technical and economic assistance. Such talk started fresh whisperings among the hotheads, not only in Tunisia but elsewhere in the Afro-Asian world.

Then there was this hideous thorn in Tunisia's side: Bizerta. The Moroccans were getting rid of French and American bases, but he, Bourguiba, had repeatedly asked the French to quit Bizerta, alternately pleading, cajoling, and threatening, all to no avail. The French presence at Bizerta was more than burden and a danger: it was a badge of continuing shame, a symbol of Tunisia's failure to achieve 'true' independence. True the Americans still had their giant base at Guantánamo, in Cuba, and this had not prevented Fidel Castro from becoming a hero to nationalists throughout the underdeveloped world. But Castro was pure, for he denounced the Americans, seized their property, and made life intolerable for American residents in his leftward-leaning republic. Bourguiba, in contrast, was suspect, for while he denounced France in public speeches, he kept looking in de Gaulle's direction for the miracle that never came.

Bourguiba was indeed becoming isolated, and the extent of his isolation was revealed to him when Morocco, but not Tunisia, was invited to the 'summit' of uncommitted leaders at Belgrade, which was to be held in September 1961. Morocco had got rid of its French soldiers and had persuaded the Americans to start leaving as well. The lesson seemed plain: Bizerta had to be attacked.

In 1962 the apparently permanent menace on Bourguiba's doorstep was removed when the Algerian War came to an end. The old fighter's reward came shortly afterwards, in July, when diplomatic relations with France, which had been suspended since the Bizerta incident a year earlier, were resumed in the midst of general felicitations. Bourguiba was free to resume his hopeful work for a united Maghreb linked, if that proved possible, with France.

4. THE SOLDIERS

I have been dividing the leaders of the new countries into militant and moderate categories. But I might equally have divided them into civilian and military. In a lecture given before the World Affairs Council of Northern California at San Francisco on 6 October 1958, Dr Guy J. Pauker of the University of California argued that in many of the emerging countries the Army is the most progressive element in the population. This argument is indeed not without force. In well-established States the Army tends to become conservative and caste-ridden. In Latin America it has traditionally intervened against social change. Revolutionary armies, however, are different in kind from the professional armies of long-established nations (although, conversely, the longer such armies are established, the more conservative they get: the Soviet Army, which was once the Red Army, has become a typically conservative, professional body, kept up to strength by conscription). In the years of revolutionary fervour the army of rebels against authority is, in a sense, born of the people, and it is certainly sustained by the people's support. This is true even of communist armies at the time of their struggle, whether in China or in Vietnam, and truer still in genuinely nationalist armies, such as Indonesia's or Algeria's.

Inevitably, such armies are the 'spearhead' of the revolution, and once the revolution is accomplished, they do not easily reconcile themselves to seeing the civilians make a mess of it. Bringing the Algerian Army of National Liberation (ALN) under civilian control was a major problem when independence came in 1962. In many other countries the Army has seized power, not, as in most of the Latin American *coups d'état*, with the object of preventing social change, but with the more noble aim of making sure that the changes envisaged under revolutionary programmes are in fact carried out.

Most of the officers who have seized power in the emerging countries have not, however, been the product of revolutionary armies. Indeed, their prototype, Colonel Nasser, was a career officer in an army that had no revolutionary tradition until he gave it one. By and large, the revolutionary armies – China's, North Vietnam's, Indonesia's, even Cuba's – were rapidly brought under civilian control once the revolutionary movements they spearheaded had been brought to power. The military take-overs in Iraq, Sudan, and Pakistan in 1958, and in Turkey and South Korea in 1960 and 1961 were accomplished by regular army officers. General Ne Win's seizures of power in Burma in 1958, and again in 1962, constitute a special case, which deserves special treatment.

If one attempts to divide the military leaders into militants and moderates, in the sense in which I have been using these terms, one runs into difficulties. Colonel Nasser, as I have suggested, is a militant who has been showing signs of turning moderate. The late Brigadier Kassim of Iraq defied classification; his revolution was certainly an anti-western one, but he was restrained from a consistently anti-western line by Iraq's economic dependence on the Iraq Petroleum Company, and by the manifest unwillingness of the Soviet Union to shoulder the burden of keeping the oil flowing in the event of his nationalizing the company. Without much discernible political talent, beyond a capacity for keeping himself in power, his régime was more notable for hysterical speeches and a disastrous attempt to repress the Kurdish minority than for social change, although a timid start was made in land reform. General Park Chunghee's revolutionary junta in South Korea has been ruthless, and indeed brutal, in eradicating corruption from official life; but the junta's first concern was to restore good relations with the United States, which had been damaged by the manner of its advent to power by overthrowing Dr John M. Chang's American-supported civilian administration. General Abboud in Sudan was more concerned to override squabbling political factions than quarrel with the West; indeed, his government's relations with Britain, for instance, could scarcely be better.

By and large, the common factor in the military *coups d'état* I have mentioned was a revulsion against civilian incompetence and corruption. This is not, whatever communist propaganda may say, incompatible with friendly relations with western countries; and whatever the permanence of such military régimes, most of them have tended towards moderation in dealings with the West.

The most interesting of the new military leaders, apart from President Nasser, are perhaps Field-Marshal Ayub Khan and General Ne Win. They share common sense, high military rank, and an exasperated impatience with the muddling or even culpable incompetence of civilian politicians. There, however, the resemblance ends. In training, outlook, and personality the contrast between them is striking.

Tall and burly – like most Pathans – and ramrod straight, General Ayub Khan has the clipped accent and moustache associated with Sandhurst; every impressive inch of him is the regular army man. Pakistan did not, of course, exist more than thirty years ago when he enrolled at the Royal Military College as one of the first group of Indian cadets admitted to that symbol of the British Raj. Promotion to Commander-in-Chief of the Pakistani Army came to him by way of the Royal Fusiliers, the Punjab Regiment, and war service in Burma. The segment of the old Indian Army that was handed over to Pakistan when India was partitioned in 1947 was already a disciplined force of proved fighting efficiency, and Ayub Khan was not the kind of man to allow any slackening of rigid standards. A strict disciplinarian, the general was capable of towering military rages (we once exchanged correspondence which, on his side, was magnificently choleric, over an article in a publication for which I was responsible). His sense of justice was, however, impartial, in that it knew no favourites. When a subordinate and admirer, Colonel Mohammad Ahmed, brought out a biography of him in June 1960, under the title *My Chief*, General Ayub Khan wrote the following letter to him:

By nature I have attachment with principles rather than with individuals. In my official dealings I have no difficulty in not allowing my personal friendship to influence my official decisions. . . . My main concern in the administration of the Army was to establish the rule of law as opposed to personal rule. The people under me found it difficult to follow this. . . . A large number of people came to petition me on official matters. I never found genuine cause for complaints in any except one case. In appealing to me they have a curious notion that I would demolish the law in their favour.

It was indeed clear enough that he was a first-class military administrator and that his army was about the only competent official body in either half of that geographical monstrosity of an Islamic State which was the late Mohammed Ali Jinnah's vision and memorial. But there had been, as far as I am aware, no sign whatever that General Ayub saw himself as a national political leader, much less that the professional military force which he commanded was to become the spearhead of a revolution imposed from above.

To a man of Ayub's uncompromising character, however, the spectacle of independent Pakistan must have been galling even before it became unendurable. In 1958, nine years after independence, there had been a Constitution for two years, but it had proved impossible to hold general elections (Pandit Nehru's India was ahead on both counts). Jinnah's Muslim League had split into squabbling factions; black marketing flourished and corruption was part of the way of life; the power of the Zamindars – the great feudal landlords – continued undiminished. There was no cohesion between Urdu-speaking West Pakistan and Bengali-speaking East Pakistan, which resented control from distant Karachi. It was nevertheless in East Pakistan that the degeneration of political life had reached its nadir (the National Parliament at Karachi preserved its dignity to the end), and the snapping point came in the violent events of the spring and summer of 1958. On 23 September the deputy Speaker of the Provincial Assembly at Dacca was set upon (he later died of his injuries) while attempting to restore order among parliamentarians who had taken to settling their differences by force instead of debate.

On 7 October, President Iskander Mirza, himself a general (and indeed the very first Indian cadet gazetted into the British Army from Sandhurst in 1919), dismissed his Cabinet, dissolved Parliament, abrogated the Constitution, suspended political

General Ne Win in Burma

Colonel Nasser in Egypt

THE ARMY TAKES OVER

LINKS WITH THE COLONIAL PAST:
The Queen as President Ayub Khan's guest in Pakistan

activity, and proclaimed martial law. The hand behind this show of force, however, was that of Ayub, whom Mirza appointed Supreme Commander and Martial Law Administrator. On 27 October Ayub sent Mirza into exile and assumed full powers, saying: 'There was no alternative to it except the disintegration and complete ruination of the country.' But the most eloquent statement of the pass to which Pakistan had been reduced was that of the departing President, in his proclamation of 7 October:

> For the last two years, I have been watching with the deepest anxiety the ruthless struggle for power, the corruption, the shameful exploitation of our simple, honest, patriotic and industrious masses, the lack of decorum, and the prostitution of Islam for political ends. . . . These despicable activities have led to a dictatorship of the lowest order; adventurers and exploiters have flourished to the detriment of the masses, and are getting richer by their nefarious practices.

By sending President Mirza into exile, General Ayub was giving notice that he intended to deal with Pakistan's evils in his own way. Before leaving, Mirza had appointed a land reforms commission; banned para-military organizations (a blow at the Muslim League's National Guard, 60,000 strong, which had been parading the streets bearing rifles and agitating for war with India); and arrested the Khan of Kalat, whose small State had acceded to Pakistan in 1948 only after the Army had marched in, and who now wanted to take it out again. General Ayub now turned on the racketeers of all kinds, whom he blamed for food shortages and spiralling prices; he had them whipped, heavily fined, and jailed. He appointed small expert committees, each one charged with a specific job and each given a time limit before turning in its report. Instant action followed in every case.

This was barracks-square government and, for a time, it brought results. Order was restored, malefactors were seen to be brought to book, and this gave the military government an initial measure of popularity; and prices did fall, at least in the

E

early months. Most of the things that were done in this period needed to be done, but they were, by their nature, emergency measures to deal with an emergency situation. The junta's problem was one which it shared with all other juntas that claim to be interested in other things but the exercise of power for power's sake: how and when to stop governing. In the early days of the revolution General Ayub had left it to President Mirza to do the talking and make the promises. He himself had merely said (on 17 October 1958):

> Let me assure everyone that, while martial law will not be retained a minute longer than is necessary, it will not be lifted a minute earlier than the purpose for which it has been imposed is fulfilled. That purpose is the clearing up of the political, social, economic and administrative mess that has been created in the past. The country has to be brought back to convalescence, if not complete health. In addition, certain major reforms have to be introduced. All these things will need the cover of martial law.

He was, however, in earnest about the reforms and right in saying they would take time. The most far-reaching of them were land reform and the drafting of a Constitution embodying General Ayub's concept of the kind of government the people of Pakistan were ready for. Both halves of Pakistan, but especially the western part, were plagued with an archaic land tenure system. At the top of the rung were the Zamindars, the great absentee landlords who enjoyed their affluence in the towns while leaving the management of their estates to tenant cultivators whom they took good care to keep in their places. Next to the Zamindars were the Jagirdars, who collected land tax on commission and in many cases acquired land of their own. There were smallholders, tilling their soil with the help of their families, but the great mass of Pakistan's cultivated land surface was thus in the hands of men who grew rich from the work of others.

In January 1959 the Government launched its land-reform scheme in West Pakistan, where the need was most urgent (a land-reform Act had been passed in East Pakistan as early as

1950). A ceiling of 500 acres of irrigated or 1,000 acres of un-irrigated land was set on individual holdings. Lands above these areas were to be offered for sale to the tenants who already worked them, with payment spread over twenty-five years. The same period was to elapse before the dispossessed landlords could redeem the interest-bearing bonds that were given them in compensation for the loss of their lands. As for the jagirs (that is, the right to collect tax on commission) they were simply abolished without compensation.

The results were spectacular. By August the West Pakistan Government had taken over some 2 million acres from a mere 6,000 Zamindars and 500,000 acres by abolishing the jagirs. Land reform was well on its way.

General Ayub's constitutional ideas deserve a few words here. The general had convinced himself of the rottenness of politicians and of the irrelevance of western-style democracy in a country with a teeming population of illiterates. He was not, however, insensitive to the need for constitutional sanction and wished the country to be ruled if not by the governed, then at least with their consent. His solution was, in effect, to perpetuate the actual rule of the 'establishment' – that is, of the officers and the officials – while keeping the masses happy by making them feel wanted and allowing them to run their own affairs in their own localities.

Casting around in India's pre-Pakistan village traditions, much as President Sukarno was doing in Indonesia, he came up with a plan for what he called 'basic democracies' – popular bodies of people's representatives who would help the authorities in rural development and social welfare. In its full details the plan was announced at a governors' conference held under the chairmanship of President Ayub (as he had become) in June 1959. *Panchayats,* or village councils, were to be set up throughout East and West Pakistan, each to consist of ten elected and five nominated members. Each council chairman would be elected and would automatically become a member of a sub-divisional council; in turn, as the pyramid of councils rose, there would be a third tier of district councils and a fourth of divisional councils.

Once again, planning was swiftly followed by action. An Order creating the 'basic democracies' was promulgated in October 1959, and in December the village councils were elected. On 14 February 1960 the President sought the approval of the 80,000 members of the *panchayats* and duly secured a dictator's majority of 95·6 per cent of the votes. Three days later he had himself sworn in at Rawalpindi, his new capital, as Pakistan's first elected President, and he immediately set up a commission to draw up a Constitution. A little over two years later, on 1 March 1962, President Ayub Khan announced his new Constitution.

These are the bare facts of Ayub's aims and of the measures he has taken to achieve them. Already it is clear enough that if, as now seems possible, Pakistan survives as a nation the credit must be given to him. Next to Jinnah, who founded it, Ayub's name will loom largest in Pakistan's early history. But this is not a history book, and it is far too early to pass a definitive judgement on the man and his work. What I can and must do is to point out that the words of praise need be tempered by passages of blame or reservations of one kind or another. The military government did make prices fall, but only temporarily; justice was meted out to speculators, but it was a rough and selective justice; some of the refugees who had poured in across the partition line years before had been resettled under special housing schemes in Karachi and Dacca, but not enough of them; economic growth was feeble; and even the régime's boast that it had eliminated corruption could hardly stand up to the experience of daily life.

These criticisms, and others, were made with suitable examples, by an acute and learned observer, Professor K. J. Newman, in an address at Chatham House that was reprinted in *International Affairs* in July 1962. Professor Newman does not make the mistake of assuming that the methods of Westminster and Whitehall can go on unchanged in an underdeveloped country from which the paternal hand of the British has been withdrawn. But he does point out that the most constructive legacy of the British presence was the introduction of legislative and educational reforms that resulted in the emergence of an able – and, despite individual excesses – an honest *élite*. It is this *élite*, with its love of liberty and its attachment to the rule of law, that is frustrated under President Ayub Khan, however popular he may be among his village councillors.

The Constitution of 1962, viewed through the eyes of this able and indeed indispensable minority, is a profoundly unsatisfactory document. It emasculates law by barring the Courts from examining administrative acts; it eliminates political opposition by banning all parties; and ensures the self-perpetuation of the régime by laying down that the régime itself will select candidates for the Presidency, to be elected in due course by the 'basic democracies'. These are serious shortcomings, which only a prolonged period of material and social progress could be held to justify.

As an officer, General Ne Win stands halfway between the regular army man of Ayub Khan's background and the revolutionary military leader, of which Mao Tse-tung and Vo Nguyen Giap of Vietnam are the prototypes. He did receive a conventional military training, but not a western one: he was one of thirty members of the nationalist Thakin group smuggled to Japan in 1940 to provide the officer corps of the anti-British Burma National Army. The Thakins saw this as an opportunity to create a force in keeping with their nationalism; the Japanese, on their side, merely wished to form a pliant instrument to further their imperialist drive. As Dr Hugh Tinker records in his standard work, *The Union of Burma* (Oxford for the Royal Institute of International Affairs), the Japanese made no effort to disguise their purpose, BNA recruits and cadets being slapped and insulted, and forced to salute all Japanese personnel, a courtesy which the Japanese were not required to return. When the time came – which was not until March 1945 – the entire BNA defected to the British side. Until then, the Japanese had mainly used it for internal security, although it had been involved in a few clashes with the British.

Despite this unheroic history, General Aung San, the real leader of the Burmese independence movement, Ne Win, and the other BNA officers did see themselves as revolutionaries and nationalists. When the new army of independent Burma came to be constituted, however, it consisted only partly of recruits from the BNA; its hard core consisted of the old Burma Rifles, which the British had created as part of the Indian Army. Beset by communalism and handicapped by its mixed origin, the new army was by no means comparable to that of Pakistan in professionalism, cohesiveness, or efficiency. Indeed, discipline and loyalty were problematical from the first, and in the summer of 1948, only a few months after independence, three of the former BNA battalions mutinied; only the fourth, which happened to be under Ne Win, then a Brigadier, remained loyal to the new State. A communist rising added to the Army's difficulties; and in 1949 two of the Kachin battalions and all the Karen battalions also mutinied. To fill the gaps, irregular forces were raised on an *ad hoc* basis. Later, many of these irregulars were incorporated into the regular army. A chronic insecurity gripped the Burmese countryside, and the largely undisciplined and truculent Army aggravated it in many cases instead of alleviating it.

The Army which General Ne Win commanded in 1958 thus scarcely seemed to qualify either as the spearhead of a revolution or as an instrument to impose military order. The need to restore order was, however, even more urgent in Burma than in Pakistan. Nor did Ne Win himself seem, on the record, to be the potential saviour which Burma had needed ever since that murderous day in July 1947 when General Aung San and all but three of his Ministers were massacred by youths armed with sub-machine-guns. Having failed an Arts course at Rangoon University, Ne Win had taken to betting at the races (like Tunku Abdul Rahman of Malaya) and had become a humble clerk in the Post Office (like the late Patrice Lumumba of the Congo). When a number of nationalist Burmans formed themselves into a group which they styled the Thakins or 'masters' (a term expressing defiance of the British rulers), Ne Win joined them. This was in the 'thirties, and the young man who joined the Thakins was called Shu Maung; it was not until his BNA days that Shu Maung assumed the more glamorous name of

Ne Win, which means 'radiant sun' (today, in his fifties, Ne Win is known as 'Ah-Ba' or 'father').

There was thus no doubt about the length of Ne Win's commitment to the nationalist cause when he first seized power in September 1958. Nor could it be doubted that the mantle of Aung San had fittingly draped itself about his shoulders. His experience of politics was, however, limited: he had served as Minister of Defence and Home Affairs in U Nu's Cabinet from 1949. Yet it must be conceded that the first, at any rate, of General Ne Win's *coups d'état* was a remarkable success, within its self-imposed limits.

That he did impose limits on his own exercise of power was in itself remarkable. Until he seized power a second time in March 1962 General Ne Win was indeed unique among modern dictators, both by the manner of his first coup in 1958 and for having voluntarily returned power to elected politicians. Even to say that he 'seized' power the first time is misleading unless the circumstances are explained. Soft kid concealed the mailed fist. For the record, U Nu was allowed to announce in Parliament that he had invited the general to assume the premiership; but this device, though it saved U Nu's face, did not fool anybody, least all the departing Prime Minister. The truth of the matter is that he had been told to get out or be deposed by force.

General Ne Win is still, figuratively, writing his biography and adding a chapter or two to Burma's history, and it is too early to see him in perspective. Did he return to power in 1962 because he had found the taste of power sweet the first time? Or because his sense of duty would not permit him to stand aside when the politicians were so patently undoing his good work? Had he, indeed, handed power back to the politicians so that they could provide proof that he, Ne Win, was Burma's indispensable man?

I'm inclined to answer 'Yes' to the second question, 'Perhaps' to the first, and 'No' to the cynical third. Ne Win unburdened himself to me with what I took to be disarming sincerity in the course of a long and informal talk in London in August 1960. This was only four months after Burma's return to constitutional rule, and the general had come to London for medical treatment. A smallish man with light-toned skin (he has Chinese blood), General Ne Win has a ready smile and a friendly, unceremonious manner. He was wearing a white shirt, open at the collar, and sandals over bare feet when he greeted me in a flat near Kensington Gardens. An aide-de-camp had opened the door to me, but he left us alone, seated side by side on a couch. It had been agreed that our talk was to be confidential, but the events of March 1962 have made this proviso irrelevant.

At the time of General Ne Win's first take-over U Nu's ruling Anti-Fascist People's Freedom League had split into two factions, which called themselves, picturesquely, 'clean' and 'stable'. U Nu led the Clean AFPFL, and his rival, U Ba Swe, headed the Stable faction. U Nu later renamed his faction the Union Party, and to many people's surprise – in view of his unsuccessful administrative record – it won an overwhelming victory in the elections of February 1960, which marked Burma's return to constitutional life. Almost immediately, however, U Nu ran into further dissension within his party, and showed alarming signs of embarking on courses that were bound to displease the Commander-in-Chief. During Ne Win's term of office Burma had been literally, as well as figuratively, cleaned up. Rangoon had been relieved of the mounds of refuse cluttering its streets; bank accounts had been scrutinized, and those guilty of corruption in any form brought to trial; hoarded grain stocks had been released. Above all, General Ne Win had made the unity of Burma a major policy goal. Indeed, the official name of the State was the Union of Burma, and the general, himself a Burmese (despite his Chinese blood), interpreted this unity in simple, soldierly terms. Whatever the Constitution might say about minority rights, including the right of non-Burmese States to secede from the Union, unity could only mean, in his eyes, a powerful, centralized administration under Burmese direction.

And now the politicians were back, having apparently learnt nothing and forgotten nothing. Corruption was returning, and U Nu was planning measures that seemed bound to undermine

Burma's precarious unity, as Ne Win conceived it, in two ways. During the election campaign U Nu had promised the Mon and Arakanese minorities the right to form autonomous States within the Union. This had won him the support of the Mon and Arakanese communities, but any attempt to fulfil his election promises to them could only intensify the naturally fissiparous tendency of the Union. Moreover, he had promised to make Buddhism the State religion, and while this promise had won him the support of the influential Buddhist monks, any attempt to implement it would alienate, for instance, the large Christian element among the Karens, and the Muslims of Arakan.

Although, on that August day in London Ne Win did not say, in so many words, that he intended to return to power, he did make it quite clear that he was deeply worried by the course of events in Burma and that he would not hesitate to take over again if the politicians allowed the country to drift once more towards ruin and disunity. One sensed a deep-seated conflict within him, however, which arose from a sincere horror of the political game, allied with a genuine reluctance to adopt unconstitutional means. While he had been Premier, he told me, the politicians of both factions of the AFPFL had asked him to form and lead a new national party, 'but I sent them away. What would be the use of forming another party? I had to stay outside politics to make sure the next elections would be fair. In Burma a political party can't win an election without being corrupt. If I had accepted the offer to form a political party of my own I would have had to become corrupt myself, and I'm not prepared to do this.'

Another reason for his reluctance, said Ne Win, was his belief in the need for constitutional continuity. 'I have closely studied military revolutions,' he said, 'especially those of Nasser and Kassim. Their mistake was to make a complete break with the past, so that they created a vacuum. This meant they couldn't hand power back to a legally constituted civilian government. I have tried not to make the same mistake. Right from the beginning, I made a point of calling in the political leaders, even U Nu and U Ba Swe (the leader of the rival faction of the ruling party), and consulting them about legislation I was planning. That way I was able to preserve continuity and make it easier to hand power back to the civilians.'

On 2 March 1962, rather less than eighteen months after this conversation, General Ne Win again overthrew U Nu's Government, this time with less ceremony than before, the political leaders being placed under house arrest. The reluctant dictator was back again, and this time without a promise to hand back affairs to the politicians, although his second-in-command, Brigadier Aung Gyi, told correspondents a few days later that the army leaders were loyal to the spirit of the Constitution, believed in democracy, and supported the socialist character of the country's economy. (In February 1963, however, Aung Gyi lost his job for saying civilian rule was better than military.)

According to press reports from Burma, Ne Win had intervened because U Nu's Government had failed to control inflation, had displayed a 'hesitant attitude' towards trade, and shown itself unable to guarantee Burma's security; but the main reason for the General's return was undoubtedly the demand of the Shan minority for the setting up of a federal system of government instead of the existing unitary one. One of the revolutionary Government's first acts was to dissolve not only the two chambers of Parliament but also the five State Councils, dealing with Shan, Kachin, Karen, Kayah, and Chin affairs. These were replaced by new State Supreme Councils, each of which was headed by men who favoured the unitary system.

Symbolically, the only casualty in General Ne Win's *coup d'état* was the teenage son of Sao Shwe Thaik, one of the principal Shan leaders and Burma's first President, who was shot dead by one of the soldiers who entered his father's residence. This incident angered the Shans, who for years had complained about the brutalities of the Burmese Army in Shan State. Some weeks after the *coup* I received a document dated 12 March 1962, and bearing the imprint of 'The Bureau of Information, the Nationalities Liberation Alliance, Headquarters, Shan States', which throws an interesting light on the attitude of Burma's minority peoples on Burmese rule in

general, and on General Ne Win in particular. It says, for
instance:

> In spite of their repeated public disavowals, both U Nu and
> Ne Win are Great Burmese chauvinists. The former is cun-
> ning and subtle, like Lenin; while the latter is blunt and
> brutal like Hitler. Their socialism is communism minus
> atheism, and neutralism is high politics blackmail of both
> Communist and non-Communist blocs.

There is, of course, no need to accept such views uncritically,
but the fact that a substantial number of Shans (and Karens and
other minority groups) hold them is a factor Ne Win cannot
afford to ignore if he is to make a long-term success of his
second attempt to run Burma's affairs by dictation.

The Ayub Khan and Ne Win experiments are interesting
examples of what soldiers can, and what they probably cannot,
do in the kind of situation that many independent countries
face within a few years of independence. (The ex-Belgian Congo
faced an even worse situation immediately after independence.
But General – then Colonel – Mobutu, who tried to seize power,
and did after a fashion, soon showed that he had neither the
experience nor the capacity to master events and impose his
authority.) What they can do is to restore order; what they
cannot do, or can do only with the greatest reluctance and
difficulty, is to restore law, thus truncating an expression – 'law
and order' – which summarizes something fundamental in the
British approach to government. True, General Ne Win stepped
down once, but he was soon back again. True again, the
Turkish officers who seized power in May 1960 surrendered it
in November 1961 to a civilian government; but very soon
afterwards, in February 1962, a group of officers tried to overthrow the new government, and though it was frustrated, there
could be no real confidence in the stability of Turkey's representative institutions.

Let us note, then, that military dictatorship is one more of the
hazards that face newly independent countries, and that there
is unfortunately little to support Dr Pauker's view (in the lecture

I mentioned at the beginning of this section) that the armies of these countries may provide a temporary period of stability enabling them to move towards the take-off stage of economic development. That they provide a period of stability is true; that this period will be short, or that it will lead to take-off seems to me to remain unproven.

Chapter 3

THE NEW COUNTRIES

I. THE BEST AND THE WORST

In many of the new countries independence has been followed, either at once or within a few years, by a decline in living standards. In many instances, though by no means in all, this has been due, at least in part, to exploding populations. India, for example, has to work hard merely to ensure that its population, increasing by 8 or 9 millions a year, does not actually get poorer. On the other hand, Burma, which is the second largest country in South-East Asia and has a population of only 29 millions, exports rice, and ought to find it relatively easy to develop its economy. Yet it has conspicuously failed to do so.

There is indeed little in the experience of emancipated colonies to support one of the favourite themes of nationalist rebels in the years of struggle and of communist propaganda at all times: that colonial exploitation had prevented economic growth and that independence would promote it. It will be seen, however, that this theme is in two parts. The first – that colonial exploitation has prevented economic growth – has, demonstrably, an element of truth in it; but it does not follow that independence automatically ushers in an expanding economy. It is true enough that not one of the western colonial powers laid the foundations of self-sustaining economic growth in their dependencies (though they did, in many cases, provide their colonies with the 'infrastructure' of an expanding economy – the roads and railways, and even the educational facilities, without which no country can hope to progress beyond a subsistence economy). It is true again, that no western colonial power took measures to forestall the impending consequences of an exploding population (India and Algeria are the worst examples of this failure). And it is true, to complete the argument, that Japan, being independent, rapidly modernized and industrialized itself after 1870, whereas India, for instance, was in no position to do any such thing. But the Japanese experience, fascinating though it is, tells us more about the ingenuity, energy, and adaptability of the Japanese people than about the benefits of independence. Siam, to take a comparable case, stayed independent throughout the period of western imperialism in Asia (apart from occupation by the Japanese during the Second World War), but remains to this day an underdeveloped country.

In principle, the achievement of political independence does remove an obstacle in the way of economic development in that it enables the newly independent country to plan for growth. In practice, performances have more often than not been disappointing, even in countries which, like India, have done their best and have had the benefit of a well-trained civil service. Failure was perhaps inevitable in the Congo, which had no trained administrators at all, and to a lesser extent in Indonesia, which had too few. But by no means all the blame can be laid at the door of the departing colonialists: the corruption, inefficiency, and plain irresponsibility of some of the new rulers must also take their share. The rest of this chapter examines examples of the best and worst that independence has brought. Among the worst: Burma, Indonesia, Algeria, and the former Belgian Congo. Among the best, that is, among those whose governments are at least doing their best: India, Cambodia, Malaya, and Nigeria; and an odd case, Mali. It is unfortunately part of the picture that even the best is not good enough.

2. BURMESE WORST

In 1951, four years after independence, the average Burman was earning no more than £13. 16s. *a year*. Twelve years earlier, under British rule, the average annual income had been nearly twice as high: £24. 14s. In pre-war years the Medical College of Rangoon University turned out between twenty and thirty new doctors every year; like the pre-war figure for national income, this one was pitifully low, but in the five years that followed independence the average output of medical graduates had fallen to just over sixteen a year.

The national-income figures appeared in a report prepared in 1951 by a group of Oxford economists who spent some months in Burma under the auspices of the United Nations. The medical graduation figures are from Burmese official sources. In 1961 – to give another example drawn from official statistics – fifteen years after independence, the country's production had only just been restored to pre-war levels.

One should resist the temptation to jump to what may seem the obvious conclusion. It is certain that conditions in Burma, as in many other newly independent countries, were worse some years after independence than they had been under colonial rule. It does not follow that the deterioration was due solely to the advent of independence. On the other hand, there is one thing the figures cannot be made to prove: that the nationalists, in Burma and elsewhere, were right in claiming that only colonial rule was keeping their country backward and that independence would set it on the course of progress.

In all fairness, one should allow for the fact that it was not the Burma of 1939 that the Thakins – Burma's nationalists – took over from the British, but a country that had been devastated by war. Education and medical care had broken down, production of minerals was virtually at a standstill, and the refugees flooding into Rangoon had turned the capital into a pestilential slum. Moreover, independent Burma had been deprived of its leadership, from General Aung San down, by mass assassination, and its unity had been threatened shortly after independence by a series of communal or political insurrections.

One should, then, allow that the Burmans had more than a fair share of bad luck. When every allowance has been made, however, it is hard to escape the conclusion that the civilian governments which ran the country between 1947 and 1958 displayed a quite remarkable incompetence. The only saving grace is that it was the incompetence of idealism and not – as for instance in Cuba before Fidel Castro took over – of political gangsterism. But the idealism of Burma's rulers brought little comfort to the ordinary Burman peoples.

The new Burma had indeed been ushered in on a wave of high ideals. Welfare and economic advance were associated with independence in the minds of the founders of the Anti-Fascist People's Freedom League, who incorporated references to such aims in their inaugural 'Naythuyein Declaration' in August 1945. The 1947 Constitution of the Union of Burma contains long passages asserting the State's right to nationalize any part of the economy and the citizens' right to work, to sickness and old-age benefits, to rest and leisure and to education. These are standard socialist aims, and though U Nu was never formally a communist – and indeed failed entirely to secure the co-operation of the communists in the early years of Burma's independence – he made it clear that he intended to fulfil them by Marxist means. Thus in his speech of 24 September 1947, moving the adoption of the new Constitution by the Assembly, he said: 'The ideology that Burma needs today is not Trotsky's "immediate action regardless of the consequences", but Lenin's "Get strong first, everything else afterwards".'

This advice, irrespective of its author, was singularly appropriate for a country in Burma's state, but in the event, U Nu did not follow it. An amiable Buddhist with literary ambitions, U Nu had a disposition that made it difficult for him to distinguish between plans and achievements. In this he was perhaps typical of a large class of indigenous politicians and administrators in South-East Asia. Dr Hugh Tinker, noting the trend in his *The Union of Burma*, wrote:

> Burma's attempt to find a short-cut to Socialism and industralization, to compel wishes to become reality may have been responsible for the development of the phenomenon of planning for planning's sake. . . . A peculiar sanctity seems to attach to reports, statistics, and, above all, to diagrams and scale models which give the desired future an illusion of immediacy. The impression is gained that planning is becoming not a prelude to, but a substitute for, actual constructional work.

Planning did indeed absorb much of the energy that ought, in the early years of independence, to have been devoted to restor-

ing and preserving law and order and stimulating the exploitation of Burma's plentiful natural riches. On 5 June 1956, after
nine years in office, U Nu resigned as Prime Minister and announced that he would devote a year to reorganizing the ruling
AFPFL. He let it be understood that his successor, U Ba
Swe (who later became the leader of a breakaway faction),
would try, in the meantime, to solve the country's economic
problems.

Nine years in office may seem a reasonable trial period, and it
is illuminating, in retrospect, to look at the situation in Burma
at the time of U Nu's resignation in 1956. Four years earlier the
Government had claimed '95 per cent success' against the insurgents and had forecast the total restoration of security within
a year. Yet in 1956 the Government's control hardly extended
beyond the principal towns. Even by day, travel was unsafe, and
by night it was still prohibited; old-fashioned dacoity – with its
complement of murders and kidnappings – was rife. Moreover,
the ill-disciplined Burma Army was itself guilty of excesses in
districts in which it was supposed to be restoring law and
order.

There were, of course, some achievements in the sphere of
social welfare, though these mainly consisted of rehabilitating
the medical and public-health services. On the other hand,
Rangoon, which, at one time, had been one of the cleanest and
healthiest cities in the Far East, remained disease-ridden and
offensive to the eye: the potholes in the streets seemed the
natural companions to the mounds of uncollected refuse on the
sides. But the most spectacular failures were in administration
and economics. Pre-war enterprises, now under government
control, were functioning at greatly reduced efficiency. The
Government had taken over responsibility for buying and dis-
tributing various foodstuffs, some categories of cloth, and
essential building materials. At the same time more than 2,000
new companies had been allowed to register as importers to
help handle less-essential goods. The great majority of these new
companies had no visibly useful economic function. Lacking
capital and experience, they seemed to exist merely to sell the
licences they obtained to the highest bidder. There remained

F

some well-established Burman firms, but nothing was done to give them the feeling of security that would have encouraged them to take a long-term view of their business prospects.

There was nothing wrong, in principle, in the Government's policy of state trading while replacing foreign traders by a local business community, but the results did not justify the policy, at least in its practical application. Money was in plentiful supply, but not goods. Administrative complications had created bottle-necks. The outcome was shortages and hoarding, high prices, and a flourishing black market in necessities.

In foreign trade government intervention was an unqualified disaster. Attached to the principles of neutralism and socialism, the Government sought to trade in the 'barter area', that is, with the communist countries. The outcome was a classic demonstration of the disadvantages of this form of commerce. The inexperienced Burmans bartered away their 1955 surplus and much of their 1956 anticipated surplus, then shipped off the 1955 instalment without arranging at the same time what they were to receive in return or making sure the value of the goods to be shipped in return would correspond to the value of their rice at prevailing world prices. The Russians shipped 60,000 tons of cement – a whole year's supply – to Burma without notice. The cement arrived in Rangoon at the beginning of the monsoon, and most of it was left in the open in the absence of storage space; when the rains came, it turned to concrete. The Russians, having taken delivery of 250,000 tons of Burmese rice, sent it straight to communist North Vietnam to relieve a near famine, thereby demonstrating that they could not provide a natural market for Burma's export surplus. In the meantime, the Burmans, having mortgaged the 1956 crop, had to turn down tempting cash offers for it.

On the administrative side, the best efforts of Burma's many able officials had been frustrated by proliferating committees, to which even the simplest inquiries had to be referred. A Bureau of Special Investigation, under U Nu's direct control, was supposed to check corruption; instead, it merely intimidated officials and reduced administrative efficiency still further. That public dissatisfaction was widespread was shown when the Prime Minister invited complaints about individual members of the AFPFL and replies came in profusion.

This public opinion poll – as it was, in effect – seems to have been the determining factor in U Nu's resignation in 1956. The change of Prime Ministers, however, made little difference. His successor, U Ba Swe, was not conspicuously more successful than he had been, and U Nu himself devoted the major portion of his attention not to reorganizing his party but to national and international Buddhist affairs. He resumed the Premiership in June 1957, but it soon became apparent that the latent split in the AFPFL was widening beyond hope of repair. On one side were Ba Swe and the party's outstanding intellectual, Kyaw Nyein – both of them socialists of a more doctrinaire kind than U Nu – and on the other U Nu and his followers. The Prime Minister had moved a long way from the Marxist theorizings he had aired in his speech of 24 September 1947. Indeed, in January 1958, opening the third all-Burma congress of the AFPFL, he denounced Marxism as incompatible with Buddhism and specifically rejected it as an ideology for the AFPFL. This offended the Ba Swe–Kyaw Nein faction, and in June both men resigned from U Nu's cabinet, taking with them thirteen other Ministers and twenty-two parliamentary secretaries. Once again, however, it would be misleading to apply western labels to Burman politics. Though 'Marxist' in ideology, the Ba Swe–Kyaw Nein faction accused U Nu of being 'soft' to the Communists, and there was some substance in the accusation, in the sense that after the 1958 split U Nu kept a narrow majority in Parliament only by accepting the support of the forty-two deputies belonging to the pro-communist National United Front, although the NUF was in open touch with the communist insurgents in the jungles.

It is hard to resist the view that Burma was becoming ungovernable by western constitutional methods when General Ne Win took over in October 1958. In a deeper sense, indeed, Burma is a singularly difficult country to govern as a national unit, even in a traditional Burmese way, let alone as a western-style nation-state. The history of Burma before the British came, first as traders then as conquerors, is largely that of a struggle for dominance between the numerous tribes or ethnic groups – the Burmese, the Arakanese, the Shans, the Karens, the Kachins, the Mons, and others – who came down to the great Irrawaddy delta from the northern mountains. Although the Burmese were the last of these groups, they became the dominant one, and in 1044 they founded the great state of Pagan, whose ruined pagodas are among the most impressive archaeological remains in Asia. Pagan was destroyed in 1287, and it was not until the conquering King Alaungpaya established his dynasty in 1755 that a semblance of unified rule returned to Burma. In the intervening centuries petty kingdoms had contended ineffectually for supremacy.

It is not by coincidence that the three examples of post-independence chaos we are considering in this chapter – Burma, Indonesia and the former Belgian Congo – are all large countries populated by a variety of national or tribal groups, each with its own language and customs. This problem is familiar enough in European history and has been solved in a variety of ways. In Britain it was solved, at least on paper, in 1707 by the union of the Scottish and English Parliaments, and though few historians would dispute that England is politically the dominant element in the United Kingdom, no impartial observer of politics or commerce in Westminster and the City of London could support the view that the Scots are an oppressed people. In Russia, both under the Tsars and under the Bolsheviks, a similar but much vaster problem has been 'solved' by the ruthless Russification of the minority peoples.

For my part, I am convinced that a federal system is the only one that can offer proper safeguards for minority peoples, and this is not only desirable but also possible in countries like Burma and Indonesia, where, by and large, each ethnic group has its own geographical area. In practice, however, the dominant race is likely to do its utmost to impose itself on its weaker neighbours. In Burma's case history has already shown that the Burmese claim a vocation to unify the geographical expression that is Burma under their own leadership. Indeed, it could be argued that in weak States with several component

groups and poor communications federalism invites further
weakness, which only a strongly centralized, unitary State could
avoid. There is some force in this argument, but it is valid, in
practice, only if the State is in fact strong enough to impose its
will on all areas within its jurisdiction. It remains to be seen
whether the Burmese State will prove that strong, even under
military rule.

If the number of ethnic communities is one of Burma's built-
in problems, so are two other legacies from the past: Buddhism
and the tradition of enrichment in office. The continuing power
of both has been analysed with great subtlety and perception
(though many passages are marred by American academic jargon) by Professor Lucian W. Pye in *Politics, Personality and
Nation Building: Burma's Search for Identity* (Yale, 1962). The
passivity of Buddhism – particularly Buddhism of the Lesser
Vehicle or Hinayana, as practised in Burma, Siam, Cambodia,
Laos, and Ceylon – is indeed a major factor in the political behaviour of the Buddhist peoples of South-East Asia. Nor is the
acceptance of favours while in office – which the West calls
corruption – confined to Burma; it is endemic throughout Asia,
western as well as eastern. The complexity and subtlety of the
Burmese mentality are, however, exceptional, even by Asian
standards. On the one hand, Buddhism is a gentle religion; on
the other, the cruelty of the later Burmese kings, many of whom
were insane, was terrifying. As Pye recalls, 'Thisi-thu-Dhamana
sought to increase his power through an elixir made of 6,000
human hearts procured by his officials.' These officials, whose
appointments were not hereditary, kept or lost their jobs entirely by favour or anger of the King – much as did the favourites of England's Tudor sovereigns – and this circumstance
greatly stimulated their talent for intrigue. Tenure being in-
secure, it was perhaps natural that officials should seek to enrich
themselves while the going was good. British rule introduced the
fresh concept that rewards should be given on merit and that
loyalty should be owed to the job and not to the richest patron.
But the period of British rule – 1886–1948 – was short in historical terms, and it can hardly be said that British concepts of
public service had superseded older traditions. (Indeed, under

British rule, as under any colonial rule, advancement was reserved to those who were prepared to co-operate with the
Government, and this must have seemed to many Burmese like
a continuation of the older system in another guise.)

Another factor in the Burmese character that has had a profound effect on the conduct of affairs since independence is a
deep distrust of, and distaste for, the profit motive. It was the
profit motive that brought the British to Burma, and it is the
profit motive that has given the Indians, and to a lesser extent
the Chinese, their dominant position in Burmese trade. The
abolition of the profit motive, through socialism, was a major
objective of Burma's nationalists. This explains why U Nu was
unwilling to allow the free play of a market economy in Burma,
though there is little doubt that only this would have enabled
the Burmese economy to recover after the Second World War.
General Ne Win's approach tends to be more pragmatic, but he,
too, announced a programme of 'Burmese socialism' and 'social
welfare' shortly after he resumed power in 1962. Since then,
indeed, he has seemed bent on carrying out U Nu's ideas more
efficiently than U Nu, including the most counterproductive
ones in economic terms. Thus, on 15 February 1963 he announced the total nationalization of the import and export
trade, and even of distribution, and a week later he nationalized
banking. These were retrograde steps that constituted so many
question-marks over Burma's future.

3. THE POLITICS OF INSECURITY

To single out Burma for special treatment was arbitrary but not
ill-intentioned. It might equally have been, say, Indonesia or
Ceylon, or – to choose examples that have more deeply disturbed the world – the Congo or Algeria. The Asian cases are,
however, different in kind from the African ones. Each of the
three – Burma, Indonesia, and Ceylon – had a long and turbulent history before the European conquerors came, bringing
unity of a kind that had not previously been achieved. All three
rapidly reverted to their traditional insecurity and disunity
(though Ceylon had made a better start than the others). In all
three, governments that proclaimed themselves socialist

wrought varying degrees of economic havoc in countries whose natural resources entitled them to prosperity.

In 1952, reaching Indonesia's capital, Djakarta, from Melbourne, I had been appalled by its discomforts: the pitted roads, the hotels – three or four to a room – the toilets that would not flush, the taps that stayed dry when turned on, the lifts that failed to respond, the telephones that brought no answer. But there was worse to come. Ten years later, in the *New Statesman* of 25 May 1962, Paul Johnson wrote:

> Djakarta is a frightening and sinister city. Nobody will go there except on inescapable business. When I arrived, there was, in addition to smallpox, a serious outbreak of cholera. The public health system has virtually broken down. . . . My hotel, once the best in the region, was in chaos. Most of the rooms had been seized by army officers and their families. A stinking mush was served twice a day in the restaurant; otherwise no food was available. In my room, the mosquitoes swarmed expectantly; gouts of red slime issued from the shower.

Shortly afterwards, in an editorial published on 9 June 1962, *The Economist* described Indonesia's general condition in these terms:

> All the earmarks of a state in collapse are present, from inflation and hoarding to corruption and administrative chaos. Exports declined sharply in the second half of last year, and by the year's end the gold and foreign exchange reserves were down to a point so near zero that no statistical sleight of hand could disguise the fact. In 1960, sugar exports had earned $3 million; last year there were none. A third of the country's tin dredges were reported to be lying idle. Slight increases in the value of petroleum, coffee, copra and palm oil exports did not compensate for the major falls in sales of other commodities. Rice imports, already the highest for any country in the world, are still rising; at least in the cities, rice is selling at up to twenty times the official price; there is malnutrition and even, in some parts of Java, famine. Distribution difficulties,

largely attributable to the persecution of Chinese traders in recent years, and therefore government-made, have aggravated food shortages. Cholera and smallpox complete a dismal picture.

The bare listing of a few of Indonesia's exported products in this paragraph is a measure of the wealth of this great arc of favoured islands. How, then, has it come to such a pass? The automatic attribution of all blame to the Dutch 'colonialists', made by almost every Indonesian politician and official, has long ceased even to sound convincing. True, the Dutch deliberately refrained from training Indonesian civil servants in the high grades. Indeed, they had no intention of surrendering their Far Eastern empire, and therefore made no provision for a successor administration. But when their lack of vision and their stubbornness have been deplored in full measure, two awkward facts remain: that they transferred sovereignty to the Indonesian nationalists in 1949, and that they were expelled from Indonesia in 1957. To an overwhelming degree, the Indonesians are to blame for their own misfortunes, and to an even more overwhelming degree, the responsibility must be placed on the shoulders of one man: President Sukarno. It is not, I think, by coincidence, that Indonesia's drift into chaos was kept relatively within bounds between 1949 and 1956 (when the President, in effect, shared power with an able and honest vice-President, Dr Hatta, and occasionally had sensible and competent men in office), but went rapidly from bad to worse after 1956, when he gradually acquired dictatorial powers. Once Dr Sukarno's power had become untrammelled, he consistently chose demagogic, irrelevant, and, in the result, disastrous courses.

The facts speak for themselves. As a community, Indonesia has a fundamental problem in that two-thirds of its 96 million people live in the overcrowded central island of Java, whereas neighbouring Sumatra, with three times the area, has only some 16 million inhabitants and large regions of fertile land. Granted that the Dutch neglected this problem (which was less tragic in size in their day) and that the Sumatrans are deeply afraid of

Javanese numbers, a policy of resettlement ought to be the first call on any Indonesian government's energies. Yet virtually nothing has been done about it since independence. Instead, Sukarno's administration has squandered the country's wealth and human resources in economically damaging exhibitions of nationalism. The expulsion of the Dutch was one; the persecution of the Chinese, who controlled the distributive trade, was another. By accepting Soviet credits of some £130 million for arms purchases in January 1961, President Sukarno saddled his already nearly bankrupt treasury with a burden that it could not afford; and by pursuing his claim to West New Guinea to the day of actual success, he saddled his overstretched administration with further tasks it should have been spared. As if this were not enough, the President invited the Russians to provide Djakarta with a grandiose stadium for the Asian Games in 1962, at a cost of £40 million in skills and in materials that could have been put to better use. If the sin of neglect can be laid at the door of the colonialists, the deadlier sins of political irresponsibility and economic lunacy can be blamed on the architect of Indonesia's independence.

In comparison with Indonesia's three thousand islands and 96 million people, Ceylon looks a manageable proposition: one island, half the size of England and with a population of only 7½ million at the time of independence in 1948. In miniature, however, its problems were much the same as Indonesia's. A population explosion: by 1961 there were about 10 million Ceylonese to feed, 2½ million more than in 1948. A communal problem: low-country Sinhalese and hill-country Sinhalese, Tamils from India, Moors and Dutch-descended Burghers. A multiplicity of parties, including some of the few officially tolerated Trotskyists in the world.

There was also, although it had seemed remote under British law and order, a past of singular turbulence and even ferocity. Ceylon's history is a long record of princely invasions from southern India, of struggles for ascendancy between the Sinhalese kings of Pihiti in northern Ceylon and the rival chieftains of the south, of colonization by the Chinese, Portuguese, Dutch, and British. The most efficient of Ceylon's oppressors was, however, native-born: in the twelth century King Prakrama Bahu, having made himself master of all Lanka (as Ceylon was then known), invaded Burma and India, built a palace of 4,000 apartments, ruined his country, and reduced his people to a state akin to slavery.

With such a heritage, it is perhaps surprising that law and order reigned even for nearly a decade after the British had handed over to an independent Ceylonese government. Indeed, an earlier generation of British administrators had tasted Ceylonese communal violence and had had to impose martial law in 1915 to quell riots between Buddhists and Mohammedans. This, however, was a dim memory in 1948, and Ceylon under its first three post-independence premiers – the Senanayakes, father and son, and the ebullient, western-looking Sir John Kotelawala – looked and felt much the same to visitors and residents alike as it had under British rule. Colombo still had its beggars, but tea-growing was prosperous, and the Sinhalese were gently Buddhist and unfanatical. The 1956 elections, however, brought the late Mr Solomon Bandaranaike and his Sri Lanka Freedom party to power. With them came the seeds of communal strife, and the accoutrements of Indian-style independence: neutralism, and half-way socialism.

Like Nehru, Solomon West Ridgeway Dias Bandaranaike came of a wealthy family. His father, an Anglican and a KCMG, had sent him to one of Ceylon's leading Christian schools, then on to Christ Church, Oxford, where his contemporaries included Sir Anthony Eden. Back in Ceylon in 1925, he renounced Christianity for Buddhism and founded the Sinhala Maha Sabha, a Sinhalese nationalist party modelled on the Indian Congress. There is no need to follow his career in detail, but it is important to know that he was brought to power mainly by Buddhist and Sinhalese extremists who hoped he would reduce Ceylon's non-Buddhist and non-Sinhalese to the status of second-class citizens. In the event, he went far enough to outrage the non-Sinhalese but stopped far short of meeting the wishes of his own supporters.

In foreign policy he asserted Ceylon's neutrality by getting the British to evacuate their naval base in 1957. In economic policy he threatened to nationalize the tea plantations (thereby making the planters doubt whether they had a future in Ceylon), but did not carry out his threat (thus disappointing his socialist followers). Another threat of his, to nationalize the life-insurance companies, *was* carried out, but not until 1960 and by his widow, who succeeded him. His most controversial measure, however, was the Official Language Act, which made Sinhalese the only official language. This pleased the Sinhalese by discriminating against the Tamils, but disappointed the extreme Sinhalese nationalists by allowing the Tamils to use their own language in residual official ways.

Communal violence in June 1956 turned out to be a mild foretaste of the violence in store. On 22 May 1958 a train carrying Tamils to a convention at Vavuniya, 160 miles north of Colombo, was stopped by a Sinhalese mob, which murdered four of the passengers and robbed and assaulted the rest. This was the signal for ten murderous days in which the unleashed Sinhalese mobs, working to what was clearly a nationally organized plan, set fire to Tamil premises, stripped Tamils naked in the streets, beat them, and robbed them. In Polonnaruwa, the Buddhist holy city, seven Tamils met death jumping down a well to escape Sinhalese rioters who had burnt their houses down. Whenever they could, the outnumbered Tamils fought back, and Sinhalese motorists venturing into the Tamil countryside were pulled from their cars and beaten. Within a few days there was hardly a corner of the island that escaped the contagion of hysteria and brutality. The Government proclaimed a state of emergency throughout Ceylon on 27 May, and order was painfully and gradually restored during the first week of June. The Tamils' Federal Party, which had announced its intention of launching a civil disobedience campaign in protest against the abrogation of the language agreement, was outlawed and fifty-eight of its members, including all its Members of Parliament, were placed under house arrest; unfairly, it seemed to outside observers, only one Sinhalese was arrested: Mr K. M. P. Rajaratna, leader of the extremist National Liberation Front (which, more fairly, was also outlawed). On

31 July Mr Bandaranaike announced that 6,302 had been arrested under the emergency regulations, together with 2,254 who had been detained for security reasons. Earlier, on 4 July, he had announced the deaths of 159 people in the rioting; but most observers thought this figure understated the truth, and estimates ranged as high as 500 deaths.

To his credit, and in the face of a high-pitched whine of disapproval from Sinhalese Members of Parliament, Mr Bandaranaike lost little time in introducing a Bill which allowed the Tamils to be educated in their own language; they were even to be allowed to sit for public-service examinations in Tamil, so long as they also knew Sinhalese. Although the Prime Minister had taken the precaution of submitting his Bill to a conference of Buddhist priests for approval, he had, in effect, signed his own death warrant by introducing it, even though it was passed by forty-six votes to three. On 25 September 1959 a Buddhist monk who had entered the grounds of his private residence in Colombo drew a revolver and wounded him in the hand, chest, and stomach. Mr Bandaranaike died the following morning.

To go from Burma, Indonesia, and Ceylon to the Congo and Algeria may seem a far cry in other ways besides geography, but there are similarities as well as differences between the two groups. Though neither Burma nor Ceylon, nor yet Indonesia, was a fully evolved nation when the western rulers moved in, each had an identifiable history and a long experience of shared cultural influences. After the colonial powers had withdrawn, traditional rivalries of culture or community reasserted themselves and there was a gradual reversion to varying degrees of anarchy or even chaos. In all three, but especially in Indonesia, the process was accelerated by the inadequacy of the leadership. Not one, however, had emerged into independence in such tragic circumstances as the Congo or Algeria. The Congo was a geographical area containing many tribes that had nothing in common beyond the accident of having been under Belgian rule (similarly, the Indonesian claim that West New Guinea was part of Indonesia rested mainly on the accident that it had been under Dutch rule). To call the Congo a nation, either before or after independence, was an abuse of language. The Algerians, on their side, could claim (on the same basis of reasoning) that they had been administered as an outlying province of the Turkish empire within roughly the same boundaries as today. But for more than 100 years from the time of the French conquest in the 1830s they had been conditioned to think of themselves as Frenchmen, albeit of an inferior kind. If (as I am inclined to believe) there now is an Algerian nation it has been forged by a certain community of effort and suffering during the harsh years of the Algerian revolution, and by the terrorist pressure of the Algerian nationalists. Algeria and the Congo have, however, something in common besides the accident of being on the same continent: both reached independence virtually denuded of the Europeans who had kept their economies running. This is fundamental.

To deal in adequate detail with either the Congolese or the Algerian tragedy would require a book in itself. It may be useful, however, to try to isolate some of the things that went wrong in the birth of these two independent countries.

To arrive in Leopoldville, as I did, on 21 November 1960, was to see the Congolese problem at its most dramatic. That evening I was one of the guests at a cocktail party given by Mr Sture Linner, the delightful, unruffled, and highly competent Swede who was running the civil side of the United Nations operation. As we sat on the balcony high above the spacious Belgian residential quarter, shots crackled in the middle distance. It was the start of a murderous incident that epitomized the Congolese tragedy. The men firing at each other were, on one side, Congolese troops, and on the other, UN troops – mainly Tunisians – who had been guarding a villa occupied by a Mr Nathaniel Welbeck of Ghana. Now Mr Welbeck claimed to be the Ghanaian chargé d'affaires and the villa, a former rest-house, had been accepted as the Ghanaian Embassy under its previous occupant, Mr Djin, the Ghanaian ambassador. Mr Djin, however, was back in Accra, and Mr Welbeck, who was very active by deed and word in Congolese affairs, had never

sought *agrément*. Was he or was he not Ghana's chargé d'affaires?
Under strict diplomatic protocol, he was not. President Nkrumah, his chief, had declined to have him accredited because he
did not recognize the existing Congolese administration. Mr
Welbeck had been calling press conferences to say that the only
legal government in the Congo was that of Mr Patrice Lumumba. At that time, however, Mr Lumumba, though still
alive, was under house arrest, and the only central administration was that of Colonel Mobutu, the Congolese Army's chief of
staff, who had seized power (a conventional phrase, there being
very little power to seize, as he soon discovered), on 15 September, and the so-called College of Commissioners which he had
set up and which consisted of fifteen young Congolese who had
had, or were having, a university education. Colonel Mobutu
had had an unexpected and intoxicating success a few weeks
earlier in expelling from the Congo the ambassadors and staffs
of the Soviet and Czech Embassies. Now he was looking around
for another success, and the bumptious Mr Welbeck seemed an
ideal candidate for expulsion. Mobutu gave Welbeck twenty-
four hours to get out, and the ultimatum had just expired on
21 November when I reached Leopoldville. When Mobutu sent
one of his Commissioners to ask Welbeck to leave quietly the
Ghanaian slammed the door in his face.

There would have been no violence if the UN, under its
Indian commander, General Rikhye, and its Indian head, Mr
Rajeshwar Dayal, had not unaccountably ordered a part of its
force to protect Mr Welbeck. On what grounds this order was
given, I was never able to discover. True, the Soviet and Czech
Ambassadors had been given UN protection on request, but
they were accredited diplomatists and Mr Welbeck was not.
Then again, had Mr Welbeck shown some awareness of the
situation he was in, violence would have been unnecessary. But
his natural arrogance was reinforced by strict instructions from
President Nkrumah not to yield an inch. As the hours of the
ultimatum ticked away, the Ghanaian leader sent his army's
chief of staff, General Alexander, back to Leopoldville (where
he had until lately served as chief of the Ghanaian UN contingent) to tell Welbeck to stay put. Arriving in an Iliyushin-14

transport, General Alexander soon saw that the situation was untenable and tried to send word to Mr Welbeck. But it was already too late: the fighting had started.

Who started it was another story. Within the next twenty-four hours I was given three entirely different versions of it by the same harassed UN spokesman, and a choice of further versions was available in Leopoldville. Somebody – a Tunisian, a Ghanaian, or a Congolese – panicked and opened fire. Soon bodies littered the garden and the veranda of the Ghanaian 'embassy'. Among them was Mobutu's closest friend, Colonel N'kokolo (who was given a state funeral two days later, in the presence of Colonel Mobutu and wailing Congolese women). During the night Congolese troops arrested several dozen UN people, molested them in various ways, and kept some of them standing all night. Next morning Mr Welbeck was flown to Accra in General Alexander's company.

'Somebody panicked'. . . . Panic was indeed the normal state in Leopoldville. Wherever one went one met fixed bayonets wielded by helmeted Congolese soldiers who bridled at the slightest imagined or genuine insult to 'our government' (the College of Commissioners) and considered ONUC (Opération Nations Unies Congo) as a particularly malevolent tribe. A group of especially ferocious-looking ones surrounded the taxi that was wandering around the residential quarter in search for the British Ambassador's home. The Congolese driver, who was quavering with fright, said to me: 'Don't put your head out, sir. They are without pity!' It appeared that we had unintentionally strayed to within a few yards of the villa where Lumumba was being detained. I disregarded my driver's advice, on the ground that the soldiers were more likely to shoot if I said nothing than if I spoke. So I put my head out and asked if they could direct me to the British Ambassador's residence. They waved me on with their bayonets and with a grunt which, I suppose, told me that I was lucky to keep my life and was being too hopeful if I thought I was going to get information out of them as well as mercy.

In the midst of this trigger-happy excitement, the Ambassador, Mr (now Sir Ian) Scott, maintained an unflappable

British presence. He had indeed chosen the moment of maximum panic, at the time of the mutiny of the Belgian-trained Force Publique, to bring out his wife to Leopoldville. He got on well with the Congolese, and his theory, which my taxi incident seemed to support, was that at all levels the Congolese were nervous or afraid and only needed to be talked to in a friendly way to relax.

One might have expected to find Leopoldville in much the same condition as Djakarta had been during the past ten years, but the reality was startlingly different. The Belgians were still running the hotels, which were clean and efficient; the restaurants, crowded by healthy Flemings, made one feel one was in Brussels (although emancipated young Congolese of both sexes frequented the bars); and one could even drink the tap-water with impunity.

To be sure, one had the feeling that the organized life of this improbably prosperous-looking city was hanging by a thread that might snap at any moment. The multi-national UN civil force was making sure the water was filtered, was tending the sick and wounded, and keeping air and radio communications open. It was even finding the money to enable the Central Government to pay its functionaries and soldiery. But, however long the UN operation was prolonged (and it was kept going, by various devices, far beyond UN's capacity or willingness to meet its costs), the UN personnel there, from Dayal and Linner down, were transients who would have to leave some day. The work they were doing was indispensable, but in no sense a permanent solution to the Congolese problem. Moreover, on the political and military sides there was much to criticize in the UN operation (even before Mr Conor Cruise O'Brien gave his controversial orders in the Katanga in September 1961). In the early months of the operation the United Arab Republic, Ghana, and Guinea had used their units in the UN force for the advancement of their pan-African policies. President Nkrumah, who considered Lumumba his protégé, had the pretention of guiding his actions from afar. Some of the letters Dr Nkrumah sent the Congo's first Prime Minister were captured when Colonel Mobutu arrested him, and Mr Welbeck publicly declared they were genuine and he was proud to say so. One of them, of which I have a photo-copy, read, in part:

My dear Patrice,

. . . Whenever in doubt, consult me. Brother, we have been in the game for some time now and we know how to handle the imperialists and the colonialists. The only imperialist or colonialist I trust is a dead one. If you do not wish to bring Congo to ruin, follow the advice I have given. Brother, have implicit faith in me, I shall not let you down. Your stand for United Congo and for African unity commend you dearly to me. Your friend, Mr Djin (Ghana's ambassador) is there to help you in every possible way.

On the administrative side, the most disquieting thing was the undisguised hostility between the Congolese administration (before Mr Adoula took over as Prime Minister) and its Belgian advisers, on the one hand, and the UN, on the other. It was a sterile and acrimonious two-way traffic, with each side obstructing the other's efforts, orders, or initiatives in every possible way. There, indeed, lies the clue to the fundamental absurdity of the Congo situation: to what went wrong and why.

The absurdity was that the only people who knew the Congo and were capable of running it, the Belgians, were not being allowed to do the job. How this happened requires some explanation. The Belgians made three fundamental errors in the Congo. They failed even to envisage the possibility of independence, and therefore made no provision for it; they then panicked and, in effect, 'dropped everything', handing over to the Congolese leaders with a haste that was as irresponsible as their previous dilatoriness; finally, they drew up a constitution – the Loi Fondamentale, which was quite unsuited to the Congo's needs. The Congo had been Leopold II's private preserve and slave-hunting ground. It became a Belgian business venture, state-supported and insulated for half a century from the political contagions of the outside world, including Belgium itself. Harsh though Belgian rule had been, the Belgians did plough back a good deal of the wealth they extracted from the Congo's

G

soil, and a good deal of it did reach the Africans (many Europeans would envy the workers' houses built for the Africans in the Congo). Primary education was widespread, if not quite universal. But secondary and university education were very hard to come by. For years after the Second World War the Congo was a huge and prosperous oasis of peace and apparent contentment in the heart of a continent that was increasingly convulsed by nationalist stirrings, and the great majority of Belgians took pride in their work, pointing to the total ban on politics as the enviable secret of their success. It could not last, however, and at least one far-sighted Belgian, Professor A. A. J. van Bilsen, saw that it could not and dared to suggest that the time had come to prepare for Congolese independence, in *A Thirty-Year Plan for the Political Emancipation of Belgian Africa*. By non-Belgian standards, Professor van Bilsen was being cautious enough, since he envisaged independence only in the 1980s; but for his pains, he was villified, ostracized, and indeed treated like a dangerous revolutionary. It is doubtful whether any Belgian government could have held the fort that long in the face of nationalist torrent that was unleashed in Africa in the late 1950s. But if van Bilsen's proposals had been adopted as official policy in 1954, when he made them, there is at least a fair chance that independence might have been delayed a few more years and that it might have come through a fruitful partnership between the Belgians and Congolese. This, however, was one of history's missed opportunities.

In August 1958 that other dangerous revolutionary, General de Gaulle, spoke in Brazzaville, and the contagion of his ideas blew across the fast-flowing Congo river into Leopoldville. The General, who was on his constitutional referendum tour of French Africa, had offered the French Congo the choice between autonomous rule within the French Community and independence. Two days later, Lumumba was asking for independence and, in the meantime, a say in Belgium's African policy. However, it took the riots of January 1959 in Leopoldville, and further disturbances throughout the year, to shock the Belgians into an awareness that something had to be done. Having taken this decision, which had become inevitable (and was therefore politically right), they went much too far and much too fast.

They invited the Congolese leaders to a round-table conference in Brussels, agreed to independence at the catastrophically early date of 30 June, and organized general elections in May, which, as might have been foreseen, produced an incoherently fragmented Parliament. Mr Lumumba, the only Congolese leader who preached against tribalism, won more seats than anybody else, but even he controlled only 33 seats out of 137. The total irrelevance of the western democratic process in an uneducated country was never better demonstrated: the elections alone would have made the Congo ungovernable from the start. Moreover, intent on preserving a unity which could exist only so long as they were there to enforce it, the Belgians drafted the constitution of a unitary state. Even more than in Indonesia (where the Indonesians themselves insisted on it) or Burma, this was a fundamental error. At the Brussels talks Mr Tshombe of the Katanga had proposed a loose federation for the Congo with strong regional autonomy for the provinces. It has become so fashionable to revile Tshombe that it is easy to forget that he made this proposal and to overlook the sense of it. Had it been accepted, there is little doubt that Tshombe (powerfully backed by the Union Minière Company) would not have proclaimed Katanga's secession from the Congo, and that some, at least, of the rich province's revenues would have reached the Central Government, instead of none at all.

It is not the least of the paradoxes of the Congo crisis that UN officials justified the protracted effort to bring the Katanga under Leopoldville's authority by constant reference to the Belgian-drafted Loi Fondamentale. In fact, the Loi Fondamentale, which was never ratified, is a poor legal basis for the Congolese State. As for Tshombe and the Katanga's secession, however much backing he may have got from powerful Belgian or British financial interests, and even though his party had won only a minority of seats in the provincial assembly, there seems no reason whatever why it should be immoral for the Katanga to secede from the Congo and moral for, say, Dr Banda's

Nyasaland to secede from the Rhodesian Federation. Yet African nationalists of all shades have had extraordinary success in persuading non-Africans, especially in Britain, that both these contradictory propositions are true.

Having said this, it was clearly desirable that part at least of the Katanga's revenues should go to the Central Government, for otherwise the Congo could not be made viable for many years, and the UN (or rather those of its members who actually paid the bills, principally the United States and Britain) would be stuck there indefinitely. We are not, however, concerned, except incidentally, with the problem of Katanga. Our concern is with what went wrong in the Congo. We have looked at some of the major Belgian errors, and it is time we looked at the fundamental error on the UN side.

Five days after independence the Belgian-trained Force Publique (later the Congolese Army) mutinied, and a wave of anti-Belgian violence swept the Congo. The Belgian Government flew in troops to protect their nationals, and Mr Lumumba's Government appealed to the UN Security Council to get the Belgians out again. This is how the UN came to be in the Congo. The Belgian move was represented as aggression, and the whole UN operation was conditioned from the start by the emotive reactions of the Afro-Asian group in the United Nations, which, of course, had just been joined by the new Congolese Government. The notion of Congolese independence was an absurdity, but the Congo had been admitted to the UN as an independent State. The prevailing atmosphere was anti-colonial and anti-imperialist, that is, in the context of the moment, anti-Belgian. The Soviet Union and its partners naturally associated themselves with the prevailing emotions (though later they were to denounce the UN operation as 'colonialist'). France was to dissociate itself from the UN operation and refuse to contribute to its cost; Britain was ready to explain and defend the Belgian action. But when the vote came, on a Tunisian draft resolution, the British and French merely abstained instead of vetoing it. The Tunisian text called on the Belgians to withdraw their troops and called on the UN—

to authorize the Secretary-General to take the necessary measures, in consultation with the Government of the Congo Republic, to furnish that Government with all the military assistance which may be necessary until, by the efforts of the Congolese Government, with the technical assistance of the United Nations, the National Security Forces are, in the opinion of the Government, in a position to deal fully with their tasks.

Perhaps inevitably, then, the whole operation was conceived as an anti-colonial operation, and this fact lies at the heart of the Congo's protracted troubles. Because of the prevailing anti-Belgian hysteria, it was unthinkable to staff the civil operation with the only people who could have made a *long-term* success of it – the Belgians. Clearly, if the Belgians had been recruited, expertise of a calibre that was simply not available outside Belgium would immediately have been put at the UN's disposal. The whole operation could have been drastically shortened, for it would have been relatively easy, within a short time, to transfer Belgian officials to the service of the Congolese Government and for the UN itself to withdraw. But given the prevailing emotions, Afro-Asian hands would have been thrown up in horror at the very idea, even though Ghana and Nigeria, to name only two examples, had retained the services of British advisers after independence and nobody had suggested that their sovereignty was being impaired. And so the Congo was subjected to the sinister futility of UN officials at daggers drawn with the Belgian officials who had, willy nilly, been recruited by Colonel Mobutu's Commissioners. Later indeed, Mr Adoula's Government engaged Belgians in suitable numbers, and even the UN quietly took on a few. But how much trouble could have been saved if this had been done right at the beginning.

In Algeria, too, it is clear enough what went wrong. There were always four main elements in the complex Algerian equation, and all the troubles of that maltreated country – including the war itself – can be traced back to the determination of some of the people concerned to ignore one or more of the elements of which they disapproved. These elements were: the French of France; the Europeans of Algeria, who called themselves French but were of variegated Mediterranean origins; the Moslems who wanted to keep the French connexion; and those who wanted to sever it. The myth of *Algérie française,* which sustained the French Army in its war against the Moslem nationalists during the first five years of fighting, rested on two fallacies: that France would never abandon Algeria, and that the population of Algeria consisted only of Frenchmen and of Moslems who supported the French connexion. The myth of *Algérie algérienne,* a phrase which General de Gaulle coined on 4 November 1959, rested on another fallacy: that the great majority of Algeria's population favoured autonomy in association with France and that the Europeans could be persuaded or forced to acquiesce in it. The myth of the 'Algerian republic', proclaimed by the nationalist Front de Libération Nationale (FLN) on 19 September 1958, also rested on a fallacy: that an overwhelming majority of the Moslem population supported independence and that a substantial majority of the Europeans could be induced to accept it as well. In other words, during the first five years of the war successive French governments dismissed the Moslem nationalists as of no account; and during the last two and a half years of it General de Gaulle ignored the Europeans. On the rebel side, the FLN dismissed the very large numbers of Moslems who were against full independence as 'traitors' and murdered them on a scale designed to make the hesitant conform. On the European side, the great majority dismissed the nationalists as a bunch of criminals and refused to the bitter end to contemplate the possibility of living under an independent, Moslem-dominated government. Taken as a whole, the Algerian war was a pitiless demonstration of the truth that in politics the longer a refusal to face facts is sustained, the worse the final retribution.

Only General de Gaulle could bring the Algerian war to an end, but in the last stages even he did it badly. It is not possible, given the scope of this book, to trace, even in outline, the zigzag course of the General's changes of front, his evasions and unkept promises, his cryptic phrases and shifting objectives. He had been brought to power in 1958 by army officers speaking in the name of 'French Algeria'; his return had narrowly averted a civil war in France itself, and his dominant preoccupation was to find a solution in Algeria (or, failing a solution, a way of getting rid of the Algerian problem) without sparking off a civil war. That the danger was real was shown by three major challenges to his authority: the insurrection of the barricades in Algiers in January 1960, the 'putsch' of the generals, again in Algiers, in April 1961, and the formation of the OAS (organisation de l'Armée Secrète) by officers who felt he had betrayed them. He did avert a civil war in metropolitan France, but not the wave of OAS excesses in Algeria itself during the first few months. And his errors of judgement, as well as those of the FLN, gave independent Algeria an even worse start than it need have had.

On de Gaulle's side there were two major errors in the closing stages of the Algerian tragedy. One was his refusal, during the Franco-Algerian talks at Evian and Lugrin in the spring of 1961, to concede that the Sahara was part of Algeria (although he finally did concede that it was, but only *after* the talks had broken down). This stubbornness on a point he was shortly to concede delayed the final agreement with the FLN by eight months and gave the OAS time to organize itself. His second major error was in refusing to release Mr Benbella, the dominant figure in the Algerian revolution, who had been in French hands since 1956, until after the negotiations with the FLN had been completed. Had Mr Benbella been released in time to take part in the negotiations, he would have been associated with them from the start; and in that event the FLN might have preserved its unity, which it lost during the first few days of independence with disastrous consequences for Algeria.

Until 1957 the French Sahara had always been administered as part of French Algeria. In 1956, however, French technicians made spectacular discoveries of oil and natural gas in the Saharan region. The following year the Sahara was detached from Algeria, administratively speaking, divided into two departments (Saoura and Oasis), and placed under a new body named the Organisation Commune des Régions Sahariennes or OCRS. The OCRS was conceived as a geographical development board, and its mandate extended to the contiguous Saharan areas of French-speaking Negro Africa: Niger, Tchad, Soudan (now Mali), and Mauretania. The FLN, not unnaturally, refused to recognize these changes, which they considered a French trick to deprive them of the riches of their own soil once independence had been won. The French, on their side, argued that the discoveries had been made by France, which had then furnished the capital and skill to exploit them; and moreover, that the Sahara belonged to all the peoples of the desert and not just to the Algerians (though the mandate of the OCRS naturally did not extend to independent Tunisia and Morocco, also Saharan countries).

During the two abortive rounds of Franco-Algerian negotiations, in May and June 1961 at Evian, and in July at the Chateau de Lugrin, not far away, the French side, led by M. Louis Joxe, the Minister for Algerian affairs, stuck undeviatingly to its argument that the Sahara was a separate question, outside the terms of reference of the talks. This was the rock on which the talks eventually foundered. Mr Belkacem Krim, vice-premier in the FLN's provisional government, who led the Algerian side, put it this way in a press conference he called on 31 July to explain why the talks had failed:

> All the African countries which have recovered their sovereignty have obtained their independence within their previous territorial limits. Why should Algeria be an exception? The French government, which has finally abandoned the myth of 'French Algeria', has invented a new myth, that of 'French Sahara'. We are asked to put the Algerian Sahara into cold storage. Knowing our determination to safeguard the integrity of our territory at any cost, was not this a clear sign of the French government's refusal to negotiate?

On his side, M. Joxe, broadcasting on 1 August, complained of the Algerians that: 'From the first session . . . they stopped at the word "Sahara" and refused to proceed any farther until they were given satisfaction and until their sovereignty over the

Sahara was immediately recognized.' And he went on to repeat the familiar French arguments about the Sahara.

Though the French attitude had been disappointing, it had, at least on the Sahara, been consistent. But only a few weeks later, on 6 September, General de Gaulle casually 'gave away' the Sahara as though it were of no consequence. He said:

> ... there is not a single Algerian – I know – who does not think that the Sahara must form part of Algeria, and ... there could not be an Algerian government, whatever its relations with France, which would not have to demand Algerian sovereignty over the Sahara all the time. The fact is that if an Algerian State is formed and is associated with France the great majority of the population of the Sahara will want to joint it, even if they have not explicitly done so before. That means that in Franco-Algerian negotiations, whether with the FLN or with another representative body, the question of sovereignty over the Sahara does not arise. .... What interests us is that if there is to be an agreement, it should provide for an association which safeguards our interests. .... It should also be clear that the peoples of the Sahara must be consulted about their fate.

These magnanimous but tardy words, had they been pronounced before or during the Evian and Lugrin negotiations, would probably have ensured their success. By delaying his Saharan 'gift' until after the talks had broken down, the General did pave the way for a resumption of the talks but did not immediately remove Algerian suspicions. And indeed the talks were not finally resumed, after intermittent secret contacts, until 7 March 1962. It was this delay that enabled the OAS to perfect its organization and lay plans for its campaign of terrorism, both in metropolitan France and in Algeria. True, the OAS already existed by the time the Evian talks began and had claimed the credit for a number of terrorist outrages, including the murder of the mayor of Evian. But the OAS became a power to be reckoned with only after the generals' putsch in April 1962, when the officers who had supported the putsch, including Generals Salan and Jouhaud, took it over. Success at Evian or Lugrin would almost certainly have wrecked its plans.

The other major error on General de Gaulle's part was to keep Mr Benbella in captivity until after his rival, Mr Belkacem Krim, had completed his negotiations with the French on 18 March 1962. For though Mr Benbella, who later became the first Prime Minister of independent Algeria, formally endorsed the agreements reached in his public statements, in private he let it be known that had he conducted the negotiations he would never have agreed to certain clauses. Moreover, he would have nothing to do with the complementary agreements reached between Mr Belkacem Krim and the OAS on 17 June 1962. As a result, Mr Krim was ousted from FLN's leadership and the European population left Algeria *en masse*. These disastrous happenings might have been avoided had General de Gaulle released Mr Benbella in time to lead the Algerian team in the negotiations. One can only surmise why he did not release the Algerian leader and his companions. It could have been out of a misplaced desire to endorse the legality of their imprisonment; but since General de Gaulle had not been in power when the French brought down the plane on which Benbella and his friends had been travelling from Rabat to Tunis at the time of their arrest in 1956, this seems hardly likely. More likely, the General may have considered Benbella a bargaining counter to be used in good time to wring concessions out of the Algerians; but there is no evidence that he did use Benbella in this way.

For the rest, the French Government and the FLN must share the blame for the tragic end of the French connexion, or, if you prefer, the dismal beginning of Algeria's independence. General de Gaulle had repeatedly made it clear, in his public statements in 1959 and 1960, that he regarded the FLN as representing only one of a number of Algerian tendencies. Others were the Europeans, who had various movements of their own, and the Mouvement National Algérien of Messali Hadj, the aged nationalist leader, which, broadly speaking, stood for equality of the communities within an autonomous, but not necessarily independent, Algeria. At a pinch, the MNA could have represented the interests of the many Algerian Moslems who had thrown in their lot with France. The FLN, however, had declared war on the MNA as well as on France, and indeed had expended perhaps as much energy seeking out and murdering MNA members as Frenchmen. To the end, the FLN refused absolutely to take part in a round-table conference at which the MNA – or, for that matter, the Europeans of Algeria – would also be represented. As for the Europeans, de Gaulle could not ignore them so long as the Army, or a large part of it, defended their cause (that the Army, even when supporting *Algérie française*, had a low opinion of the Europeans does not affect the point). Once he had smashed the generals' putsch, however, he evidently felt strong enough to ignore the Europeans. In the event, then, neither the MNA, nor the Algerians who had opted for French Algeria, nor the Europeans themselves, were represented at the negotiations that led to Algerian independence. Nor were they even consulted. As Professor Maurice Allais pointed out in *L'Algérie d'Evian* (L'Esprit Nouveau, Paris, 1962), this was one of the great injustices of the Evian agreements.

To say this is not to espouse the cause of the Europeans uncritically (Allais himself was one of the few Frenchmen who, as early as 1955, publicly defended the right of the Algerian Moslems to independence). The Europeans of Algeria, whether the relatively few great landowners of French descent or the great mass of lower-middle-class or working-class people of Spanish or other non-French origin, were a privileged minority. Volatile, turbulent, and, with obvious exceptions, unenlightened, they refused to countenance change of any kind. Indeed, it was because they had successfully resisted change that the Algerian revolution became inevitable. But the fact remains: Algeria was their country, not France. On the Moslem side, the FLN's highly efficient propaganda machine persuaded people in many countries that their movement was 'the revolution of an entire people', but this claim was disproved by the number of Moslems they found it necessary to murder, especially in the first three years of the insurrection. The fact is that many Moslems, probably hundreds of thousands, were in favour of maintaining the French connexion. These included many of those – and they were numerous – who had achieved a roughly European standard of living, the tens of thousands of 'harkis' who had served in the French Forces and who (rightly, as it turned out) feared the FLN's vengeance, and the many Moslem officials and others who had believed French promises that Algeria would be French for ever. This last group included the Moslem deputies elected to the French Parliament in the elections of 1959. In the eyes of the FLN all these men and women were traitors. But the fact remains: Algeria was their country, too, and there was no moral justification for the proposition that they should be condemned to be a persecuted minority in Algeria.

On the FLN side, some consideration was given to the European point of view, but absolutely none to that of Moslems who did not happen to share the FLN's demand for independence. On the surface, the FLN's attitude towards the European minority was indeed fairly reasonable. The FLN leadership recognized the fact that the Europeans were essential to the economic well-being of an independent Algeria. They were unwilling to allow them to retain their privileges (indeed, it was to end these that they had taken up arms), but they were willing to offer them what sounded like a fair place in the new Algeria. During the first round of negotiations at Evian Mr Saad Dahlab, who later became the provisional government's Foreign Minister, and who was one of the principal negotiators, explained the FLN's attitude to me in these words:

> Those who feel themselves Algerians can have full citizenship without distinction or discrimination. Those who feel French can either go home, or stay in Algeria, where they can be given every facility for working, practising their professions, etc. But we will not allow the continued existence of a privileged minority. We are not communists, but we *are* revolutionaries. A top limit will be fixed for the area of land holdings. The land reform will be applied to Moslems and Christians without distinction.

This was reasonable enough and, in the event, is essentially the offer that was incorporated into the Evian agreements of 18 March 1962. Why, then, did the Europeans reject it, as they

did, first by terrorism, then by mass exodus? to answer these
questions is to find reasons for the wave of frightfulness unleashed by the OAS in the cities of Algeria in the spring of 1962.
The exercise is worthwhile and yields illuminating conclusions,
but to attempt it does not imply, in the slightest degree, support
for terrorism. I was as sickened by the terrorism of the OAS as I
had been by that of the FLN, perhaps slightly more, because in
earlier days, in Indochina, I had known and liked such men as
Colonel Jean Gardes, who became one of the leaders of the
OAS. But moral disapproval, though comforting to the dis-
approver, does not alter the fact that political terrorism is the
last resort of desperate men who feel that other means of expression have become futile. This was true of the FLN, and it
was true of the OAS. Of course, the OAS included adventurists
and sadists and army men who embraced the cause of French
Algeria for their own ends. True again, only a few of its
leaders, including General Jouhaud and the civilian, Jean-
Jacques Susini, were of Algerian birth. Nevertheless, it is beyond
argument that the great mass of Algerian Europeans regarded
the OAS as an organization protecting their interests and supported it in all possible ways. Publicly, the OAS had proclaimed
its determination to destroy Algeria, leaving it as the French
had found it in the 1830s. While its campaign lasted, Algerian
Moslems were murdered in large numbers, and every day
brought news of installations blown up, from the University of
Algiers to docks and factories. In secret, however, the OAS had
on more than one occasion sent emissaries to the FLN proposing
negotiations. The arguments of these emissaries are worth re-
counting. They declared that the Evian agreements were valueless because they had been concluded by the 'wrong' partners,
that is the French and Algerian Governments. The 'right'
negotiating partners would have been the two communities of
Algeria, that is, the Europeans and the Moslems. Just as the
FLN was the true representative of the Moslems, so the OAS
was the true representative of the Europeans. The OAS was not
anti-Moslem and had supported French Algeria only because
that seemed the only way to preserve the unity of the Algerian
people. If the FLN refused to negotiate, then it would indeed

inherit the Algeria of 1830, that is, the land minus the Europeans and all they had brought to Algeria.

During the first few weeks of OAS terrorism the FLN turned a deaf ear to these arguments. The Moslem nationalists knew that they would soon be taking over anyway, and they believed that General de Gaulle was now irrevocably committed to smashing the OAS. Clinging to the belief that the majority of the Europeans would be ready to stay on in Algeria as a minority in a mainly Moslem state, they declined to accept the OAS claim to represent the Europeans. In the end, however, a section of the FLN became alarmed by the scale of the destruction unleashed by the OAS and by the increasing rate at which Europeans were leaving Algeria for France. In mid-June Mr Belkacem Krim, the negotiator of the Evian agreements, met Jean-Jacques Susini of the OAS at Rocher-Noir, the French administrative centre near Algiers, in the presence of Dr Mostefai, one of the FLN's representatives in the provisional executive set up after the Evian agreement, and of M. Jacques Chevallier, the liberal Frenchman who had been Mayor of Algiers and who was one of the first Frenchmen to opt for Algerian citizenship. On 17 June Susini and Belkacem Krim announced agreement; there was to be an amnesty for all who had taken part in acts of violence on either side; the Europeans would be allowed to join the local security forces; in return the OAS would call off its terrorism and encourage the Europeans to stay in Algeria and help to build the Algerian republic. On both sides this agreement (which had not been enshrined in an agreed text) was hailed as marking the final reconciliation between the two communities of Algeria.

The agreement, however, was still-born, although the OAS terrorism did stop. It soon became clear that Mr Belkacem Krim had taken part in the Rocher-Noir discussions against the wishes of an important section of the FLN leadership, headed by Mr Benbella. Within a few weeks the revolutionary movement, which had held its cohesion through the hard years of fighting, was split from top to bottom. There had always, of course, been latent dissensions within the movement: between those who saw the future of Algeria in terms of links with the Arab world and those who saw the value of French assistance and were willing to pay a price for it; between those who had fought in Algeria and those who had organized the rebellion from abroad; between the Kabyles (principally Mr Krim) and the Arabs (mainly Mr Benbella); between those who had been captured by the French and those who had kept their freedom. In all these aspects, Krim and Benbella were on opposite sides of the fence. Krim, the tough little ex-NCO who had fought in the field in Algeria, had broadened out into a diplomat and a statesman. Although never the titular head either of the FLN (which had none) or of the provisional government, he had been the dominant figure in the revolution after Benbella's capture. He had rallied international support to the Algerian cause and successfully negotiated Algeria's independence. He had the vision to see that unless the Evian agreements were complemented by agreements between the two communities, Algeria would indeed begin its sovereign life under the worst conditions. Benbella, in contrast, had learnt nothing and forgotten nothing during his years of captivity (this indeed is another reason for deploring the fact that de Gaulle kept him captive so long). He emerged to freedom in March 1962 determined to reassert his leadership and convinced that his colleagues had already given away too much at Evian. He saw the Algerian revolution in Egyptian and Cuban terms and hero-worshipped Nasser and Castro. True, he had been kept informed of the progress of the negotiations and had approved them, but he had not taken part in the talks and was in no position to veto their outcome. And if he was prepared, in the end, to swallow Evian, Rocher-Noir was more than he could stomach.

There is no need to recapitulate the unedifying and well-publicized struggle for power that took place before and after the advent of independence on 3 July. The important thing, in the context of this chapter, is that Benbella was the victor and Belkacem the loser. The knowledge that Benbella refused to endorse the Rocher-Noir understanding had already undermined the fragile confidence of the Europeans. His victory and that of the anti-western Colonel Boumedienne, who controlled the Algerian Army, broke it altogether. The exodus of the

Europeans continued uninterrupted, and within a few weeks of independence more than 800,000 of them had taken refuge in France, leaving about 100,000 who might or might not stay on. The Moslems, too, were leaving for France by the ship load – not necessarily as a political protest against Benbella's republic but because they were afraid of starving to death in Algeria. By November, half of Algeria's labour force of about 4 million were unemployed and starvation had, in fact, come to certain regions. Business was at a standstill and the administration was busying itself with plans to redistribute land and nationalize industries, except gas and oil (which came under the Evian agreements). The public services were hardly functioning and taxes were going uncollected. There was virtually no local government, and the FLN ministers, in their new-found administrative splendours in Algiers, had nothing to lose but their slogans. In the countryside the FLN had found work to do, however: it was dealing with the forgotten and unprotected men – the harkis – in its own way. Within three months of independence, 10,000 of them had been put to death, according to reports that have not, to my knowledge, been denied by the Algerian authorities.

Against all this, France was still contributing about £700,000 a day to the running costs of the Algerian administration, 12,000 French teachers had gone back to Algeria and thousands of French technicians were being sent there; and the United States was delivering food enough for 3 million people. At the beginning of December Benbella sent his Foreign Minister, Mr Khemisti, to Paris for talks on the implementation of the Evian agreements. Though the French Government was disposed to be reasonable, the fact was that it had promised £200 million a year for technical aid and development mainly to make it easier for the Europeans to stay in Algeria. Now most of them had gone and the promise seemed unnecessarily large. Was France to continue to finance an anti-western Moslem State in North Africa? The question was left unresolved on that occasion, but after only a few weeks of reflection, the French decided to honour their promise which, as it appeared in the Evian agreements, was to grant aid 'at a level equivalent to the programmes

at present under way'. The hardy minority of French shop-
keepers and others who had stayed on began to congratulate
themselves. Between them, General de Gaulle and Mr Benbella
had presided at the birth of an underprivileged infant. But at
least mother France looked like providing bread, and even a
little jam, for some time to come.

4. MALI'S BEST

Bamako is an agreeable little capital that reminds me of
Vientiane, in that both are overgrown villages made to do the
work of administrative centres. Both are set in red-earth country
near great rivers, the Niger in Mali and the Mekong between
Laos and Siam. But beyond that, a common heritage of French
rule and a high illiteracy rate, they have as little in common as
one would expect.

Both, however, are good examples of what underdevelopment
means in its administrative sense. We shall return to Laos more
than once in these pages; for the moment, Mali has the stronger
claim on our attention.

I reached Bamako by air in November 1960, reasonably
secure in the knowledge that a reservation had been made for
me at the Grand Hotel. The management, however, had no
record of any reservation, and I found a room in a smaller
hotel, where I spent the night in the company of giant cock-
roaches. I returned to the Grand Hotel next morning, and the
man who had looked blank the previous day consulted his books
and remarked: 'Yes, Monsieur Crozier. Your reservation was
from yesterday, but you didn't claim it.'

Within twenty minutes of reaching the previous day's temporary haven, I had made contact with the Information
Ministry. The Minister was in Prague, but his assistant invited
me to drop in. He was an amiable, bustling young man, who
carefully noted all my requirements during my stay, starting
with my projected interview with President Modibo Keita, and
told me all arrangements would be made. I have never set eyes
on him since that day.

Tiring of fruitless telephone calls and visits to an empty office,
I dropped in to see the head of Radio Mali, M. Corneille Dia.
H

He had, visibly, French blood in his veins, and was bitterly anti-colonial, but listened to my predicament and undertook to rescue me. I had only to telephone him that afternoon and he would give me the time of my appointment with the President. When I telephoned, however, the voice at the other end said: 'I regret, Monsieur, but I have not had the honour of meeting you.'

'Are you M. Corneille Dia?'

'Himself.'

'Then you must remember the conversation we had this morning in your office.'

'No, Monsieur. You must have made a mistake.'

In the end I made my own appointment with the President, by the simpler device of telephoning his Directeur de Cabinet.

On my last evening in Bamako I went to a French reception, where I saw M. Corneille Dia. I asked him for an explanation. He listened carefully, then said: 'I regret. You must have spoken to somebody else on the telephone.'

I have not told this story, which is authentic in all details except certain names, with pejorative intent. One does not have to leave London, Paris, or Washington to experience the frustration peculiar to relations with officials. Nor is inefficiency an African monopoly. Two things, however, make the story relevant to this study. One is the fact that in Bamako, as in any other truly 'underdeveloped' capital, Parkinson's Law has not had time to do its work. I discovered later that the bustling young man at the Information Ministry was required not only to do all the executive work at the Ministry but also to produce, practically single-handed, Bamako's only daily newspaper, *L'Essor*. This discovery softened my anger; indeed, I was probably lucky to have seen him at all.

In another respect, however, my frustrations in Bamako were marked by that amiable irrationality which seems to be characteristic of Africa. Different in kind from the irrationality of, say, Europe or South-East Asia, it consists, I think, of the cheerful coexistence of incompatible ideas. It is conceivable that this quality adds to the charm of Africa in the eyes of its visitors. It is certain that it adds to the difficulties of the handful of trained men trying to bridge the gap between tribal Africa and western technology.

That gap is as discouraging in Mali as almost anywhere in Africa. In the South, Mali (the former French Soudan) is part of the great savannah belt that sweeps across Africa north of the rain forest; its arbitrary northern boundaries cut a wide swathe across Saharan sands, encompassing the legendary Timbuctoo. If Mali has mineral riches they still lie undiscovered. Where the vegetation grows, the Malian peasants grow millet, rice, maize, and peanuts by primitive methods, although much progress has been made under the admirable guidance of the Office du Niger, whose former head, M. Wibaux, became France's first Ambassador to independent Mali. This was one of the more sensible appointments made by General de Gaulle in Africa. M. Wibaux was well liked among the Soudanese and soon established relations of mutual confidence with President Keita and his ministers. Probably nobody else could have done this at a time when the Malians were bitterly blaming the French for the break-up of the short-lived Mali Federation between Soudan and Senegal. Neither Modibo Keita nor General de Gaulle, however, wished the break between their two countries to become as complete as that between France and Guinea. Thus, French economic aid continued even after the new Mali had proclaimed its independence; the Office du Niger continued its work, under Malian control but with French technical and financial assistance; and Mali stayed within the Franc zone, whereas Guinea launched a currency of its own.

The past may have provided inspiration, but it could not offer relevant advice. Geographically, the Mali of today can at least claim to lie on part of the territory that constituted the medieval empire of Mali (which is more than can be said of Ghana, modern and ancient). The Sudanic peoples, the peoples of the savannah, have a distinctive way of life, which the accretion of Islam enriched but did not destroy. But nothing now remains of medieval Mali, whose 'power, wealth, and good order' aroused the admiration of visiting Arabs, according to

Roland Oliver and J. D. Page in *A Short History of Africa* (Penguin African Library, 1962). But one likes to think that somewhere in the ancestral memories of the contemporary Soudanese there still stirs that 'horror of injustice' which the traveller Ibn Batuta noted during his tour of Mali in 1352 and 1353 when the empire was at its peak.

In a curious way, one gets the impression, in Modibo Keita's presence, that it does, and that it conditions the superficially Marxist methods of Mali's single ruling party, the Union Soudanaise. During our talk in Bamako I had expressed the view that his party was organized on Marxist lines and this had provoked an explosion of mirth that was certainly unfeigned. My observation was not unfounded, but the President's laughter was justified. What significance could Marxism have, he asked, in a country 92 per cent of whose inhabitants could neither read nor write? (What, for that matter, could be the significance of western-style parliamentary democracy in such a country?)

Mali's massive illiteracy is indeed a central fact as crushing as the country's material poverty, which it reflects. It justifies a system of government that would be found repugnant in the West, but which, when Modibo Keita explains it, acquires a certain dignity and 'horror of injustice'. It was the role of the party, said Modibo, to explain decisions *before* they became law, to people who would not understand these if they first learned of them, say, by radio. He gave me an interesting example.

One of Mali's unexploited potential sources of revenue at that time was a small surplus of rice, which could have been exported to its neighbours had its price not been prohibitively high. As it was, the Ivory Coast, which needed rice, imported it from Indochina, many thousands of miles away. The State was still, in fact, paying the rice producers the same artificially high price the French had paid them for economic reasons that had lost their relevance once Mali had broken away from the French Community. The party, examining this situation, had concluded that the price had to be cut by a third. Its problem was how to convince the producers of the need for this cut. To this end, the producers had been invited to a conference organized by the Union Soudanaise. When the need for a natural outlet – as distinct from the 'colonial market' France had provided – was explained to them they accepted the cut, with what measure of good grace I cannot say. But Modibo Keita's argument that their reactions would have been 'adverse' had they learnt of the cut without prior notice can hardly be disproved.

It was disheartening, but hardly unexpected, to see Mali get into acute financial difficulties in 1962 and 1963. As we have seen, French aid continued, but this was not all, for others rushed in to help and, if possible, to influence the Malians with their advice. The Grand Hotel dining-room became a living theatre of neutralism and co-existence, with the Communists tactfully arranged on one side and the Westerners on the other, and those difficult to classify – such as Jugoslavs and Israelis – at the central tables (a touch of amphitryonic genius). In no time, Mali was getting aid from thirteen countries. To feel so wanted is a demoralizing experience. Falsely secure in the knowledge that their backers were so numerous, the socialist-minded Malians plunged into ill-conceived State ventures: an airline, the symbol of independence, 'people's shops', a State trading organization, a (worthless) currency of their own. Though poor, Mali would have been capable of paying its modest way without such extravagances. With them, it achieved a soaring trade deficit ($26 million in January 1963), dwindling reserves (only $5 million about the same date), rioting merchants, and an exodus of the French businessmen who had been keeping the economy going. For Mali, as for other newly independent countries, there was a clear way out of such man-made difficulties. Clear but painful, as all fundamental rethinking is. It involved breaking out of the vicious circle implicit in the equation: anti-colonialism = socialism = State control. At the time when these lines were written there was no sign that any such rethinking was on the way. But there was at least the consolation of knowing that if the time ever came, it would be easier to change course in a country with a structure as simple as Mali's than in the more complex countries that now have their national sovereignty.

5. HOPEFULLY ALONE

Daily newspapers, even when accurate, are inevitably misleading in that bad news makes better copy than good. Disturbances and scandals, rape and violence, political crises and wars fill their columns. Can this be the world as it is? The answer, of course, is that these things do happen, but so do better and duller ones. But good news is often dull news, and dull news ends up on some sub-editor's or copy-reader's spike. That is why the Scandinavian countries, for instance, offer such poor competition to Katanga for headline space (although Sweden occasionally makes it through the allegedly depraved morals of its teen-agers).

Though an author ought to try and keep his readers alert, he ought also to feel the need to strike a balance. That is the purpose of this chapter. I have devoted a good deal of space to disheartening examples of independence in action, and the dismal picture I have painted so far will be out of focus unless it is seen in the perspective of some of the countries where independence seems to be working out rather better than in Indonesia or the Congo. The space we devote to these hopeful cases need not be long, for the good things about them can be told economically.

Two are very large and two rather small. Not one of them is an unqualified success story, for all are fighting against adverse circumstances. But the point is that they *are* fighting, on the whole intelligently and well, to improve their lot.

India and Nigeria have size in common, though India's problems are much the graver: with a population more than ten times as great, it could scarcely be otherwise. Malaya and Cambodia are in some respects favoured lands: their people are not yet, by a long way, short of living space. But they, too, have their built-in problems.

India is certainly the most important of the 'new' countries, if only by its size, and the achievements of the man who has guided its destinies since 1947 are of staggering magnitude when measured by the scale of India's inheritance of squalor and overpopulation, social intolerance and religious taboos. Though in the autumn of 1962 Mr Jawaharlal Nehru had the bitterness of seeing his foreign policy of neutrality collapse around him on the bayonet points of the advancing Chinese Communists, probably only he could have done all these things: restored order after the violent partition of the Indian sub-continent; preserved the unity of a country rent from within by linguistic, caste, and communal divisions; set about, with remarkable success, to create a secular state with Pakistan as a theocratic neighbour; and to have done all this while preserving parliamentary democracy and the fundamental liberties. Like all great men, however, Mr Nehru has to be swallowed whole, with the faults to flavour the virtues. And the faults have naturally attracted attention. The holier-than-thou sanctity of utterance when wagging an admonishing finger at the great powers, especially the western powers, coupled with a curious reluctance to condemn the communist powers; the woolly reliance on irrelevant theories of 'socialism' to lift India from its tragic poverty; and, above all, the great blind spot of Kashmir – 'Nehru's country' as the banners said when Mr Bulganin and Mr Khrushchev visited that unhappy province on their tour of India in 1955. These things are large enough to be recorded, and there is no point in denying that they belong to the record. Nehru's greatest failure was surely a product of the general attitude which his faults reflect: that of failing to see to it that India was adequately defended against the communist giant to the north. His most irritating idiosyncrasy was the persistence with which he supported his one-time Defence Minister, Mr Krishna Menon, against all opponents, until, under the pressure of the marching Chinese, he fired the man who had airily dismissed the notion that India could have any enemy but Pakistan. But in the perspective of history, even such faults and failures will probably be dwarfed by the achievements.

In its more modest way Malaya, too, is a hopeful case, and mainly for the same reason, for it has been blessed, in Tunku Abdul Rahman, with a natural leader able to unite a fundamentally disunited country. Malaya is, of course, a small country of not much more than 7 million people, but it has a formidable communal problem, and the fact that it was peaceful and orderly early in 1963, when these lines were written, owes as much to the presence of 'the Tunku' as to the fact that it has living space and two great economic assets – rubber and tin.

Independence came on 31 August 1957, after nine years of a murderous Emergency provoked by a communist insurrection. Most of the Communists were of Chinese origin, and this fact complicated Malaya's already tangled communal question. Today and tomorrow the Tunku's biggest problem is that the Malays – his own community – are a minority in their own country. But though they are outnumbered by the two other principal communities combined – Chinese and Indian–Pakistani – the Malays are the largest of the three. This, and the fact that the British encouraged their political advancement, gave the Malays a privileged position under the independence Constitution. The question is: how long can they, or should they, hold it? Broadly speaking, the formidably efficient Chinese community has given more of its attention to commerce – in which they are supreme – than to politics, in which they remain handicapped by a very limited suffrage. The Indians or Pakistanis, again broadly speaking, form a proletariat, largely on the rubber plantations, and find a semi-political outlet in trade-union activity. The Chinese are the larger problem, for a variety of reasons. Many of them are rich and some very wealthy; they cling tenaciously to their cultural traditions, especially in their insistence on having their own schools. Moreover, they have their own subdivisions. One of these is by province of origin and spoken dialect. The Chinese of Malaya, and of Singapore, may speak Cantonese or Hokkien, Hakka or Teochew or many other tongues incomprehensible to Chinese outside the appropriate group. True, they can all read the same newspapers in the universal ideographic language that is written Chinese. But it is an everyday experience in Kuala Lumpur or Singapore to find two Chinese of different provincial ancestries communicating in English or Malay because they have no common Chinese tongue.

Another, and politically more disturbing, division among the Chinese is by allegiance or loyalty. I remember raising this point with Tunku Abdul Rahman when he was in London for the final talks on independence. It is invariably a pleasure to meet the Tunku. Warm, friendly, and courteous, his authority is unforced – the logical reward of natural charm. He will, I hope, forgive me if I say that on this occasion I found him disquietingly starry-eyed (I have since seen him become noticeably tougher and more realistic). 'There are three different sets of Chinese,' he said. 'There are the Straits Chinese or Queen's Chinese. They are with us, partners in our Alliance party (which unites Malays, Chinese, and Indians), so they're no problem. Then there are the Chinese who sit on the fence or who feel loyal to Formosa. With them, it's just a question of getting them off the fence and over to our side. Then there are those who look towards Peking, and *they* can be ignored.'

The realities of power and of South-East Asia modified the Tunku's simple confidence. On one point his preoccupations coincided with those of the retreating British. Britain's problem was how to get rid of the remaining bits of empire in that area: Singapore and the three territories of British Borneo – North Borneo, Brunei, and Sarawak. The Tunku's problem, in the same context, was Singapore's future. Apart from the existence of a British naval base on Singapore, there seemed to be no special reason why Singapore should not become independent at the same time as the rest of what was once British Malaya. (Although old Malayan hands pointed out, with more logic than relevance, that Singapore was just a swamp when Raffles became interested in it, so why give it independence at all?) Although an island, Singapore is the geographical extension of the Malayan peninsula and its natural commercial entrepot. Economically, they are complementary. But at first the Tunku would not hear of union with Singapore, for the island's population is overwhelmingly Chinese, and in a straight merger the Malays would find themselves swamped by the Chinese. It was these circumstances that gave birth to the idea of a Greater Malaysia Federation, to consist not only of Malaya and Singapore but also of the three territories of British Borneo, where Malays or related peoples are numerous enough to overcome the Tunku's fears of Chinese domination in a wider federation.

From the beginning Tunku Abdul Rahman's opposite number in Singapore, Mr Lee Kuan-yew, supported the Greater Malaysia idea, just as at first he had argued in favour of a straight union between Malaya and Singapore. It would be hard to imagine a greater contrast than that between Mr Lee and the Tunku. Overcoming an early reputation as a playboy, the Tunku took his law exams late in life and just scraped through. Mr Lee, who has rare intellectual gifts, took a first at Cambridge (not, as is often said, a double first: that was his wife's accomplishment) and was a successful advocate in Singapore before going into politics. The Tunku trusts his instinct; Mr Lee calculates moves and consequences. At first he aroused great distrust among the British business community, for his People's Action Party was frankly anti-colonialist and included a number of Communists who had been interned during the Emergency. I once asked him where he stood, and he replied, with undeniable pertinence: 'Anybody who wants to succeed in politics in Singapore must win the support of the Chinese-educated Chinese (he himself was English-educated, though he has taught himself to make speeches in Mandarin Chinese). This often means that you have to take the wind out of the sails of the Communists.' In fact, Mr Lee turned out to be a moderate and rather pragmatic socialist. He clamped down on Singapore's more offensively visible vice and increased welfare-state measures. But he also isolated and finally got rid of the Communists and other anti-British extremists within his party. This gained him the support of the business people, but weakened him dangerously within his Parliament. It was this circumstance that made the Tunku change his mind about a merger with Singapore. It was bad enough to have a relatively stable, mainly Chinese island at his doorstep; it would be much worse to have a communist one. Singapore's Communists and other extremists were agitating for Singapore's complete independence (it had been a self-governing State since 1959, with defence and foreign affairs in British hands), and Mr Lee was politically in danger. One way out would have been a merger with Malaya, but for the ethnic reasons we have mentioned, Borneo had to be brought in as well, into a federation of Greater

Malaysia. In the summer of 1961 the Tunku himself launched the Greater Malaysia idea, and in August he invited Mr Lee to Kuala Lumpur, where the two men jointly signed a statement outlining a Greater Malaysian plan in which Singapore would run its own affairs in labour and education, but the new federal government would take over security and defence (and the naval base) from the British.

Though the Communists immediately labelled the scheme 'neo-colonialist' it was the only conceivable way out of the built-in dilemmas I have mentioned. For Mr Lee, it offered a path to independence within a wider ensemble; for the Tunku, it offered control over Singapore's defence and internal security and a dosage of Malaysians to compensate for Singapore's Chineseness; and for the British it gave a chance to pull out of Singapore and Borneo painlessly and honourably. Unfortunately, there were snags as well as advantages. One was a fiercely vocal opposition among many of the Peking-orientated Chinese of Singapore. This Mr Lee overcame in September 1962 by means of referendum that offered voters only a choice between three different forms of federation without an option to say No, and in which those who would have liked to say No were told in advance that blank votes would be counted in favour of Greater Malaysia. In the event, however, the blank vote opposition amounted to less than 30 per cent of the total – small enough to show that there was no need for such dishonesty. But there were other snags. The worst was the existence of considerable opposition to the scheme in British Borneo, especially in the semi-autonomous Protectorate of Brunei. In December 1962 this opposition exploded in a sharp and very nearly successful *coup d'état* against the authority of the Sultan of Brunei. Clearly it was going to be no easy matter to establish a politically stable federation of Greater Malaysia.

If I have appeared to digress from a theme of independence at its most hopeful it is because any optimism that is expressed about Malaya or Singapore has to be tempered by an awareness of their dangerous problems and of the difficulty of solving them, even by a scheme that looks as sensible on paper as does the plan for a Greater Malaysia. But whether or not the federation explodes in the faces of its creators (as did the West Indies Federation) or is involved in a war with its aggressive Indonesian neighbour, or gradually establishes itself, it has to be said that Malaya itself was making a success of independence six years and more after the event. Though handicapped by fluctuating world prices of rubber and tin, it had managed to maintain the colonial achievement of a high standard of living, probably the third in Asia after Japan's and Formosa's. And this it would probably not have done without the unifying, tolerant, and conciliatory presence of the Tunku.

In a more humble way, Cambodia, too, has been making a success of independence. Once again, this would have been unlikely without outstanding leadership – in this instance that of a mercurial but gifted figure, Prince Sihanouk, whom we met at some length in Chapter 2. King Norodom, as he was when independence came in 1954, had the originality to abdicate and turn himself into a political leader. He founded a party, the *Sangkum Reastr Niyum* or People's Socialist Community, and swept the board with it at general elections in September 1955 (indeed, with characteristic candour, he later apologized for his party's 'too complete success'). Surviving plots from within and without, and pressures from his larger and more aggressive Siamese and Vietnamese neighbours, the Prince has brought stability and progress to Cambodia.

In terms of national or individual income, Cambodia is a poor country (though not a hungry one, for it has plentiful rice for export). Moreover, the Khmers, Cambodia's original inhabitants, are the poorest of its communities; the large Vietnamese and Chinese minorities are noticeably more prosperous. When one speaks of progress or raises hopes for the future, therefore, one must bear in mind that Sihanouk's Cambodia started in a very humble way of business, most Khmers never having given any thought to the desirability of accumulating wealth, and tilling their fields to feed themselves and only incidentally to make money out of crop surpluses. Dysentery, malaria, and tuberculosis affect most of the population at one time or another, and add their debilitating quota to a steamy and oppressive climate.

Bearing these things in mind, Cambodia's achievements under Prince Sihanouk have been remarkable, as a few facts and figures will show. In 1953, a year before independence, there were just under 249,000 little Cambodians in primary schools and only 2,268 bigger ones in only seven secondary schools; there was only one centre for higher education, with 190 students. By 1962 the changes were dramatic; the number of primary schoolchildren had more than doubled, to 563,000, and those at secondary schools had increased by more than twelve times to over 27,000, attending forty-six colleges or lycées (nearly seven times as many as before independence). As for higher education, the one establishment of the old days had multiplied to five, with 1,120 undergraduates. The government was spending less on defence than on either education or public health. By 1962, Cambodia had five times as many doctors as in 1955, four times as many midwives and twice as many health officers and nurses. Four new hospitals and thirty-eight new infirmaries had been built. In the meantime, that is from the 1953–57 average to 1962, rice production had grown from 1,250,000 to 1,500,000 metric tons, and agriculture was being rapidly diversified by the cultivation of maize, tobacco, kapok, and other crops.

It is sad to have to add that in the autumn of 1962 Cambodia's budget was in the red to the appalling extent of 1,700 million Riels (which works out at between $30 million and $50 million according to whether one uses the official or the free exchange rate). Sadly also, four factories built and run with Chinese communist assistance were working well below their theoretical capacity. The budget deficit was the kind of trouble a developing country almost invariably runs into: the production difficulties were typical of the kind of trouble a new country buys when it puts its faith in state enterprise. But there was a hopeful air about Cambodia, the air of a little country on the move and quite possibly with a reasonably happy future, if only its larger and more aggressive neighbours would leave it in peace.

To turn from Cambodia to Nigeria is to jump in more ways than mere longitude. By any measurement, Nigeria is the most hopeful, as well as the biggest and most important country in black Africa. Its population of about 38 million outnumbers that of all the former French colonies in Africa put together, and includes some of the most gifted and technically advanced Africans in the whole continent, notably the astute and go-getting Yorubas of the Western Region. Its mineral wealth and economic potential are impressive.

There is, of course, a reverse side to this shining coin. One is a catastrophic gap between rich and poor. Free enterprise is both free and enterprising in Nigeria, and in time the wealth it is rapidly creating will spread to the less fortunate. But today the contrast between the magnificent public buildings in Lagos and the homes of the wealthy and successful, on the one hand, and on the other, the dismal corrugated-iron shacks of the poor is a pain to the eye and the mind. Of every ten children born, death claims four before puberty. Many of those who live on will be plagued by intestinal parasites or worse afflictions. Kingsley Martin of the *New Statesman*, whom I bumped into in Lagos's splendid Federal Palace Hotel (£6. 15s. a day, bed and break-fast), described to me in depressing detail the appalling sights he had seen in Nigerian hospitals, and seemed to think – one hopes wrongly – that the Nigerian authorities didn't really care very much.

Politically, Nigeria's greatest asset is also its greatest problem. It was an act of wisdom on the part of the British to lead Nigeria's three regions (Northern, Western and Eastern) towards a Federation. Had the same thing been done in the Congo, there might never have been a Katanga problem. But if federation was the most reasonable way of meeting Nigeria's twin chal-lenges of size and diversity it contained, almost by definition, the seeds of future dissolution. Inevitably, there was no nation-wide political party. Each Region has its own party and, again inevitably, each party won in its own Region in the pre-inde-pendence election in 1959, so that Nigeria started its inde-pendent life the following year with a regional (Western Region) opposition instead of a national one. Two years later, in May 1962, the opposition leader, Chief Awolowo, was arrested and his Action Group Regional government suspended. In July a financial scandal, again in the Western Region, was uncovered: the Action Group, it was alleged, had made little attempt to keep its own funds and those of individual supporters separate from those of its Regional government.

Such happenings might have been expected severely to shake the Federal Government or even to provoke a secessionist agitation in the Western Region. But the encouraging things are that the Federal Government – under its able, moderate, and golden-voice Prime Minister, Sir Abubakar Tafawa Balewa – kept its head, and that law and order prevailed in the Western Region throughout the crisis. To a large extent this was doubtless due to the fact that the Federal Government, for all its determination to weaken the Action Group, had taken care to handle the proud Yorubas (who controlled the Action Group) with diplomatic tact. A Yoruba had been appointed from Lagos to be the Regional Administrator, and welcome reforms, such as the reorganization of the tribal courts, had been introduced. Moreover, the financial scandal was dealt with much as a similar scandal might have been in Britain, by the appointment of a commission of inquiry, which did its work with quiet competence and without vindictiveness.

It was Nigeria's misfortune to join the queue for economic aid very late in the day. The ambitious six-year plan announced in 1962 assumed that half of the total projected investment of £676½ million would come from abroad. In September of that year I heard Sir Abubakar complain in London, in his disarming way, that foreign governments were being slow in responding to Nigeria's appeals. At that time only half the money had been promised, mostly from the United States, Britain, and West Germany. Since then, however, more American money – including private capital – has come in, and the Nigerian assumptions may, in the end, turn out to be less extravagant than at one time they had seemed.

Poverty and tribal rivalries, domination by the backward but populous Northern Region under the formidable personality of the Sardauna of Sokoto (Sir Abubakar's real boss), and the pan-

African notions of a turbulent student body are among the question-marks that hang over Nigeria's future. It is much too early to say whether or how they will be answered. But there is an impressive common sense and dynamism about many Nigerians that seem to promise solutions of a kind in good time. If success comes, Nigeria could be a solid anchor of stability in Africa; the contagion of failure would be correspondingly disastrous. But I am not among those who expect Nigeria to fail.

INDEPENDENCE AT ITS WORST:
The mob and the soldiery between them made Leopoldville a
hazardous capital in 1960

Lee Kuan-yew
of Singapore

Tunku Abdul Rahman
of Malaya

MALAYSIA'S LEADERS

Chapter 4

THE ASSERTION OF
INDEPENDENCE

I. IDEAS AND CONFERENCES

Recognition of independence improves the morale of nationalist leaders, but some naturally feel the need to go farther and prove that they really are independent. There are many possible ways of doing this. Most of the new countries being poor, financial independence is relatively hard to assert. The favoured ways of demonstrating independence are therefore concerned with foreign policy. As soon as a government is recognized (not necessarily by *all* other governments) it has a choice of ways of proving, at least to itself, that it has an independent foreign policy. The first proof, more often than not, is a public declaration of non-involvement, which shows that the government concerned does not take its orders from the major western or communist powers. Another favourite proof is taking part in conferences with the governments of other new countries. These do little harm, as a rule, and often some good. A more controversial, perilous, and unpredictable method consists of making some spectacular gesture of defiance of the former imperial power, such as the Indonesian expulsion of the Dutch in 1957 or the Tunisian attack on Bizerta in 1961.

The first two of these methods need not detain us very long. Non-involvement, or non-alignment, was Mr Nehru's idea. By such terms, the Indian Prime Minister meant that his country should not 'commit' itself to this side or that in the cold war and should keep out of all military alliances. To this extent, it was a form of neutrality, but it differed in important respects from the traditional neutrality of such European countries as Sweden or Switzerland, whose governments carry their concept of the neutral State to the extent of not expressing views on most

I

important international conflicts or controversies (Switzerland is not even a member of the United Nations as such, though it does belong to some UN agencies). Mr Nehru's India, in contrast, has frequently asserted the right to moralize on international issues (though rather less since India swallowed Goa in 1961 and became involved in frontier fighting with China). Non-alignment, moreover, is different in kind from, say, the neutrality that was imposed on Austria under the State Treaty of 1955 when the Russians withdrew their occupation forces. The 'uncommitted' nations did not have non-involvement forced on them; they chose it for themselves. Indeed, the choice, as I have said, was one of the ways in which they asserted their independence. During the 1950s the terms 'neutralism' and 'neutralist' came to be applied to these unaligned countries, partly to distinguish them from the European 'neutrals' and traditional 'neutrality', but partly also as slightly pejorative references to what many western statesmen and journalists considered to be a lack of courage on the part of India and other non-communist countries in refusing to align themselves with the West. The unaligned leaders took up this implied challenge, however, and the term 'positive neutralism' (implying that those who professed it would 'positively' work for peace) gained currency in the speeches of President Nasser of Egypt.

With few exceptions, the leaders of the newly independent countries adopted non-alignment as their basic foreign-policy doctrine. This was not true, as one would expect, of the divided countries, such as Vietnam or Korea, for the communist half being, by definition, part of the communist bloc, the anti-communist half naturally sought protection from the western powers, especially the United States. Ceylon started off, under the government of Sir John Kotelawala, with a pro-western bias and British bases, but Mr Solomon Bandaranaike, who was elected in 1956, quickly de-aligned his island state. Independent Morocco, which had inherited French and American bases from its dependent years, negotiated their withdrawal as soon as practicable. The rulers of the new Indonesia, though they had always professed non-involvement, departed from the principle in 1952, but caused themselves such embarrassment that they soon reverted to it. The then Foreign Minister, Dr Subardjo, as Dorothy Woodman recorded in *The Republic of Indonesia* (Cresset Press, London, 1955), secretly signed an aid agreement with the American ambassador, Mr Merle Cochran, which contained military clauses. When the agreement became known this brought the Cabinet down, and the next Cabinet negotiated an alternative agreement, without military clauses.

Such examples show clearly enough the state of feeling and the force of opinion in the new countries. But two quotations will explain better than I can the strength of the uncommitted concept, and of the reasoning behind it. The first is from Mr Nehru's speech of 22 April 1955, before the political committee of the Afro-Asian Conference at Bandung:

> So far as I am concerned, it does not matter what war takes place; we will not take part in it unless we have to defend ourselves. If I join any of these big groups I lose my identity; I have no identity left, I have no views left. . . . If all the world were to be divided up between these two big blocs what would be the result? The inevitable result would be war. Therefore every step that takes place in reducing that area in the world which may be called the unaligned area is a dangerous step and leads to war. It reduces that objective, that balance, that outlook which other countries without military might can perhaps exercise.

This speech appears in full, together with other valuable documents, in George McTurnan Kahin's useful little study, *The Asian-African Conference* (Cornell, New York, 1956). An equally significant statement is quoted by Erskine B. Childers in *The Road to Suez* (MacGibbon & Kee, London, 1962). It is the reply Colonel Nasser, then thirty-five, gave to John Foster Dulles in the spring of 1953, when the American Secretary of State visited Cairo and tried to persuade him to bring Egypt into a Middle East Defence Organization:

> We are opposed to alliances with any outside Power because we have strong cause to suspect them, and because our peoples will not support any government that makes them. You are

asking to defeat your own aims. The defence of this region must come from within, from something that can bind its people together. That force, that internal front, is our nationalism, social reform, progress. If the strength of this internal Arab front, which we have still to build, is weakened by even more unpopular alliances, there is only one political force that can gain. The greatest danger from communism in this region is from an attack from inside this region. And what use will 'linear strategy' be, if the attack comes from inside?

Time seems to have shown the wisdom of Nasser's words and the irrelevance of Dulles's proposed pact, at least to the *Arab* countries of the Middle East. The defence organization was born, eventually, however in 1955, though without American participation, and called itself the Baghdad Pact; but Iraq, its only Arab member, left it after the 1958 revolution that deposed Nuri es-Said, the only Arab leader who had been willing formally to bind his country to a western alliance; and later, its remaining members (Britain, Turkey, Persia, and Pakistan, with the Americans as participating observers) gave it the more innocuous name of Central Treaty Organization. That such pacts were indeed unacceptable to the Arabs anywhere was shown when King Hussein of Jordan had to withdraw his acceptance of a British invitation to join the Baghdad Pact after violent rioting had broken out in various cities at the end of 1955.

In the Far East, too, military pacts proved unpopular. When Mr Dulles tries to bring South-East Asian nations into an anti-communist alliance after the French defeat in Indochina in 1954 only three responded: Siam, which had not been colonized and had no anti-western bias; Pakistan, which had a quarrel with India over Kashmir; and the Philippines, which retained strong links with the United States. Burma, India, and Indonesia were among those that stayed out, and Mr Nehru denounced the pact that did emerge, named the South-East Asia Collective Defence Treaty and usually known as Seato. So did Prince Sihanouk of Cambodia, who repeatedly protested that his country did not wish to be protected by Seato against its will.

It is natural enough for the leaders of newly independent countries to wish to meet each other in conference. Before independence, such meetings were impossible, except on an unofficial level, or perhaps for cultural purposes. Independence removes the prohibition, and participation in international conferences thus demonstrates the fact that independence has indeed come. In a less exalted way it is fun to travel, especially at public expense. There is, however, another and more important reason for the profusion of international gatherings among the new countries. Most of them, including those that most loudly proclaim their freedom and denounce their former oppressors, are desperately conscious of their own weakness. Individually, with the exception of such giants as India or Indonesia, they carry little weight. Together they look more convincingly like a pressure group.

It was Mr Nehru who started the fashion of anti-colonial conferences by calling a meeting of Asian leaders in 1947. But at that time only some of the Asian colonies had won their independence and virtually none of the African ones. It was Bandung that really made the world conscious of what came to be known – rather misleadingly – as the 'Afro-Asian bloc'. The Bandung Conference was the brain-child of a former Indonesian Prime Minister, Dr Ali Sastroamidjojo, who first proposed it to the Prime Ministers of Burma, Ceylon, India, and Pakistan when they met in Colombo in April 1954. After initial misgivings, notably Mr Nehru's, the idea snowballed. In the event, exactly a year later, twenty-nine Asian and African countries sent representatives to Bandung. Only six of these were African: Egypt, Ethiopia, the Gold Coast (before it became Ghana), Liberia, Libya, and the Sudan. The rest ranged over much of Asia, with some interesting omissions and one towering inclusion: the Chinese People's Republic. Both North and South Vietnam were there, but Korea, another divided country, was left out, many participants having lately been engaged in the Korean war. Since communist China was to be there the Chinese Nationalist Government (Formosa) was kept out. Israel was not invited either, because if it had been, the Arabs would not have turned up. Apart from the official delegations, a largish host of unofficial observers found their way to Bandung. These included Archbishop Makarios of Cyprus and various African nationalists.

As might have been expected, this large gathering was far from homogeneous. Only twelve of the participating countries had reached independence since the Second World War; the others were more or less free from the anti-imperialist neuroses or scars of the newcomers. Most of the participants were un-committed, but communist China (at that time) and North Vietnam were firmly aligned on the Soviet side of the cold war, and Turkey, Iraq, Persia, Pakistan, Siam, and the Philippines had military alliances with the West. The search for common ground was therefore far from easy. Mr Nehru, who had in-sisted on China's inclusion and was co-existing affably with Mr Chou En-lai, was shocked by Sir John Kotelawala's anti-communist speeches, and told him so. So, too, was he shocked by the militancy of the Turkish delegates, and he chided them repeatedly in his speech before the political committee of the conference. Mr Chou, whose endearing eyebrows and warm smile had made many friends for the distant government in Peking, whose real intentions few of those present either under-stood or wished to understand too well, was all mildness and peace. Together, he and Mr Nehru 'sold' the famous five prin-ciples of peaceful co-existence, which they had jointly drafted some months earlier during a break in the Indochina Confer-ence at Geneva, to the twenty-seven other delegations. But by the time they appeared in the final communiqué, the five principles had grown to ten, and various delegations had made it clear that they would interpret controversial clauses as they chose. The most controversial of all was the fifth, which read:

> Respect for the right of each nation to defend itself singly or collectively, in conformity with the Charter of the United Nations.

This clause clearly met the views of the Siamese, Pakistanis, Turks, and other aligned Asians. But Mr Nehru and Mr Chou had made it clear that they thought it could not possibly apply to Seato, and Colonel Nasser argued that it could not possibly include the recently concluded treaty between Iraq and Turkey (the beginning of the Baghdad Pact) because of the ensuing clause, which he had drafted. The first part of this fifth clause read:

> Abstention from the use of arrangements of collective defence to serve the particular interests of any of the big powers.

By such private interpretations or public reservations, the participants came to feel they had achieved unity. And many western governments and observers, who rightly sensed that the majority bias of the conference had been anti-western, allowed themselves to use the terms 'Afro-Asian bloc' or 'the Bandung powers' as though such unity had in fact been achieved. But this view was only an approximation of the truth, as the wayward course of African and Asian votes in the UN in the ensuing years clearly showed.

If Bandung did not really achieve the unity of the African and Asian world, however, it did give the participating countries – and especially those that had achieved independence only lately – an entirely new concept of their own importance and of the potential power for peace of their massed opinions. It also persuaded many of the more sceptical delegates that Mr Chou En-lai's peaceable reasonableness was the true face of communist China; and conversely, it may have persuaded Mr Chou that China had a good deal to gain by cultivating the goodwill of fellow-Asians, many of whom were clearly terrified of the prospect of war between China and the United States. At any rate, shortly after that the Chinese Communists and American diplomats sat down together in Geneva to discuss their differences in the first of an interminable series of abortive exchanges that was later transferred to Warsaw. And for the next four years, until the flight of the Dalai Lama from Tibet to India in 1959, the Chinese Communists behaved reasonably well. This alone was an encouraging outcome of what at first had looked like an unwieldy and incoherent gathering.

Bandung was thus, or seemed to be at the time, an educational occasion, almost a graduation course in international realities, from which students of diverse ideological persuasions had benefited. From the communist standpoint, however, it must have been regarded as a defeat, since communist views, though they had been taken into account, had not prevailed. Hence the Communists made a determined and partly successful effort during the next few years to gain control of the Bandung movement, through the Afro-Asian solidarity organisation set up in Cairo in January 1958 with an Egyptian Secretary-General and Soviet and Chinese participation. It seems hardly necessary to go into the details of the innumerable other conferences, both Asian and African, that have taken place since Bandung.

One conference that does need to be mentioned, on the other hand, is a permanent or recurring one: the United Nations. One of the many unfortunate things about the UN is that it has given the new countries an unprecedented opportunity for creating an illusion of strength. It is, of course, only human for the men in charge of newly independent countries to wish to demonstrate the fact of their independence by sending a delegation to the UN. Nor is there any harm in it, so long as they do not fall victims of the illusions that flourish in the international organization. Many of them do, and this is unfortunate, from their point of view as well as from that of the great powers which really do have the strength, for the temptations of publicity are often not resisted by this or that delegation as they make their often dreary speeches or combine in often pointless resolutions. Such energies could, in many cases, be more intelligently employed coping with the hard realities of independence at home than seeking the limelight in New York; so, too, could the money used to finance their journeys and maintain a presence at the General Assembly.

There is no originality in saying, as so many others have, that the UN's voting system is an absurdity, since each nation, no matter what its size, carries one vote. But original or not, the absurdity remains; poverty-stricken Gabon, with less than half a million people, carries the same weight in the Assembly as the Soviet Union or the United States. Thus, illusion is piled upon illusion. Sixty small countries combine in voting for an anti-British or anti-French resolution and shout for victory when it is carried, often by virtue of fortuitous circumstances, such as the fact that each of the pieces of Africa that were carved up for convenience' sake by the colonial powers, happens to get its separate independence. Since in nearly all cases such resolutions are unenforceable in a world of sovereign States, the achievement of getting a resolution passed is of little value.

This is not the place for a reasoned argument of the merits and disadvantages of the UN. Certainly the superb General Assembly building is one of the best clubs in the world, and that is perhaps the most sensible way of looking at it. As an instrument for the assertion of national independence its value is almost purely psychological (at a high cost in financial terms). As an instrument for the maintenance of peace – its primary original function – it is more often than not irrelevant. In most real crises, such as Berlin or the Chinese invasion of India, it is powerless. And most of its few near-successes have been due to special circumstances. One instance was the Korean war crisis, when the UN, under American leadership, was able to intervene only because the Russians happened at the time to be boycotting the Security Council and were therefore not present to use their veto. Similarly, the UN operation in the Congo was possible only because the Russians boycotted the whole exercise, but did not feel like actually sabotaging it in the face of the unanimous support of the Africans and Asians. The Suez crisis is an example of another kind of rarity: that of Russia and America being on the same side of the fence. Though the British and French made a show of conforming to UN resolutions calling on them to quit the Canal area, however, the real reason, in Britain's case, was an American threat to cut off oil supplies and credit; and France could not stay on alone once Britain had decided to cut its losses. In contrast, the Russians ignored UN resolutions on Hungary, even though all the uncommitted countries voted against Soviet intervention. There is at least an element of truth in General de Gaulle's lofty dismissal of the world organization (as it has developed) as a just a *machin* or 'thingummybob'.

2. ACTS OF DEFIANCE

One of the recurring themes at the Bandung Conference was the complaint that the colonial powers would persist in treating their former colonies like children even after they had become independent. As with the Barretts of Wimpole Street, the complaint was not without substance. The mother countries, like Victorian fathers, did on occasion argue that though their children had reached their majority, they were still not grown up, since they had not yet learnt how to stand on their own two feet. The resentful daughter, on being battered with this argument, has been known to elope in secret; and the resentful son to turn around and kick father hard on the shins before dashing out of the front door to make his unaided way in the world.

This, in effect, was what King Hussein of Jordan did when he dismissed his almost legendary British adviser, Glubb Pasha, on 1 March 1956. If one stretches the metaphor a little it is also what happened when Nasser nationalized the Suez Canal Company, when Sukarno expelled the Dutch from Indonesia, when Bourguiba attacked the French at Bizerta, and when Fidel Castro seized American properties in Cuba. These acts of defiance were assertions of independence, and it is worth finding out just how successful some of them were.

By far the most rational of these actions was the nationalization of the Suez Canal Company, although no other event in recent memory has so stirred atavistic emotions latent in the phlegmatic British people. The story of the Suez expedition has been told so often that there is no need to tell it again in detail. What concerns us is whether Nasser's original act of defiance paid off, and the answer clearly is that it did. It follows, though some people have found this part harder to admit, that the Franco-British attempt to foil Nasser was a failure.

The simplest way to verify the truth of these two propositions is to ask what each side was trying to do. Nasser, in his important but often misinterpreted little book, *The Philosophy of the Revolution,* had listed three sources of strength for the Arabs: the fundamental unity of the Arabs through Islam and a common language; their geographical position 'at the world's cross-roads'; and oil. The first of these was a condition which Nasser could and did exploit through the efficient Egyptian propaganda machine, but only to the extent that the underlying oneness of the Arabs transcended their many discords. The third, oil, was largely outside Egyptian control. Egypt was, however, supremely well placed to exploit the second of the Arab 'sources of strength', for the Suez Canal, the main link in the 'world's crossroads', ran through Egyptian territory.

Nasser may or may not have intended all along to nationalize the Canal Company at some time or other. There is no way of knowing. But there is no mystery about why he nationalized at a certain moment. On 19 July 1956 Mr Dulles had abruptly and publicly withdrawn an American offer to help finance the building of the proposed Aswan High Dam. The circumstances were particularly humiliating for the Egyptians, in that until that moment the arrangements for the dam had appeared to be secure. On 9 July the President of the World Bank, Mr Eugene Black, had reaffirmed the Bank's offer of a loan (which in turn was contingent on American and British offers of grants). On 17 July, the Egyptian Ambassador, to the United States, Mr Ahmed Hussein, returning to America, declared that Egypt accepted the western offers. And two days later a Foreign Office spokesman in London reaffirmed the readiness of the British government to carry out its end of the deal. True, Mr Dulles had told the Press on the 10th that it was 'improbable' the grants would in fact be made. But less than a week later he had written to the Senate Appropriations Committee to say that neither he nor President Eisenhower would be bound by a committee rider on the current aid Bill forbidding the use of aid funds for the dam unless the Congress specifically authorized it. Nor had the Egyptian Government been given an inkling of the Secretary of State's real intentions. His announcement of 19 July – only a few hours after the Foreign Office's affirmative statement – was therefore a public and deliberate snub to Nasser. A week later, on the 26th, Nasser nationalized the Canal Company. It was a clear enough case of cause and effect.

It should not have been surprising that the manner of

Nasser's 'grab', as the Press called it, was offensive and provocative. Nasser's speech of the 26th was peppered with references to the 'flames' of Arab nationalism. He had given the Canal Company no previous notice of his intention to take over its assets, much less offered to negotiate suitable terms. On the other hand, he had formally pledged compensation to the Company's shareholders, not in vague generalities but in specific terms: at the prices ruling on the Paris Bourse the previous day. Moreover, the company he had nationalized, however international its ownership might be, was registered in Egypt, and its principal asset – the Canal – was in Egyptian territory. And he had made it clear that his object in seizing the Canal, and placing it under an Egyptian state authority, was to use the income from Canal tolls to help finance the building of the Aswan dam.

Now a number of British and French statesmen claimed at that time to see in Nasser's action the sinister beginning of a dictator's foreign adventures, and in *The Philosophy of the Revolution* the *Mein Kampf* of a new Hitler on the Nile. The comparison was made by Sir Anthony Eden (as Lord Avon then was), by his Foreign Secretary, Mr Selwyn Lloyd, and by the French Premier, M. Guy Mollet, and it was hard to tell whether it was the outcome of cynicism or self-deception. At any rate, the comparison was always grotesque, given the disparity between the means at Hitler's disposal and those at Nasser's, even after he had seized the Canal Company. Since there were Arabs outside Egypt, and since Nasser did see himself as their leader, it is reasonable to suppose that he had foreign ambitions; but absurd to imagine that he intended to fulfil them by military conquest (though he did, much later, interfere by force on the side of the Yemeni republicans). There is indeed no reason to question the prosaic truth of the reason Nasser himself gave for taking control of the Canal: this was, as Nasser must then have seen it, the only way left of raising revenue to build the dam. Nor was this vast project to be simply a monument to Nasser's grandeur, a modern pharaoh's pyramid. The dam was necessary, not to provide Egypt with the material basis for a policy of conquest, but simply to keep Egyptians from dying of starvation.

When Nasser seized the Canal Company Egypt's population stood at about 23 millions. By 1962, six years later, it had probably reached 25 millions. And the relentless explosion of new mouths goes on, with the ever-growing pressure of disease and hunger on the thin strip of fertile land the Nile has wrested from the desert.

The motives of the British and French in invading Egypt were never as clear as Nasser's in furnishing them with the pretext for their intervention. The confusion arose from the fact that their stated motives were not the same as their real ones. Eden had kept even the Foreign Office in the dark about his intentions. Sir Humphrey Trevelyan, the then British Ambassador in Cairo, had not been consulted; the assistant Under-Secretary of State in charge of all the official information services had not been told what to say. I well remember calling on the head of the Foreign Office news department with two colleagues from *The Economist* a few minutes before Eden made his fateful speech in the House of Commons on 30 October 1956. He told us he had a draft of Eden's speech, but saw no point in giving it to us, as the actual text would soon be coming over the agency tapes. In our impatience we pressed him to give us the general theme the Prime Minister would be expounding, and he replied: 'He will invoke the Tripartite Declaration.' These were comforting words: this document, issued by the United States, Britain, and France in 1950, pledged the maintenance of the 1949 armistice line between the Arabs and Israelis, as well as the balance of armaments between them. A few minutes later, however, Eden was throwing the Tripartite Declaration to the winds by issuing one of the most curiously conceived ultimatums in history. The head of the Foreign Office news department was not trying to deceive us; there would have been no point in trying, since the text of Eden's speech was about to reach us all. The point is that he had no idea Eden was about to tear up the Tripartite Declaration, because he, along with the rest of the Foreign Office, with the one exception of the permanent Under-Secretary, had been deliberately deceived. There is no other possible interpretation of the facts.

The Eden–Mollet ultimatum was addressed both to Israel,

which had invaded Egypt, and to Egypt itself. Its stated aims were to separate the combatants and protect the Canal. There was no mention, however, of the 1949 armistice line; instead, the combatants were told to withdraw to ten miles from either side of the Canal. Failing compliance within twelve hours, the British and French were to occupy Port Said, Ismailia, and Suez – that is, the three main points along the Canal from north to south. Since the combatants were far to the east of the Canal at the time the ultimatum was issued, the objective of separating the combatants cannot be taken seriously. Even the stated aim of keeping the Canal open was a subsidiary purpose. The real aim of the expedition was left unstated: it was to bring down Nasser's revolutionary régime. Eden and Lloyd were coy about overtly admitting this aim, which deviated from a public image of a law-abiding senior member of the United Nations. It was, however, clearly implicit in the whole build-up of the notion that Nasser was a Hitler on the Nile. Indeed, the evidence, as assembled by Erskine Childers, in his able study, *The Road to Suez* (MacGibbon & Kee, 1962), is overwhelming. In Paris, moreover, there was no real attempt to disguise the fact that the object of the exercise was to bring Nasser down. The logical French, rationalizing a series of dubious propositions, justified their intervention on the following grounds: (1) that Nasser was another Hitler who had to be stopped before it was too late; (2) that the Algerian insurrection was directed by Nasser; and (3) that Nasser, and through him the Algerian rebels, were the instruments of communist expansion in North Africa. That the first and third of these propositions were mutually contradictory made no difference; that the second was untrue, I have tried to show in some detail in *The Rebels*. Whatever the reasoning, however, the French were determined to bring the Nasser régime down, and were frankly in alliance ('collusion', as most commentators like to call it) with Israel; whereas the British, who could not have failed to know what was going on, preferred to appear not to know.

It should not be inferred from this highly condensed account of the Suez crisis that I was one of the indignant opponents of the Anglo-French expedition; nor, from this last remark, that I was one of its flag-waving supporters. In fact, I was neither for nor against it. I thought of it as an unusually interesting exercise in power politics. Since that is what it was, I was disappointed by Eden's hypocrisy in failing to disclose his real aims. As a student of international affairs, I was also disappointed that the expedition ended inconclusively. Either it should never have been launched or it should have been seen through to the end. Since Eden's nerve failed him (not because of the rocket threats from Bulganin and Khrushchev, but because the Americans had threatened to deny Britain finance and alternative oil supplies once the Canal had been blocked), we shall never know whether Nasser would have been brought down or whether a durable alternative to him would have been found. The probable answers are Yes to the first question and No to the second. But these are surmises. What of the facts?

The first is that Nasser did get away with his act of defiance. Indeed, he defied not only two great powers but even the UN, which had rescued him, for once the Canal was reopened to shipping, he kept Israeli shipping out of it, in defiance of UN resolutions.

In one sense, indeed, Nasser scored an undeniable triumph. He exploded for all time the myth that only Europeans could run the Suez Canal. The myth had been sedulously and unscrupulously fostered. Childers records (on page 218 of *The Road to Suez*) that:

> To demonstrate that Egypt could not in any case keep the Canal running, it was arranged that pilots of the old Company on leave should stay on leave . . .; that the western press should publish grave descriptions of the expertise purportedly needed to steer ships through; and that Egyptian advertisements for new pilots should be rejected by amenable western newspapers.

I remember listening to one of the pilots in a radio interview, describing the years it had taken him to acquire the skill to steer heavy ships through the narrow channel without hitting the sides. It sounded convincing at the time, but Egyptian, Jugoslav, and other pilots were soon running the Canal as before, without loss of efficiency, and shipowners were soon paying tolls to Egypt, in defiance of Eden's warnings.

On the British and French sides the expedition had been a total failure. It had failed to dislodge Nasser or keep the Canal open; oil supplies had been disrupted and imports of raw materials for industry, especially in Britain, had been severely reduced. Moreover, the Egyptians and Israelis had been separated, after Israel's lightning victory, not by Anglo-French military force, but by the pressure of the super-powers and of the United Nations. In short, Nasser had won, and the western powers had failed.

We have seen something of the state of mind President Bourguiba was in when he ordered the Tunisian attack on Bizerta on 19 July 1961. Our concern now is to look at this tragic incident as an act of defiance against the former colonial power. As such, it was a disastrous failure, even though Bourguiba later got what he had wanted.

Nuclear strategists have long doubted the value of air–naval bases like Bizerta in the nuclear age. But the French, who had been fighting a sub-nuclear war in Algeria and did not rule out the possibility of other such wars, dissented. At the time of the attack Bizerta was one of the four principal bases of the French Fleet, the others being Mers-el-Kebir in Algeria and – in France itself – Toulon and Brest. The town and commercial port of Bizerta stand at the mouth of a $1\frac{1}{2}$-mile canal which links the Mediterranean with the Lake of Bizerta. The massive French installations were along both sides of the lake, but mainly on the western shore.

Bizerta was the last French thorn in Bourguiba's side, but it was deeply embedded and painful. In 1958 he had negotiated a phased withdrawal of French troops from Tunisia, which began on 3 July and was completed on 11 October. Only Bizerta remained. In July 1961, when Bourguiba ordered the attack, the French garrison numbered 7,400 men, of whom 5,000 were technicians. The defending troops were an infantry regiment, armed with artillery and tanks, and supported by a squadron of Mistral jet fighters.

THE VIOLENT MORNING AFTER:
Les Paras do their worst at Bizerta

AFRO-ASIANS DISCOVER THEMSELVES:
The Bandung Conference, 1955

HOME FOR NEW NATIONS:
The UN General Assembly in session

Bourguiba had always admired General de Gaulle, but until 1961 had never met him. In the face of Algerian bitterness and cynicism, he had continued to believe that only General de Gaulle could bring the Algerian war to an end, and that he *would* do it. Although he had repeatedly tried to get the French out of Bizerta, and was under continual pressure from his ruling Néo-Destour party to get results, he had always refrained at the last moment from taking desperate measures, partly because the memory of the French bombing of Sakiet inhibited him, and partly because he was aware of the delicacy of de Gaulle's relationship with the French Army, and did not want to do anything that might prejudice an Algerian settlement.

Then, out of the blue, in February 1961, came an opportunity for Bourguiba to meet de Gaulle in private. The Tunisian chargé d'affaires in Paris was one of the guests at a reception on 1 February at the Elysée Palace. General de Gaulle told him he would like to invite President Bourguiba to Paris. After various diplomatic preliminaries the invitation was officially confirmed on the 21st, in communiqués issued in Paris and Tunis; and on the 27th General de Gaulle, towering over his Tunisian guest, greeted President Bourguiba at Rambouillet, his official country house. The two men were closeted for six hours, and Bourguiba emerged both flattered and elated. Later that evening the two men met again in the presence of the top advisers. Undoubtedly Bizerta must have been discussed, but the communiqué was as cryptic as a communiqué can be. It noted joint hopes about Algeria and the future of North Africa, but without saying what these hopes were.

As everybody knows, de Gaulle is the greatest living master of the sibylline utterance, the subtly worded allusion that requires expert exegesis before it can be assessed at its true value. This seems to have been a case in point. Bourguiba, delighted and flattered as we have seen, seems to have emerged with the feeling that a promise had been made about Bizerta; but de Gaulle must have known that he was still making no promises. The confident feeling that negotiations were on the way, however, clearly played an important part in President Bourguiba's miscalculation of political and military risks.

K

The crisis really started at the end of June when the French began extending the runway of the main Bizerta airfield, Sidi Ahmed, so that it could be used by the latest *Mystère* jet fighters. The Tunisians said this was a provocative act and claimed that they had learnt of the work in progress only by accident. The French, on their side, claimed that the Tunisians not only had been consulted but had given official permission for the work to proceed. Whatever the truth, the Néo-Destour's political bureau went into secret session in an atmosphere of growing tension and announced on 4 July that priority would be given to 'the evacuation and liquidation of the Bizerta military base'. Mr Bahi Ladgham, the Tunisian Secretary of State for Defence, called on the French chargé d'affaires, M. Raoul Duval, that day, and raised two questions. One, of course, was the evacuation of the base. The other was a Tunisian frontier claim which showed, better than anything else, the never-wracking delicacy of Bourguiba's relationship with his Algerian guests.

More than two years earlier, in a letter to the French Government dated 24 January 1959, President Bourguiba had staked an unexpected claim to a few thousand miles of desert on the Algerian side of the *de facto* frontier between Tunisia, Algeria, and Libya. The merits of this claim do not concern us; the interesting point is that since 1959 an American oil company (Esso Sahara) had been prospecting in this area, admittedly without success at the time of the crisis, and that Bourguiba clearly wanted his claim to be recognized by France *before* Algeria became independent. The Algerians, on their side, had always made it clear that they claimed the whole of that part of the Sahara that lay within French jurisdiction and control, including areas claimed by Morocco as well, as the region now claimed by Tunisia. Clearly they were not prepared to weaken their bargaining position *vis-à-vis* France for the sake of Maghrebin unity.

Bourguiba had raised Tunisia's Saharan claim during his talk with de Gaulle in February, again it seems, inconclusively. Now he wrote to the General, on 6 July, restating it and calling for the evacuation of Bizerta. He had devoted thirty years of his life, he wrote, to working for free co-operation between Tunisia

and France; but 'there is one thing I place above this co-operation and in fact above everything – Tunisia's complete sovereignty, without any limits except those to which we have freely
agreed'. He had tried repeatedly to get a peaceful settlement,
but now France was increasing the military potential of the
base, a clear sign the French wanted to hold on to it. He then
added the warning which the French Government found hard
to take as seriously as it was intended:

> . . . the French government apparently holds our national
> dignity in contempt, does not take our just claim seriously,
> and does not believe in our determination to achieve the
> liberation of our national territory at all costs. I am therefore
> obliged to assure you of our firm and irrevocable decision to
> put an end to this situation.

The die had been cast, but it remained for these national
aspirations to be translated into action. The Néo-Destour,
united and assured of popular support, organized mass demonstrations throughout Tunisia from 6 July. Three days later
thousands of volunteers enrolled by the party were sent to
Bizerta, where they started building a trench around the Sidi
Ahmed airfield; and four days after that the French Government announced that there could be no negotiations 'in an
atmosphere of disturbances and demonstrations'. Two warnings to this effect were delivered to the Tunisian Government
by M. Duval. President Bourguiba, however, had made up his
mind. On the 17th he told the National Assembly that a blockade of the Bizerta base would begin on the 19th; at the same
time Tunisian troops would be sent into 'Tunisia's' Sahara to
plant a flag, whatever the consequences and even though the
Algerians refused to concede the Tunisian claim.

A further French note, this time couched in the gravest terms,
reiterated that there could be no negotiations under threat, and
warned Bourguiba of the consequences of the actions he was
proposing to take. It was delivered on the 18th, and a few hours
later, just after midnight, 10,000 Tunisian volunteers began to
erect barricades of sandbags and rocks on all roads leading to
the French installations. The blockade had begun. Unknown

to the Tunisians, however, the French were preparing a dreadful revenge.

The form this French counterblow was to take emerged clearly enough during the day, when the Government announced after a Cabinet meeting that paratroops were being flown to Bizerta from Algeria. The dreaded *paras*, perhaps the toughest combat troops in the world at that time, who had cleaned up Algiers of terrorists with brutal efficiency in 1957, ought to have been a deterrent. The mere threat of dropping them on Paris a year later had toppled the Fourth Republic and brought General de Gaulle back to power. But Bourguiba did not waver. At 2.15 p.m. Tunisian National Guards, armed with rifles, opened fire on a French helicopter. Three hours later Tunisian anti-aircraft guns fired at French reconnaissance aircraft. At 7.5 p.m., French aircraft machine-gunned the Tunisian anti-aircraft posts, and at eight three French cruisers, *Colbert*, *Bouvet*, and *Chevalier-Paul*, were reported off the coast. The Tunisians, who had blocked the channel leading to the lake with chains, announced that the warships would not be allowed in. The battle was on, but the Tunisians, as yet, hardly knew it.

The full force of it hit them the following day, when the French troops opened fire on demonstrators in Bizerta, then launched an offensive against the Tunisian barricades, supported by rocket air raids and naval shelling. At the end of the day the Tunisians counted 110 dead and 500 wounded; the French had lost five men.

At 2 a.m. on 21 July the Tunisians rejected a French ultimatum calling on their forces to evacuate Bizerta and make way for French troops. During the morning French bombers struck at military targets. Then at 2 p.m. *les paras*, reinforced by a third regiment from Algeria, moved in for the kill. Their main target was the Tunisian barracks, which had been machine-gunned from the air and whose occupants had ignored surrender leaflets. By all accounts, the Tunisian defenders fought with desperate bravery, resisting from room to room. In one of these thirty men died at their posts and many others were wounded. At 11.30 p.m. Vice-Admiral Amman, the French Commander, announced that Bizerta had fallen. The streets were littered with the bodies of men, women, and children machine-gunned by the invaders, but though Bizerta had officially fallen, fighting continued the next day. The Tunisian defenders fell back into the Casbah – the medieval Arab quarter, where they felt safe in the narrow, winding streets. Indeed, the French made no attempt to follow them in, but they mortared the Casbah, causing still more civilian deaths and wounds. In all, 1,300 Tunisians had been killed and 639 taken prisoner. The French lost only 21 dead and 101 wounded.

To these Tunisian casualties should be added about 100 others, killed or wounded. These were some of the volunteers who had crossed the Algerian border on the morning of the 19th to plant a Tunisian flag at a spot of their own choice. They never made it.

Why had Bourguiba brought such destruction down on the heads of his people? I have already mentioned Bourguiba's fears and preoccupations in general terms, but I can now be more specific. The dominant consideration was undoubtedly the fear that the whole Algerian situation was turning sour again. French and Algerian negotiators had had one unsuccessful round of negotiations at Evian in the spring, and a second round at Lugrin just before Bourguiba ordered the Bizerta action. One of the causes of the collapse of the Evian talks had been a French refusal to discuss the future of the naval base at Mers-el-Kebir. The French had given no indication that they might be more forthcoming in the second round of talks, and Bourguiba rightly supposed that Lugrin would be as unsuccessful as Evian had been. This seemed to foreshadow a further prolonged period during which the French would refuse to discuss Bizerta as well. Indeed, Bourguiba's information was that the French military planners regarded Bizerta and Mers-el-Kebir as part of a permanent system of Mediterranean bases which France would continue to hold on behalf of Nato. Partly for reasons of personal conviction, partly because of Tunisian political opinion, and partly because of the state of feeling among the African and Asian countries, Bourguiba was determined to demonstrate that he would have no part of any such conception. His determination was reinforced by a subsidiary fear, which, to some observers, seemed ill-founded, but which he and his advisers took seriously: that if the French were involved in war over Berlin the Tunisians would be dragged in as well because of Bizerta.

But these considerations, though they explain Bourguiba's urge to 'do something', do not explain why this born politician, this master calculator of possibilities, so miscalculated the consequences of his chosen course of action. Memories of Sakiet ought to have made the savagery of the French reaction predictable. Metaphorically, the French Army – and especially that arrogant elite, *les paras* – was like a snarling dog, best left alone, for when kicked it could be relied upon to bite. *Cet animal*, as the French say, *est très méchant; quand on l'attaque, il se défend.* The British, who were aware of the state of mind of the French, had sent Bourguiba a friendly warning that any blockade of Bizerta would bring serious consequences. Bourguiba, however, had been convinced right till the end that de Gaulle would open negotiations on Bizerta despite his fear that Bizerta, like Mers-el-Kebir, was not negotiable from a French viewpoint. Indeed, he would probably have been content to bring the French to the conference table, even in the knowledge that the talks might be prolonged and abortive, for the opening of talks would have removed the political pressure on him to 'do something' about Bizerta.

It is now known that at the time General de Gaulle had no intention of discussing the evacuation of Bizerta. Indeed, on 5 September, long after the events, General de Gaulle stated that it had been agreed to postpone a decision until after the Algerian war was over. In one of his messages to the Tunisian Government – dated 16 July – the General had conceded, however, that the Tunisian blockade of Bizerta was evidently not directed against French lives and property; he was therefore not disposed to reply to Bourguiba's letter of 6 July – the warning letter which the French had not taken seriously. On receiving the message of 16 July, Bourguiba, rubbing his hands in misplaced glee, told his friends: 'I am completely optimistic. There will be negotiations and they will lead to the evacuation of Bizerta.' Optimism had thus temporarily replaced the general pessimism about Algeria and relations with France which had dominated Bourguiba's mood for so long. But on the 18th came a further message, which dashed Bourguiba's fragile hopes; so long as the atmosphere remained disturbed, said de Gaulle, he could not reply to the Tunisian President's letter. By this time, Bourguiba had committed himself too far for withdrawal, in the eyes of his party and his people. Next day, the Tunisian forces opened fire.

Ironically, the first shots, fired at a French helicopter, did not even hit their target. Even later, when French aircraft started machine-gunning Tunisian posts, the Tunisians seem to have thought that all they had provoked was a mild skirmish. And indeed, the violence of the French reaction surprised even the French Commander, Admiral Amman, who is said to have twice asked for his instructions to be repeated before he would agree to carry them out. Although it must always be assumed that a decision of such importance would be taken by General de Gaulle himself, it must be recorded that the instructions came directly from the office of the then Prime Minister, M. Debré.

My friend Lucien Bodard, reporting the Bizerta massacre on the spot for *France-Soir*, allowed himself to question the need for so violent a retaliation, but this comment, which was out of tune with official policy, appeared in only one of that day's editions of his newspaper, as some of its more careful readers noted.

Two remarks made by President Bourguiba during those turbulent days have been handed down by those who heard them. One was made after he had read General de Gaulle's discouraging message of 18 July: 'I now realize that to come to terms with de Gaulle, one must be either a Brazzaville black or an Algerian.' Decoded, this meant that one must either be prepared to collaborate wholeheartedly or to make war. The second remark, sadder in tone, came on 21 July after confirmation of the news of French brutalities in Bizerta town: 'I had wanted little Tunisia to become the West's (postage) stamp on the African continent. Now all that is over.'

One of the most spectacular acts of defiance by a newly independent country was the expulsion of the Dutch from

Indonesia at the end of 1957. By devious ways which we shall examine, the purpose of this action was to hasten the day of the 'liberation' of West New Guinea from Dutch rule. The Dutch did finally quit West New Guinea, but not until 28 September 1962 – nearly five years later. The length of time elapsed suggests that there was little connexion between the two events, and indeed it can be shown fairly clearly that the decision of the Dutch to quit New Guinea was made for reasons that had relatively little to do with Indonesian actions. The whole unhappy episode is, however, an interesting study in the assertion of independence.

The Indonesian Government wanted Dutch New Guinea because it had been part of the Dutch East Indies empire. The Dutch had clung on to it for a variety of reasons: originally, no doubt, because they had not reconciled themselves to the loss of that empire and nursed the secret hope that they might regain it, if only they kept a foothold and waited for the Indonesian Republic to collapse; because they hoped the territory would prove economically profitable; and also for the nobler motive of protecting the interests of the primitive people who live there. A further motive was plain, old-fashioned Dutch stubbornness. There are many accounts of the Dutch–Indonesian dispute, both in its wider aspects and in connexion with New Guinea, but perhaps the best, for concision and impartiality, is Dr Leslie Palmier's *Indonesia and the Dutch* (Oxford for the Institute of Race Relations, London, 1962). There is no need to go into the full details of the problem here, but some essential facts have to be mentioned.

New Guinea is huge and inhospitable, as the Japanese, Australian, and American soldiers who fought there during the Second World War will never forget. The eastern half of the island is under Australian rule, and the Indonesians have never claimed it. The western half remained under Dutch control after the Netherlands had formally handed over sovereignty over the rest of their East Indies empire to Indonesia in December 1949. It is a country of swamps, impenetrable jungle, and towering mountains. About 700,000 people live in West New Guinea; they are Papuans, and therefore belong to the

Melanesian ethnic group and are not racially akin to the
Indonesians (whose origins are diverse, but who are mostly
Malaysians). Each little tribal community has developed – or,
better, remained static – on its own, isolated from others by lack
of communications. As a result, there are some 200 languages in
what used to be the Dutch half of the island. Often the Papuans
in one place cannot understand a word of what is said to them
if they wander into another tribal area a few miles away.

It has always been hard to see why the Dutch wanted to keep
West New Guinea and just as hard to see why the Indonesians
wanted to take it away from them. Politics, however, are only
occasionally rational. What matters is not whether a thing is
important in itself, but whether politicians think it is important.
Both in Holland and in Indonesia the politicians did think it
was important, and in both countries they went to considerable
lengths to persuade the people that it was important and to keep
the issue alive. As a result, feelings – especially in Indonesia,
which felt itself the aggrieved party – became more and more
inflamed. Whatever the merits of the case, there is no doubt that
the West New Guinea issue poisoned relations between the
Indonesians and their former rulers. The British were soon on
good terms with the peoples and governments of their former
colonies, such as India, Ceylon, and Burma; and even the
French, who lost their Indochina empire after a long and
disastrous war, managed to establish amicable relations with
the Vietnamese, Laotians, and Cambodians. Only the Dutch
failed in this respect, and West New Guinea was by far the biggest cause of this failure.

From the beginning, the Indonesian politicians treated West
New Guinea as an 'anti-colonial' issue. They argued that the
Dutch East Indies had constituted one colony, West New
Guinea being administered as part of the Moluccas; since the
Indonesian Republic had taken over as successor State, there
was no reason why West New Guinea should remain in Dutch
hands. The Dutch replied that West New Guinea was a special
case, as a backward area, inhabited by primitive, non-
Indonesian people to whom they felt a sense of obligation.
Moreover, the legal position was ambiguous. Article 1 of the

Charter of Transfer of Sovereignty, agreed by the Dutch and Indonesians after bitter and protracted negotiations, transferred 'complete sovereignty over Indonesia' to what was at that time the Republic of the United States of Indonesia. But Article 2 laid down that the *status quo* in Dutch New Guinea was to be maintained, pending negotiations within one year to determine its political status. Negotiations did follow, but they proved sterile. In August 1950 a mixed commission reported that it had failed to reach agreement; deadlock was the outcome of further negotiations in 1951 and 1952.

In a way, Dutch New Guinea *was*, as the Indonesians argued, a colonial issue. Certainly the Dutch were there by right of conquest and they were ruling over a dependent people. On the other hand, if the Dutch transferred their authority to the Indonesians, would not the Papuans be exchanging one form of colonialism for another and less-efficient form? That is how the Indonesian claim looked, in the eyes of many people in the West; and indeed if imperialism is the domination of one people by another that was at least a possible interpretation of what was in store for the Papuans. Imperialism or colonialism, as the former colonies of the West conceived it, was very narrowly defined. It was simply the domination of black, brown, or yellow peoples by western whites. The domination of white by white (e.g. Hungarians by Russians) or yellow by eastern whites (e.g. Central Asians by Russians) did not arouse emotions; even that of yellow by yellow (Tibetans by Chinese), though it might provoke moral searchings, was hardly a cause for excitement. As for the proposed domination of the black Papuans by the brown Indonesians, so lately freed from Dutch rule, that could scarcely be regarded as colonialism. ('Even if the Papuans aren't racially the same as we are,' one Indonesian diplomat used to say to me, 'we are more like them than the Dutch.' This was unanswerable, but irrelevant.)

The Indonesians naturally sought their friends among the like-minded, and these were naturally to be found among the other colonies or ex-colonies. One of the underlying motives of the Indonesians in organizing the Bandung Conference in 1955 was undoubtedly that of winning friends and influencing people. In this they were, on the whole, successful, for the final communiqué of the conference had this to say about West Irian (West New Guinea):

> The Asian-African conference, in the context of its expressed attitude on the abolition of colonialism, supported the position of Indonesia in the case of West Irian, based on the relevant agreements between Indonesia and the Netherlands.
>
> The Asian-African conference urged the Netherlands government to resume negotiations as soon as possible, to implement their obligations under the above mentioned agreements and expressed the earnest hope that the United Nations would assist the parties concerned in finding a peaceful solution to the dispute.

The Dutch, however, took no notice. Refusing all further negotiations, they maintained a course best calculated to inflame Indonesian feelings to their eventual snapping point. The man who, more than any other, was responsible for this unblinking policy was Dr Joseph Luns, who became Foreign Minister in 1956 and held that post through successive Dutch administrations. Thus huge, genial man, who is roughly tall enough to look General de Gaulle in the eye, has an emotional blind spot about Indonesia, much as Nehru has about Kashmir, but with far less justification. Unlike many Dutch high officials, he never served in Indonesia. A career diplomat, and therefore not a politician, he served with the Dutch delegation to the United Nations before being offered his first Cabinet post in 1952. From 1956, when he became Foreign Minister, he was in the thick of a political fight, both at home and abroad. It is said of him that at one stage in the interminable dispute with Indonesia he was deeply offended, both personally and nationally, by President Sukarno's refusal to meet him (though his own comment is that he never officially requested a meeting). But this, by itself, seems an inadequate explanation of the stubborn passion with which he opposed the notion of a Dutch withdrawal from Holland's last Far Eastern possession. We once had a talk at the residence of the Dutch Ambassador in London, Baron Bentinck, and he opened by haranguing me for five minutes on the wickedness of the British in holding up the return of the Dutch forces to Indonesia in September 1945, after the Japanese surrender. True enough, the British commander, General Christison, who was in charge of the British landing under Admiral Mountbatten, had said: 'I am stopping all Dutch troops coming until we are well established. We shall hand over all internal security to them when their forces come in, and then dispense with the Japanese.' True also, this British decision had hindered the Dutch and helped the Indonesian Nationalists. But the Dutch had underestimated the force of Indonesian nationalism, which would have driven them out even without the slight and temporary assistance it received from the British. Such an error of judgement was perhaps forgivable in 1945, when the Dutch were emerging from German occupation. But it was hard to understand how Dr Luns could seriously advance the same arguments fifteen years later, when our conversation took place.

Many Dutchmen, however, thought the same way as Dr Luns; and indeed the Dutch might still be in New Guinea or, alternatively, locked in combat with Indonesian invaders, had their residual economic hopes not collapsed in the mid-'fifties. Minerals had been found on the island, but the forbidding physical conditions made exploitation commercially unattractive. There had been one important exception: oil. But in the event, even oil turned out a disappointment. From 1936 to 1955, says Dr Palmier in *Indonesia and the Dutch*, the Netherlands New Guinea Oil Company invested £40 million ($112 million), but recouped only £10 million ($28 million). At its peak in 1954 oil production did reach a respectable 550,000 tons, but thereafter it fell fairly rapidly, and by 1958 it was down to 267,000 tons – a drop of more than 50 per cent. This collapse of economic prospects was naturally reflected, from 1956 on, in a movement among Dutch business men in favour of finding some way out of New Guinea. The ancient appeal of 'patriotism' and 'national honour', however, continued to be stronger than the counter-appeal of commercial accounting, although by 1958 Dutch New Guinea was costing the Dutch taxpayers £10 million ($28 million) a year more than it was bringing in.

Although stubbornness and Dr Luns's refusal to draw the right inferences from contemporary history were important elements in Holland's policy, they did not entirely account for it. One cannot simply write off another element: a genuine concern for the future well-being of the almost inconceivably primitive people who remained under Dutch rule. There was, of course, no such thing as 'Papuan nationalism' until the Dutch themselves created it by training two or three thousand Papuans in various minor administrative capacities. Scarcely half West New Guinea's scattered population was really under Dutch control, and in the interior were many tribespeople who had yet to see a white face. These facts alone made West New Guinea a special case, as the Dutch had said it was in 1949. On the Indonesian side, tame pro-Indonesian Papuans could be produced, as tame pro-Dutch ones could be by the Dutch. In neither case did it mean much. The Dutch, however, had involved themselves, as administrators, doctors, and teachers in the lives of the Papuans and did not feel they could just abandon them. Moreover, they felt a special responsibility towards the the 2,000 or 3,000 more or less educated Papuans who formed the administrative *élite*, much as the French had felt responsible for the safety of the far greater number of Moslems who had thrown in their lot with France in Algeria. Given the circumstances, statehood of any kind seemed inconceivable in either half of New Guinea for perhaps fifty years. Self-determination, on the other hand, had a respectable ring and offered the merit, from Dr Luns's viewpoint, of allowing the Dutch to retire gracefully, in their own good time, without handing their half of New Guinea to the Indonesians.

Since the inhabitants of western and eastern New Guinea were racially identical, the logical course for the Dutch seemed to be to concert their policy with Australia's. This they did, and in November 1957 the Dutch and Australian governments jointly announced that they intended to strengthen co-operation between them in leading the people of New Guinea towards self-determination. The Indonesians had got wind of this agreement some weeks before it was published (I remember startling some high officials of the Dutch Foreign Ministry in The Hague in

October by asking for details of the agreement which, at that time, had not yet been disclosed).

If the last straw had been needed, this would have provided it. But President Sukarno had probably already made up his mind that his patience was exhausted. Hard though the Indonesians had worked among their African and Asian friends, either they had not worked quite hard enough or the composition of the United Nations did not yet automatically provide a strong enough majority in favour of *any* anti-colonial resolution. At any rate, on 29 November, a resolution affirming Indonesian sovereignty failed, as on previous occasions, to secure two-thirds of the votes in the UN General Assembly. Even this setback, however, was a signal for action rather than a final, unbearable affront, for ten days or so earlier, on the 18th and 19th, representatives of political, youth, and military organizations had been brought to Djakarta from all over Indonesia to 'urge the Indonesian Government' (as the resolutions they passed worded it) to take various retaliatory measures against the Dutch, should the UN fail to give the Indonesians satisfaction. Dutch-owned enterprises were to be nationalized and all Dutch nationals who were not contributing to Indonesia's 'reconstruction programme' were to be repatriated. In addition to the increasingly active 'Action Committee for the Liberation of West Irian', two militant organizations were to be set up: the West Irian Reconstruction Brigade and a West Irian Liberation Fund.

On 1 December, two days after the UN vote, the first blow fell. The Indonesian Information Minister announced a general strike in all Dutch enterprises, and a ban on all Dutch language publications, while the Royal Dutch Airlines (KLM) planes were forbidden to land and even to fly over Indonesian territory. Within the next few days (and, to be fair, in the face of repeated official warnings against unauthorized acts), groups of Indonesian workers and youths had seized Dutch concerns of all kinds, including banks and merchant houses in many parts of Indone-Whsia. en the management of the KPM or Dutch Packet Navigation Company refused to sign an 'instrument of transfer' all Dutch employees were forced out of its buildings. Red flags were then hoisted overhead and over other seized buildings. The colour of the flags was a reliable clue, for most of these apparently spontaneous, but remarkably synchronized, actions had been organized by the Indonesian Communist Party, which was determined to demonstrate that it was even more patriotic than the Government. Everywhere, services of all kinds, from the sale of food to rides in taxis, were refused to anybody who was visibly Dutch. But hungry, footsore, and scared though they were, the Dutch were at least allowed to keep their lives and stay unbruised: discomfort and hardship were widespread, but there was no violence.

The Government on its side was doing well enough. On the 5th the Ministry of Justice announced the impending expulsion of 50,000 Dutch citizens – the entire Dutch community except certain categories classified as 'experts'; and the Foreign Ministry announced that all Dutch consular and diplomatic missions throughout Indonesia – except only the consular section of the Embassy in Djakarta. On the 9th all 500 Dutch-owned estates and plantations throughout the islands were placed under government control. Many of these had already been seized by Communist-led bands of peasants, much as the offices has been taken over in the towns. But now the Government stepped in, forbidding harmful activities on the estates and calling on Indonesians to stop their economic boycott of the Dutch and, in particular, to sell food to them. The Army Chief of Staff, General Nasution, forbade further take-overs and announced that military administrators would take over all expropriated enterprises.

To understand the pointless harshness of the expulsion order one has to remember that three-fifths of those who were being thrown out of Indonesia were Eurasians who had never known any other country. Some were full-blood Indonesians who happened to be Christians. After the transfer of sovereignty in 1949 they were told to choose between Dutch and Indonesian nationality, and most of them, who liked to think of themselves as Dutch although they had never seen Holland, misguidedly chose to be Dutch citizens. Now, in their tens of thousands, women and children, old people and breadwinners, boarded ship for the rainy, distant, overcrowded little country that had once been the metropolitan power. To their honour, a number of prominent Indonesians publicly protested against the anti-Dutch measures.

In one concentrated blow, Dutch influence had been eliminated in the islands where the Hollanders had first settled more than 300 years earlier. As in war – and this was a kind of war – the cruellest hurts had befallen the innocent; but the political purposes of the attack remained unaccomplished. West New Guinea stayed in Dutch hands until five years later, when a combination of circumstances that owed nothing to the expropriation of properties or the expulsion of citizens brought Sukarno his elusive prize.

Since we are examining acts of defiance as the instruments of policy of newly independent States, we shall have to look at the consequences of the anti-Dutch campaign and at the circumstances that did bring West New Guinea under Indonesian control. No doubt the managements of expropriated firms were put to great inconvenience and expense, but the greater losers were the Indonesians, not the Dutch. The seizure of the KPM shipping line had brought inter-island traffic to a standstill throughout Indonesia. The price of rice – the staple food – trebled in three months in Java, while stocks rotted on the docks in less-crowded islands. Thereafter, the economic consequences to Indonesia of the anti-Dutch action became blurred, for in February 1958 a rebellion against the Indonesian Government broke out in Sumatra and Celebes, and it was difficult to know how much of the continuing deterioration was to be attributed to the departure of the Dutch and how much to the seizure of the export market by the rebels. Whatever the precise allocation of causes, however, the ordinary people of Indonesia were having a thin time. The *Indonesian Observer*, a Nationalist newspaper supporting President Sukarno's Government, put it in these words:

If shortly after the West Irian action, during the early part of 1958, people willingly sacrificed luxuries for the national cause, nowadays almost everything has become a 'luxury'.

... Home produced bathsoap is no longer within reach of
the lower paid groups. ... A city worker who only makes
Rp. 6.50 daily can never afford a litre of rice as this com-
modity is only available at 8 Rupiahs a litre. He therefore
cannot even support a family on the wages he earns. ...
This cannot go on much longer.

On the Dutch side there was, as I have said, a great deal of
individual hardship, much of it affecting people who had never
been to Holland in their lives. One should perhaps distinguish
between the losses of individuals and those of Holland as a
nation and a State. Among individuals, the careers of thousands
of Dutchmen were wrecked, and the life-savings of many
families who had invested all they had in Indonesia were wiped
out. On the national side, the value of the Dutch-owned enterprises seized in 1957 was about £550 million, and the prospect
of compensation at anything like an equitable figure, or at all,
were exceedingly dim. As for Holland as a State, it showed itself – to the surprised discomfiture of Indonesian officials – able
to take the financial loss in its stride. In 1958, according to the
Dutch Finance Minister, the additional financial burden directly
attributable to the Indonesian action was about £30 million –
a loss which the thriving Dutch economy could stand without
excessive strain. Indeed, the guilder retained its value and
Holland remained one of the most prosperous countries of
Europe. In contrast, the Indonesian budget ran up a deficit of
9·7 billion rupiahs in 1958, by official reckoning, and 12 billion
by unofficial estimating (there is no point in trying to convert
these figures, as the official valuation of the rupiah bore no
relation to its true value); in one year currency in circulation
rose by 50 per cent; many industries had to close down for
lack of raw materials owing to drastic import cuts; and the
family budgets of middle-class officials rose by 80 per cent, again
in 1958. Whatever the precise causes of this catastrophic decline,
one thing was clear: the expulsion of the Dutch had not brought
prosperity to Indonesia, just as it had not brought ruin to the
Dutch economy.

Nor did it yield the political dividend it was supposed to

L

bring: instead of handing over West New Guinea, the Dutch government became, if anything, more determined than before that even if they left, the territory should not be allowed to pass into the hands of the Indonesians. A year after the expulsion, as we have seen, the Dutch and Australian governments agreed on a joint approach to self-determination for the Papuans. In April 1961 Dutch New Guinea's first representative central body – the New Guinea Council – started functioning; and shortly afterwards, in December that year, the territory was given the less-colonial-sounding name of West Papua. In October the Dutch Government had announced far-reaching proposals offering self-determination to the Papuans leading to sovereignty over their own country, and continued financial assistance at the rate of $30 million a year – all under the auspices of the United Nations, which was invited to send a fact-finding commission to West New Guinea.

Almost exactly a year later, however, the Dutch policy lay in ruins and Holland was handing West New Guinea over to the Indonesians, via the UN. What had made the Dutch government change course? Certainly nothing that could be traced back to the expulsion of the Dutch from Indonesia. Historians will almost certainly find that the determining factor was Senator John F. Kennedy's victory in the American Presidential elections in 1960. That the Dutch, nearly a year later, were still advocating a policy which had ceased to have the slightest chance of success merely showed that they were trying not to face the facts. President Kennedy brought to office with him a team of brilliant intellectuals who were determined that the United States should swim with and not against the anti-colonial tide of contemporary history. Men like Chester Bowles, a former Ambassador to India, John Kenneth Galbraith, a future Ambassador to India, or George Kennan, perhaps the foremost Sovietologist in the United States, were tired of seeing their country tarred with the imperialist brush, as it had been consistently under the Eisenhower Administrations. Their advice, which President Kennedy accepted, was that wherever anti-colonial claims did not conflict with American vital interests, the US Government should support them. Clearly this advice created a dilemma, in that the United States was in military alliance with all the western colonial powers – Britain, France, Holland, Belgium, and Portugal – within the North Atlantic Treaty Organization. Britain, however, had a first-class record in ridding itself of its colonial burdens; France was doing brilliantly in the same field in Africa, with the one exception of Algeria. The major allies could therefore be supported in most issues; and the colonial interests of the minor allies were judged, by and large, to be expendable (the Congo being a special case). There was never the slightest chance, for instance, that the United States would defend Portuguese Goa against the Indians; and the Kennedy Administration soon made it clear to the Dutch that they could not count on American military support should the Indonesians invade West New Guinea. This was a bitter pill for the Dutch to swallow, but it was presented to Dr Luns with unfailing regularity each time he went to the United States. The Australians, concerned about their half of the island, found President Kennedy's attitude equally unforthcoming. The Australian Prime Minister, Mr Menzies, dropped in on the President at the end of February 1961, on his way to the Commonwealth Conference in London, and found him unreceptive to his two main arguments: that New Guinea as a whole was a key area in strategic terms, which the United States as well as Australia had fought to defend during the Second World War; and that Mr Kennedy, who had himself served in the Pacific war, should turn a deaf ear to the sentimentalists who wanted him to hand Dutch New Guinea over to a potential enemy. Mr Menzies supported this view by drawing the President's attention to facts of which he was certainly aware, such as an enormous purchase of Soviet arms by the Indonesian government a few weeks earlier, and the growing power of the Indonesian Communist Party (PKI).

The President's mind was made up, however. When the New Guinea Council was inaugurated in April he refused to send a representative (although Britain did). Not long afterwards on 17 August, the US ambassador to Indonesia, Mr Howard P. Jones, was heard shouting *Merdeka* ('freedom') in Jakarta when the Indonesians celebrated their independence day. More constructively, the Americans set out to bring the Dutch and Indonesians to the conference table.

This proved as stubbornly difficult as might have been expected. The symbol of unredeemed West Irian had acquired an obsessive urgency in Jakarta. To 'recover' it had become an imperative necessity, justifying any financial folly or military adventure. In January 1961 an Indonesian mission had committed itself to buying some £130 million worth of arms in the Soviet Union. The enormity of this purchase contrasted with Indonesia's depleted treasury and argued either that President Sukarno had decided on a military solution or that he wished the Dutch to believe he had. Shortly afterwards, however, a major internal development in Indonesia forced the chancelleries to take the country's militant mood more seriously. In April a number of major leaders of the 1958 rebellion surrendered to the central government, bringing their forces with them. Others were to follow suit. These surrenders transformed the military outlook. An Indonesian invasion of West New Guinea had been unthinkable so long as the bulk of the Indonesian forces was tied down in the rebel areas of Sumatra, Celebes, and the Moluccas. It became at least credible after the rebels had laid down their arms.

The Indonesians had still not committed themselves to an invasion, however; indeed, they thought they had reason to hope for a change of heart on the part of the Dutch. Between the spring and autumn of 1961 there were repeated, though unofficial, discussions between Dutchmen and Indonesians, on the possibility of reaching a peaceful settlement in New Guinea. The contacts took place in Washington, London, Bonn, and other places. The Dutchmen involved were mostly business men and politicians, and the Indonesians, politicians, officials, and army officers. One of the Dutchmen was a brother of the Dutch Prime Minister, Professor de Quay, who happened to be a Catholic missionary in Indonesia. His participation alone encouraged the Indonesians to believe West New Guinea would soon drop into their laps like an overripe fruit. Dr Luns, the Foreign Minister, strongly disapproved of these peace-making contacts, however, and his influence within the Cabinet and

Parliament was strong enough to frustrate them. Hence the Dutch self-determination proposals of October, which, as Dr Luns had rightly calculated, were angrily rejected by the Indonesians.

During the ensuing few weeks a note of heightening militancy, and indeed hysteria, came into the public statements of the Indonesian leaders, whose intention was clearly to whip up popular feeling in favour of military action against the Dutch. There was a grand double climax in two bellicose speeches by President Sukarno. In the first, on 19 December, he announced the setting up of a 'command' for the liberation of West Irian, and in the second, on 26 December, he rejected a Dutch offer of unconditional negotiations, which had been made a few days earlier after a Cabinet meeting in The Hague. Shortly afterwards he decreed general mobilization, and the impression grew that Dr Sukarno would prefer to 'liberate' West New Guinea by force than gain it by negotiation. One factor in this intransigence was probably the Indian seizure of Goa in December 1961. By refusing to condemn India, the United Nations had appeared to sanction aggression, so long as it was for the purpose of 'recovering' a colony. The fact that the aggression had been committed by Gandhi's political heirs seemed to provide an additional dispensation.

The awkward fact was that whereas Goa could be swallowed in one military mouthful, West Irian was bound to make a heavy and indigestible meal. The Dutch defences were strong, and had been reinforced at various times during the previous eighteen months. Although Indonesia's forces were, at least on paper, much stronger, they faced many potential difficulties, from the mountains, jungles, and swamps of the territory to a possibly hostile reception from tribespeople who had never heard of Holland or Indonesia. Something, however, had to be done, and on 15 January 1962 three Indonesian motor torpedo boats were sent to patrol the waters off the West New Guinea coast. The outcome was painful to Indonesian pride. The Dutch coastal batteries opened fire; one of the Indonesian boats was sunk, and the deputy chief of the Indonesian Naval Staff, Commodore Sudarso, was killed; fifty-two Indonesians were taken prisoner.

This incident was probably a turning-point. It brought home to the Indonesians that the Dutch were prepared and that an invasion was not going to be a walk-over. It gave the Dutch a confident feeling that if they did negotiate it would demonstrably not be out of weakness. On the other hand, it brought home to them, too, the prospect of an interminable series of incidents, to cope with which would involve them in a mounting spiral of defence expenditure – and the end of which could not be victory.

In London and Washington, also, the incident had its effect. On 23 January, Lord Home, the British Foreign Secretary, announced the suspension of British exports of arms and military equipment to Indonesia 'as a temporary measure until the situation over West New Guinea has been clarified'. The Americans, on their side, were made to realize the urgency of bringing the Dutch and Indonesians together, for the incident seemed to show that the Indonesians would be unable to make a clean military job of an invasion and would be driven into increasing dependence on supplies, advice, and perhaps direct military aid from the Soviet bloc. This fear was underlined shortly afterwards when the Indonesians sent a further mission to Moscow, to arrange for deliveries of heavy arms, including jet aircraft, under the previous year's arms agreement.

There was still, however, a stubborn gap between the negotiating positions of the two sides. As we have seen, the Dutch had already offered to negotiate without prior conditions. This had been the Dutch Government's response to a telegraphed appeal from U Thant, the acting Secretary-General of the UN, sent at the end of 1961 – just after President Sukarno's two provocative speeches. U Thant had also sent a telegram to President Sukarno, but the Indonesians kept on saying that they would talk with the Dutch only if it were clearly understood in advance that the talks would lead to a transfer of authority in West Irian from Holland to Indonesia. Now, after the incident of 15 January, U Thant sent off further telegrams to both sides. Within twenty-four hours the Dutch Government replied, again expressing willingness to negotiate without pre-conditions under the auspices of the UN, while reserving the right of self-defence.

President Sukarno did not reply until the 20th. He did not rule out peaceful negotiations; nor, on the other hand, did he welcome them.

This was the position when, in February 1962, President Kennedy sent his brother, Mr Robert Kennedy, the US Attorney-General, on a diplomatic journey to Jakarta and The Hague. Little has been disclosed about the arguments Mr Kennedy used in either place, but it is clear that they were potent, and something of their nature can be deduced from later developments. He probably pointed out to the Indonesians the wider international dangers of the violent course on which they seemed set, and argued that the principle of self-determination on which the Dutch case rested could not lightly be cast aside. To the Dutch, he probably pointed out that they were in danger of allowing themselves to be drawn into a pointless colonial war in which they would find themselves isolated and friendless from the start. To both, he must have offered the good offices of the United States in reaching a settlement.

Though on paper, the two sides were still far apart, it was clear from private conversations that they had been moving closer to an agreement. By offering to negotiate without prior conditions, the Dutch had tacitly, though not explicitly, retreated from their earlier insistence on self-determination for the Papuans. On their side, the Indonesians had been saying privately since the beginning of the year that they would be willing to consider some form of self-determination, so long as it was preceded by a long enough period of Indonesian rule. They argued, rightly enough, that self-determination under Dutch rule would simply produce a pro-Dutch result. Their unspoken implication was that a period of Indonesian rule would produce a pro-Indonesian vote. Thus the outline of an agreement – at the expense of the Papuans, the most expendable of the three peoples concerned – was beginning to emerge.

It took several more months of patient American diplomacy to produce a document acceptable to both sides. Mr Ellsworth Bunker, a former State Department man, was called back out of retirement to act as 'good officer'. An old country house in Virginia was put at his disposal, and there he acted as host to

the Dutch and Indonesian negotiators. As a gesture of concilia-
tion, the Dutch had announced that no further reinforcements
would be sent to New Guinea, and had begun to repatriate the
prisoners captured on 15 January. President Sukarno, however,
still felt the need to make his public believe that West Irian was
being wrested from the Dutch by Indonesian force. In May and
June, and in five separate operations, 600 Indonesian paratroopers were air-dropped at scattered points on the island. A
number of them died after landing awkwardly on trees; others
were drowned in swamps; many more were killed in subsequent
fighting with the Dutch. Altogether, about 200 Indonesians and
five Dutchmen lost their lives. The most disappointing thing of
all, however, from the Indonesian point of view, was the reception the liberated Papuans reserved for the paratroopers. The
Indonesians had been ordered to avoid direct clashes with the
Dutch and organize the Papuans for guerrilla warfare. The
smiling friendliness of the natives encouraged them to think
their mission would soon be accomplished. In many cases, however, the Papuans, after providing them with food and guides,
led them straight into Dutch ambushes. Other groups of
Indonesians waited around for further reinforcements and
supply drops, which had been promised, then became dis-
couraged and surrendered. By death, capture, or surrender,
then, more than half of the 600 had been put out of action by
July, and the others were a diminishing threat.

These Indonesian actions inevitably raised the temperature,
both in Jakarta and The Hague, and delayed the inevitable
settlement. Agreement was finally reached, however, on the
night of 15 August 1962. Predictably, the Dutch gave away
more than they had hoped. Control was to be handed over, first
to UN officials, then from these to the Indonesians. The first of
these operations was to take place as soon as possible (it actually
took place on 28 September), and the second not later than
May 1963. A referendum was to be held not later than 1969,
giving the Papuans a choice between independence and incor-
poration into Indonesia.

This was a stony end to a long and bitter road. By their stubbornness, the Dutch had lost the bulk of their international

interests in Indonesia, Indonesia's goodwill and West New Guinea into the bargain. By their folly, the Indonesians had compounded their own bankruptcy to acquire a wilderness sparsely populated by Stone Age people who did not want them. Only the Papuans had got nothing out of the deal, except the prospect of up to five and a half years of Indonesian rule to condition them for a state of more permanent dependence. Perhaps, on the other hand, the Indonesians had not heard the last of Papuan nationalism.

It had all been tantalizingly avoidable.

PART II

The Frailty of Independence

Chapter 1

THE COLD WAR

As soon as colonies become independent, and sometimes sooner, their survival begins to be threatened. The threat may be local, as in the case of Togo, which is claimed by Ghana, but it is as likely to be global. The greatest and most persistent threat to the survival and independence of the new nations undoubtedly arises out of the cold war which, in its simplest terms, means the rivalry between the Soviet Union and the United States, and at its most complex involves the allies of each.

The leaders of the new countries are, of course, aware that the cold war presents a threat to their independence, but they do not always see the nature of that threat as clearly as they might. One reason for this is that all the new countries were until lately colonies of western nations; they therefore tend to think of colonialism as a purely western phenomenon. Another reason is that during the years of struggle for independence the new leaders mostly found their friends among left-wingers, who encouraged them to associate colonialism with western capitalism and anti-imperialism with communism. Communist imperialism is, however, on a gigantic scale, and unlike the western colonial powers, the communist ones have kept what they grabbed.

The facts of communist – especially Soviet – colonialism are important but are often overlooked, partly because of the mental blockage I have just described, partly because the communist empire forms a vast land mass stretching from East Germany to North Vietnam, and the outlying bits are less visible than were those of the overseas empires of the western powers, and again partly because of the communist monopoly of media of information. Those who want to go into the question more fully than I can here might turn to Professor Hugh Seton-

Watson's *The New Imperialism* (Methuen, London, 1961) or to
Robert Conquest's *The Last Empire* (Ampersand, London,
1962). All I can do is to summarize the essential facts. The Bolsheviks had promised to free the 'enslaved peoples' of the
Tsarist empire, but they lost no time in substituting their
authority for that of the Tsars. Independent governments had
been set up in Azerbaidjan and Georgia, and farther east in
Khiva and Bokhara, in the confusion that followed the defeat of
the Russian armies in 1917. By 1921, the Bolsheviks had overthrown them all and supplanted them by governments controlled from Moscow. Within the next three years the Russians,
taking advantage of anti-Chinese sentiment among the Mongols
of Outer Mongolia, set up a satellite government there. In 1921
they brutally suppressed an anti-Russian uprising in Armenia;
and in 1924 in Georgia. Under Stalin the Soviet régime annexed
Bessarabia and Northern Bukovina, the independent Baltic
States of Latvia, Esthonia, and Lithuania, Tannu Tuva, parts
of Finland, and nearly half of Poland. These were war-time
acquisitions, and they were simply swallowed up inside the
Soviet Union after ruthless suppression of the local populations:
thus, well over 700,000 Balts were deported to Siberian labour
camps. After the war, between 1945 and 1950, the Russians and
local Communists trained in Moscow, took advantage of the
presence of the Red Army in 'liberated' eastern Europe to seize
power in Poland, Czechoslovakia, East Germany, Albania,
Rumania, and Bulgaria (and in Jugoslavia, too, though that
was a special case). These countries became true satellites and
colonies of Russia, ruled indirectly by men appointed by Moscow and exploited by unequal trade treaties. The Soviet hold on
Poland was, however, considerably diminished by the revolution of 1956, even though it left Poland under communist rule;
in Hungary, however, the anti-communist revolution was ruth-
lessly suppressed by Soviet force. In the Far East the Chinese
seized Tibet by force in 1950 and mercilessly suppressed an
anti-Chinese uprising in 1959. Two satellites were set up: in
North Korea by the Russians and in North Vietnam by the
Vietnamese Communists with Chinese help.

This is the basic picture that must be remembered if

American and allied actions are to be seen in perspective. In pursuance of their own security and that of friendly peoples, and in the face of the Soviet advance into eastern Europe, the United States, under Presidents Truman and Eisenhower, created a world-wide system of alliances which, in effect, ringed the Soviet and Chinese empires. In the course of establishing this system, the United States acquired a large number of client states – régimes which supported the US connexion and adopted anti-communist policies, in return for which they were propped up, more or less successfully, by American money and military support.

Clearly such régimes – for instance, those of Chiang Kai-shek in Formosa (Nationalist China), Syngman Rhee in South Korea, or Ngo Dinh Diem's in South Vietnam – cannot be considered wholly independent, by the yardstick of absolute independence which I have been using in this book. All independence, however, is relative, and in comparison with Russia's satellites, America's client states have retained considerable freedom of manoeuvre, most notably, perhaps, the freedom to ignore American advice and – when necessary – to blackmail the United States. Certainly, at crucial times the US Government has been quite incapable of influencing events in its client states. Nor should this seem surprising; by force of history the United States has an anti-colonial bias, and by democratic tradition it is against intervention by force in the affairs of small countries. (There are, of course, exceptions to this general rule, of which the most notable was Guatemala in 1954, where the United States was largely instrumental in removing a leftist government and replacing it by one that met Washington's approval. But this does not invalidate the rule.)

The Russians – and more lately the Chinese – have made, and continue to make, strenuous efforts to subvert governments beyond the confines of their empires. By and large, as the next chapter will show, these efforts have been curiously unsuccessful. This does not mean, however, that there is no such thing as a communist threat. What it does mean is that the gap between communist theory and the real world is constantly widening, so that the Communists find it increasingly difficult to adapt their plans to reality. What it also means is that communism has little chance of establishing itself where there is no Red Army to cow the non-communist majority. Communism spreads outward from a hard centre; it has never yet established itself anywhere by free elections. And the only country where it *has* established itself far from the Sino-Soviet land mass – Cuba – is not so solid a satellite as some people may have supposed.

Chapter 2

THE COMMUNIST THREAT

A great deal of nonsense has been written about communism both by those who fear it and by those who do not. The first tend to see a Communist under every bush and to exaggerate the capacity of Communists to undermine non-communist societies. The second, even when they are not themselves Communists, find it hard to believe that Communists could be guilty of the things that are attributed to them, and therefore underrate the danger of communism. Those who underrate the danger leave themselves wide open to communist thrusts; those who overstate it raise false alarms, institute witch hunts (as Senator McCarthy did in the United States), dissipate energies better employed on legitimate objectives, and, in the end, play into the hands of the Communists. The truth of the matter, briefly stated, is that there *is* a communist danger, but that the Communists, by and large, are less successful than many people think.

I hope to prove both these propositions in this chapter, which, however, is not concerned with every aspect of the communist threat but only with those aspects that affect the emerging countries. Since the first concern of every newly independent country is to preserve its independence, its leaders ought to be aware of the nature of the communist threat to that independence. Fundamentally, that threat arises from a simple fact: communism is an expanding, proselytizing movement. The Communists argue that in time the whole world will embrace communism. In itself, this could be an innocuous belief: it becomes dangerous because the Communists are not content to sit and wait for others to embrace communism, but reserve the right to hasten the event. Since they consider the end to be not only predestined but also an essential condition of universal

M

peace and happiness – an end, indeed, that justifies the means – they have no compunction about the methods they use to bring it about. These methods include subversion, terrorism, and armed insurrection. By its nature, then, Marxist communism is dangerous in itself; but it is even more dangerous, from the viewpoint of the new countries, because, in practice, it is used as an instrument of foreign policy in the service of two great imperial powers: the Soviet Union and China. The Soviet Union is the Tsarist Empire, expanded and consolidated; the Chinese People's Republic, shortly after it was founded, set about re-establishing the frontiers of imperial China, by invading Tibet, and resumed its advance by invading territory which the Indians claimed as theirs in 1962. This imperial background is of fundamental importance; if the international communist movement had its headquarters, say, in Belgrade instead of in Moscow and Peking it would present a much feebler threat to the non-communist world.

Since the Communists themselves attach great importance to theory, one ought to look at some of the documents that guide and determine their actions, before turning to the actions themselves. The most relevant of these documents from the standpoint of the emerging countries are: the Declaration of twelve Communist parties (Moscow, November 1957); the Declaration of eighty-one Communist parties (Moscow, December 1960), and a booklet by Professor I. I. Potekhin, the foremost Soviet Africanist, entitled *Africa Looks to the Future* and published in Moscow in 1960. The purpose of international communist declarations nowadays is to reconcile doctrinal differences between national communist parties. In the days of Stalin this was unnecessary: Moscow laid down the law and the other parties obediently followed instructions. The rise of communist China as an independent fount of Marxist wisdom, and Mr Khrushchev's flexible approach to dogma, have changed all this. As a result, international communist gatherings now produce bitter wrangling, much of it incomprehensible to those not initiated in Communist jargon. The 1957 Declaration attacked 'dogmatism' (i.e. excessive orthodoxy) to please Mr Khrushchev and 're-visionism' (i.e. insufficient orthodoxy) to please Mr Mao Tse-tung. From the point of view of the emerging countries, its most important section was the one dealing with 'imperialism', which accused the 'aggressive imperialist circles of the United States' of seeking 'to bring most countries of the world under their sway, hamper the onward march of mankind, and enmesh liberated peoples in new forms of colonialism'. It praised as 'powerful peace forces' what it called 'the peace-loving countries of Asia and Africa taking an anti-imperialist stand'.

These sweeping generalizations were given a good deal more precision in the 1960 Declaration. This was a much more important document than the 1957 one, not only because it embodied the consensus of opinion among eighty-one parties but also because it went a good deal further in formulating an agreed communist policy to hasten the advent of communism throughout the non-communist world. The conference of communist parties that gave birth to the Declaration had been convened to thrash out doctrinal differences between the Russians and the Chinese. Since 1956, the Russians, under Mr Khrushchev's leadership, had argued that communism might, in certain cases, be ushered in by non-violent methods, for instance, through western-style parliamentary elections. The Chinese, however, had continued to argue that violence was the only road to communism. The Moscow conference lasted three weeks, during which, according to western Communists who attended it, there were lively exchanges between the Soviet and Chinese delegates. In the end the Declaration, which stretched to 15,000 words, incorporated ideas from both sides, without regard for consistency.

The 'uncommitted' leaders of the world, under Mr Nehru's guidance, have attached so much importance to the 'five principles of peaceful co-existence' which the Indian and Chinese Prime Ministers drafted in 1954, that it is illuminating to read how the 1960 Declaration defined 'peaceful co-existence':

> Co-existence between States of differing social systems is a form of class struggle between socialism and capitalism. . . . (It) does not mean a reconciliation between the socialist and

bourgeois ideologies . . . it implies an intensification of the struggle.

The Declaration called on Communists and their sympathizers in the newly independent countries to work from within to make their governments adopt Communist-type policies. To this end, Communists and like-minded people were told to form a 'national-democratic front', carry out various communist aims, such as land reform; liquidating the 'remnants and survivals of feudalism' (meaning, for instance, religious observance, tribal customs, or the power of local chiefs); forcing 'foreign monopolies' (that is, companies) out of the economy; and developing economic and cultural relations with communist countries (that is, trade and aid pacts on the economic side, and on the cultural side, exchanges of visits on a group basis, sending students to communist institutions and allowing Communists to distribute their propaganda). Countries that did all these things, embarked on what the Declaration called the path of 'non-capitalist development' and allowed full liberty of action to local Communist parties were to be known as 'national democratic States'. This was a new category of States in the communist dictionary, and apparently applied to countries such as Castro's Cuba and Sékou Touré's Guinea, which seemed promisingly anti-western and might, with encouragement, turn in a communist direction.

The Moscow Declarations were, of course, of general application. Professor Potekhin's booklet, on the other hand, shows how a Marxist applies the principles of the Declarations to a special case, that of 'black' Africa, south of the Sahara. In many ways, as Potekhin's booklet shows, Africa baffles Marxist theorists; for one thing, there are no 'classes' in Africa, as Marxists understand them; for another, Soviet experience of Africa was indirect or second-hand until African countries began to get their independence in the 1950s and 1960s. Before that, the Russians worked through the communist parties of the colonial powers, especially those of France and Britain. As a result, their usual preconceived notions are even more remote from reality in Africa than they are in other places. *Africa Looks to the Future* nevertheless represents the culmination of years of specialized study by Professor Potekhin, and deserves to be read closely, both by non-Marxists and by those who form its subject matter: the Africans themselves.

Professor Potekhin starts off by arguing that Africa has a 'vocation for socialism'. One by one, he quotes African definitions of socialism: those of Senghor and Nyerere, Nasser and Nkrumah, and the rather special one of Jacques Janvier of Senegal, who wants Africa to take Jugoslavia for a model. One by one, he gently takes them to task and argues that the Marxist variety is the only possible socialism for Africa. In particular, he criticizes the concept of an African socialism based on the peasantry. Though 'class formation' is still not complete in Africa, he writes, millions of Africans already work for hire. These constitute a proletariat and are being organized into trade unions. Because the industries are owned by foreign companies, the 'formation' of the proletariat is more rapid than that of the bourgeoisie. Africa, he maintains, cannot be an exception to Marxist–Leninist theory.

The professor goes on to expound an argument that has dominated Soviet propaganda during the past few years: the view that 'the advent of independence does not complete the process of decolonization'. This needs a word or two of explanation. Marxist–Leninist theory holds that the imperialist powers never willingly surrender their hold over subject peoples. Since the opposite has happened (whereas neither the Soviet Union nor China shows the slightest sign of freeing its own dependent races) an explanation had to be found, so that the facts could be made to fit the theory. The explanation is therefore that a country does not become independent just because it has an internationally recognized sovereign government. To become truly independent it must go on to remove 'the last vestiges of colonialism'. Independent economies must be built, with communist economic assistance. This means, among other things, that a new country must issue its own national currency (a dig at most of the former French colonies which use money tied to the French franc, and a bow in the direction of Guinea, which set up its own bank of issue, with notes printed in Czechoslovakia – and almost worthless on the international money market). 'Imperialist' political influence and military bases must go; so must the artifical linguistic divisions, for instance between French-speaking and English-speaking States. To this end, African national languages must be re-established (even though most of them have no written form).

It is clear enough that any African State which did all the things that Professor Potekhin advocates would find its affairs being run by Soviet or other communist experts, and would have lost its means of communicating with the outside world. Its reward, presumably, would be to be classified as a 'national democratic State'.

Some of the foreign activities of communist governments are legitimate, and there is no point in confusing the issue by lumping them together with the less-legitimate ones. Much of the trade of the communist countries serves a genuine commercial purpose, and not all the work of communist diplomatic missions abroad consists of spying (though much of it does). Subversion and terrorism, however, are a different matter. There are so many examples of both that only the choice is difficult.

In his brilliant study *World Order and New States* (Chatto & Windus, London, 1962), Peter Calvocoressi defined subversion as 'the clandestine attempt to undermine a régime or a society beyond one's own borders'. One form of communist clandestinity is the 'front' technique. Europe has long memories of the 'popular fronts' of the 1930s. These were alliances, mostly between Communists and Socialists, for the purpose of achieving parliamentary power. A front need not be overtly political, however. Any organization, national or international, which comes under communist control and is used for communist purposes is a front. The term 'communist' never appears in the names of these organizations, for the whole idea is that their communist purpose should be disguised. After the Second World War the Communists established a very large number of these organizations, with names like the World Federation of Democratic Youth, the International Union of Students, the World Federation of Trade Unions, and many others.

Many western trade unions, youth federations, and other mass organizations became affiliated to these front organizations, without, at first, suspecting their true purpose. They soon discovered it, however, and in most cases broke away to form their own non-communist international bodies. The fronts carry on, however, and during the past ten years, especially, have been concentrating on enrolling Asians and Africans, in the hope that they will prove more receptive to communist ideas than the Europeans did.

To read the resolutions passed unanimously (as they always are) by communist-controlled fronts is to venture into a dreary desert of stereotyped jargon, covering by now many square miles of paper. Some of the front meetings, however, have been of momentous importance. One such was the World Youth Conference held in Calcutta in February 1948. It has been known for some years (mainly through the disclosures of Communists who were there) that its main purpose was to transmit marching orders issued in Moscow to the Communist parties of South-East Asia. Shortly afterwards, communist-led insurrections began, almost simultaneously, in the Philippines, Indonesia, Burma, Malaya, and India. I have described these insurrections in some detail in *The Rebels*, but two aspects of them are of particular relevance to this chapter. One is the fact that they did indeed start as the result of a preconceived communist plan; the other is the no less curious fact that they all failed. Why they did is a fascinating illustration of the limitations of communist methods.

Insurrections against established authority succeed only if the insurgents enjoy overwhelming popular support or get material help from abroad, or preferably both. Now the most deep-rooted of communist fallacies is the belief that the Communists represent the people. Holding this belief, Communists easily deceive themselves into supposing that they have popular support (even if they find themselves forced to terrorize ordinary people into giving it). This fallacy lies at the bottom of the communist failures in South-East Asia. In Burma and India the communist insurrections were pointless, because these were anti-colonial insurrections in countries that had already gained their independence; in Indonesia the Dutch had still not transferred sovereignty to the Indonesian nationalists, but the national movement had its own leadership, and by challenging it the Communists merely bewildered the people, who had been told for years that their enemies were the Dutch. The Philippines, too, were already independent when the Communists launched their rebellion; and both there, and in Malaya, where independence was still a long way off, the Communists gained startling initial successes, only to be defeated in the long run. The reasons for their successes and their final failure are easy enough to find. In the Philippines independence had done nothing to relieve the hardships of the peasants, who were shamelessly exploited by the State and by absentee landlords. There was a long background of peasant unrest, and the Communists exploited it for all it was worth. In Malaya the British had lost prestige by their defeat at the hands of the Japanese (as indeed the white man had everywhere in South-East Asia), and there was widespread dissatisfaction at the slow progress towards either independence or a higher standard of living. This, again, the Communists exploited at first with success. Both in the Philippines and Malaya, however, the Communists were defeated, and in each case by a combination of military–police action and political progress. In Malaya the pace of the march towards independence was drastically accelerated. In the Philippines the peasants were given a new deal. As soon as the Communists were deprived of the grievances they had been exploiting, their support melted away and they were defeated. An additional and very important point is that in all these places the communist insurgents were without a friendly supply base.

It is instructive to compare these communist failures with one great communist success: the defeat of the French in Indochina. Unlike the insurrections in neighbouring countries, the Indochina war began as a great patriotic movement, with which the Communists identified themselves, and which they eventually came to control. The refusal of the French to give true independence to the three countries of Indochina (Vietnam, Cambodia, and Laos) played into the hands of the Communists.

Moveover, from December 1949, when the Chinese communist armies reached the Indochinese border, the Vietnamese Communists had the advantage of massive supplies of arms and short communication lines. In combination, these factors proved irresistible.

Towards the end of 1960 – more than six years after the French defeat – the Vietnamese Communists started a fresh insurrection, this time directed against the anti-communist government of President Ngo Dinh Diem in South Vietnam. One has to remember that Vietnam was partitioned into roughly equal halves as part of the Geneva settlement that ended the Indochina war, the northern half being a communist republic under President Ho Chi Minh. The anti-Diem insurrection was still raging when these lines were written, and this is not the place to consider it in detail. But one aspect of it is another illustration of the way Communists use the front technique. When terrorism and guerrilla ambushes had brought the Communists their first successes they felt the need to create a front that would conceal the communist leadership of the insurrection. Accordingly, they set up a 'National Front for the Liberation of South Vietnam' in January 1961. In the autumn of 1962 an important document giving instructions from the Vietnamese Lao Dong (Communist) Party to district committees of the front fell into the hands of the South Vietnamese Army. In it, the Communists disclosed that the front had been set up 'with the object of attracting into its ranks capitalist and intellectual classes, including the capitalist youth, students, and intellectuals of the cities and the middle and rich farmers of the countryside'. It added the following revealing observation:

> Although the Front unites a wide range of classes, the workers and peasants are its first-line troops. City youth, students, intellectuals and capitalists are only the second line and are dependent upon the first. They are used only to lend prestige to the NFLSV and to the revolution to liberate South Vietnam.

This was candid enough. Youths (if not working class), intellectuals, and capitalists were held to be expendable, and would be discarded if ever the Front brought the Communists to power. As might be supposed, the published documents of the Front were less forthcoming. The interest of this one lay in the fact that it was not intended for publication.

In Africa, as in Asia, the Communists have made extensive use of the front technique – so extensive indeed that one could easily fill a book the size of this one with a mere selection of the proceedings of various front conferences. But there is no need for such tedium.

The purposes of this chapter will be better served by mentioning two more tangible evidences of communist interference in the internal affairs of African States. One concerns Cameroun (French Cameroons) and the other Guinea, the one Republic that broke away from France in 1958 after General de Gaulle had returned to power. In Cameroun the inevitable front was the Union des Populations du Cameroun, a terrorist organization set up under communist control in the 1950s and first heard of by the general public in May 1955, when the French authorities declared it illegal after an outbreak of murderous rioting which it organized. The UPC went on to mount a campaign of terrorism, sabotage, and murder, first against the French, in the name of nationalism, then against the independent Cameroun Republic that emerged in 1960. It might well be asked why a nationalist organization fighting for independence should go on fighting after independence has been gained. The answer lies in the communist definition of independence which Professor Potekhin spelled out, and which I have mentioned. An ex-colony, even if it is recognized as independent and has a seat in the United Nations, is not really independent until it has got rid of western influence and accepted communist guidance. Hence the fight must go on, even after independence has been won.

We are concerned, however, with Russian and Chinese interference in the affairs of African States. Interesting evidence came to light when six Camerounians who had been to China tried to re-enter their country in 1961, and were arrested as they crossed the border. They disclosed that about 100 Camerounians, including themselves, had been trained in Moscow and

Peking. They had belonged to a group of nine who left Cameroun secretly without travel documents, but with Soviet and Chinese help. In Moscow they were welcomed by Soviet members of the World Federation of Democratic Youth, who registered them at a hotel and took them on a sightseeing tour. Peking, however, was their destination. There, discipline was strict. They were kept apart from other Africans, to the extent of having their meals served to them in a separate room. The first ten days were devoted to sightseeing and to looking at propaganda films. Then the serious work began. It consisted of a thoroughgoing training in sabotage and the use of explosives, in weapon training and maintenance, in guerrilla warfare, including night combat and the capture or assassination of sentries. Fully trained as instruments of communist policy, they were sent back to Cameroun, but were captured before being able to apply the lessons they had been taught.

The Guinean example is even more illuminating, if only because the exposure of communist methods and aims was more public. I am not concerned here with the normal activities of the communist government missions of one kind or another that swarmed over Guinea shortly after Sékou Touré said No to de Gaulle. Finding himself friendless, Sékou Touré turned to the communist countries, and naturally enough they responded. This was perfectly legitimate so long as the aid and technical missions confined themselves to their overt official duties.

On 16 December 1961, however, the Soviet Ambassador in Guinea, Mr Daniel Solod, left Conakry for Moscow with his wife in circumstances that made it clear he had been expelled. Some attempt was made, both by the Russians and by the Guineans, to hush up the facts, but they came out in various ways. For instance, on 19 December Conakry radio, in a broadcast in Soussou (one of Guinea's tribal languages), said Mr Solod had been expelled and accused him of having been behind serious disturbances that had taken place in Guinea the previous month.

The disturbances had begun at Labé, 300 miles north of Conakry, on 23 November; on that day five Guineans had been jailed for plotting against the Government, and the Labé riots were in sympathy with the accused. The following day students rioted in Conakry itself, where they tried to march on the Presidential palace. Now the interesting thing is that the jailed 'plotters' were Communists or sympathizers. On 11 December President Touré himself made a speech in which he blamed the disturbances on intellectuals who had espoused the communist cause. More interestingly, he said they had been in touch with the diplomatic missions of communist countries (which he did not name) in Conakry. He also revealed the existence of a secret communist organization at Labé, where the riots started. Shortly after the President's speech the heads of all the communist missions in Conakry were summoned to a meeting with the Guinean Foreign Minister in connexion with Sékou Touré's charges. Moscow's agents had shown their hand too blatantly. It was the beginning of the end of Sékou Touré's flirtation with the communist bloc.

The late Walter Kolarz, in a lecture republished in *International Affairs* (London) in April 1962, sagely observed that the term 'fellow-travellers' is not as reassuring to the Communists as it is disquieting to the anti-communists; and he recalled Trotsky's anxiety lest the fellow-traveller should change into a train going the other way. People like Mr Robert Welch of the John Birch Society in the United States, and others who ought to know better, have been far too ready to write off countries like Guinea or Mali as 'communist'. The Communists themselves can never be so sure. Orthodoxy – that is, doctrinal purity – is a constant and dominant concern of all Communists, as anybody who has followed the Sino-Soviet ideological dispute knows. Concepts like Nasser's 'Arab socialism' or the 'African communism' of a Sékou Touré are anathema to them, for such terms imply that there may be a non-Marxist road to 'socialism'. To the extent that such home-grown ideas are anti-western, Moscow and Peking will welcome them and will play along with them, hoping that when the time is ripe they will find a way of gaining control of the local ruling party and turning it in a Marxist direction. That is what they tried to do in Guinea, but

failed because they underestimated the force of Sékou Touré's
personality and his hold on Guinea's ruling party. They can
hardly have forgotten that the Guinean President bitterly denounced communism in a speech which *Le Monde* reported on
4 April 1960.

If the orthodox Communists have cause to be worried about
men like Nasser and Sékou Touré, then they can hardly feel
secure in the company of so mercurial and unpredictable a
figure as Fidel Castro, even though he might proclaim that he is
a Marxist. American right-wingers, who had said from the start
that Castro was a Communist, were delighted when he publicly
exclaimed in one of his interminable speeches, on 2 December
1961, that he was a Marxist–Leninist. This, they felt, entitled
them to say: 'We told you so.' But if they had taken the trouble
to read right through this speech – perhaps the most fascinating
Castro has ever delivered – they might have found cause to
wonder, as the Communists must have, just how Marxist Castro
really was and how far back his conversion went. For these
were some of the things he said:

> Recently, looking for some books on *Das Kapital*, I found
> that in my years as a student I had read up to page 370 of
> *Das Kapital*. . . . I intend to continue to study Karl Marx's
> *Das Kapital*. . . . Did I believe (in Marxism) on July 26th (the
> date of his first attempt to overthrow the Batista régime in
> 1953)? I believed on July 26th. . . . Did I understand it as I
> understand it today? No, I did not understand it as I under-
> stand it today. . . . Did I have prejudices? Yes, I had
> prejudices. . . . Could I call myself a complete revolutionary
> on July 26th? No, I could not call myself a complete revolu-
> tionary.

Anti-communists might brush all this aside as of no consequence, for what did it matter that Castro did not consider
himself a true Communist in 1953 if he now proclaimed his
belief in Marxism–Leninism and said (as he did in the same
speech) that Cuba was heading for communism? But Soviet
Communists could not allow themselves to be so blissfully uncritical. What were they to make of this impassioned giant, the

leader of a successful revolution, who, like a diligent schoolboy, said he was going to continue to study *Das Kapital*? Were they to overlook the fact that Castro has built his revolution on the dissatisfaction of a group of middle-class intellectuals and on peasant grievances, leaving the sacred proletariat out altogether? (They must indeed have gone deeper into the question and asked themselves what the proletariat was doing while Castro was revolting against Batista. They would then have found that Eusebio Mujal, the Secretary-General of the Cuban Confederation of Labour, loyally supported Batista and kept his members at work when Castro tried to call a general strike in April 1958.)

As for Castro himself, what was he to think of his chosen alignment with communism when the Russians meekly agreed to dismantle the rocket bases they were setting up on Cuban soil on being faced with President Kennedy's threat to do the dismantling for them in October 1962? Indeed, the assumption, so widely made in western capitals, that Cuba was one of communism's great successes, needs to be critically examined. It *was* a success, of course, but hardly in a way that would please communist theoreticians. The revolution was the work of Fidel Castro's 26th of July movement, not of Cuba's Communist Party, the Partido Socialista Popular. As the American writer Theodore Draper convincingly argued in some remarkable articles in *Encounter*, later reprinted in book form, Castro betrayed his own revolution. Its original purposes had been western-style democracy and constitutional government. Swept away by his own *folie de grandeur*, Castro soon forgot his earlier promises and started jailing his original companions, such as David Salvador, the outstanding labour organizer of the movement, or driving them into exile. The offence these men had committed was to remember Castro's promises and remind him of them. Megalomania turned Castro into a dictator, and anti-Americanism made him turn to the communist bloc for economic and military help. At home his only friends or supporters left were stooges or Communists; abroad, only the communist States and the more revolutionary régimes, such as Guinea. By this time, the Communists had their men in key positions and were ready for the take-over which Castro's betrayal had pre-pared.

It is important that such situations as Cuba's should be properly diagnosed by policy-makers in the western capitals, especially in Washington, for in diplomacy as in medicine faulty diagnosis leads to worthless prescriptions. By prematurely labelling Castro and his revolution communist, men like Senators Eastland and Dodd of the Senate Internal Security Sub-Committee, and the bulk of the American Press, played into the hands of Cuba's Communists. Similarly, by sending hard-core supporters of the ex-dictator Batista as well as disillusioned ex-Fidelistas to give battle against Castro's forces in the Bay of Pigs in the spring of 1961, the American Central Intelligence Agency made sure the expedition would fail, even leaving its military inadequacy out of account.

For the leaders of the new countries, the contrasting examples of Guinea and Cuba are instructive. Each shows the nature of the communist threat to their countries' independence, but while the Guinean case shows how to deal with the threat, the Cuban one shows how not to. Once Castro had handed his revolution to the Communists, Cuba became an instrument of Soviet foreign policy. Hence the installation of Soviet rocket bases. Once the Americans had shown they would not tolerate this disturbance to the nuclear balance of power, however, the Russians demonstrated that Cuba was expendable. In Guinea, however, Sékou Touré showed that he was unwilling to hand his revolution over to the Communists and sent the Soviet Ambassador packing. There is no doubt which of the two was the wiser.

Chapter 3

CLIENT STATES AND SATELLITES

I heard myself whistling as I stepped out of the plane that had brought me back to Laos from communist North Vietnam, and I realized that I was expressing joy in breathing the air of a free country again. That evening, at a cocktail party, I told this brief story to an official of the Laotian Foreign Ministry, and he rewarded me with an unreserved Laotian smile. He then asked me my name, smiled again, and said, apparently without the slightest guile: 'Oh, yes, I saw your dossier this morning.'

Freedom being relative, Laos remained freer than North Vietnam, even after the discovery that I already had a dossier at the Laotian Foreign Ministry. If the story has a moral it is that the existence of a security service is indispensable to the preservation of countries threatened from within and without, as Laos was.

Laos had a security service, and much else besides: American aid in bottomless quantities, an army of 25,000–30,000 men, help from France, and moral encouragement from Britain, not to mention formal protection from Seato (the South-East Asia Treaty Organization). All this did not save it from the corrosion of a powerful communist acid distilled in neighbouring North Vietnam. It is not my purpose, however, to look at the Laotian problem in detail, but more simply to consider a single question: did American aid, on which the Laotian State was utterly dependent, turn Laos into a satellite of the United States?

Certainly it was a client state. Between July 1954, when the Geneva agreements brought independence to Laos, till July 1962, when a further set of Geneva agreements brought the blessings of the great powers on the formation of a neutralist government in Vientiane, the United States paid virtually all the expenses of the Laotian government, civil service and army. It would hardly be surprising if, having paid the piper so handsomely, it also called the tune. And in fact it did so, with intermittent success, until mid-1960. Thereafter the situation slipped out of the control of the Americans, and though they made strenuous attempts to recapture the initiative, and appeared to do so once or twice, they never held it for long.

The whole purpose of the American effort in Laos was to set the country on a non-communist course – or, for preference, an anti-communist one. It was, however, far from easy to set Laos on any course at all. Although Laos is nearly the size of the United Kingdom, its population probably does not greatly exceed 2 millions. It is convenient to call the people as a whole Laotians, but only about two-thirds of them are Lao, that is, members of the Lao branch of that Thai family to which the Siamese and the Shans of Burma also belong. The rest are more or less primitive tribes: Meo, Man, and Lolo to the north, Kha in the south. The Lao are Buddhists, practising the simpler form of that faith also found in Burma and Ceylon, Siam and Cambodia; the rest are animists. The Lao are gentle, subtle, and pleasure-loving, though hard-working enough in the fields when necessity demands. If ever a people deserved to be left to pursue in peace an idyllic way of life, it is the Lao. But history has made them weak and disunited. In 1353 the petty states of Laos did unite to form the Kingdom of the Million Elephants, with its capital at Luang Prabang, where to this day, the King of Laos has his palace. But in the eighteenth century southern Laos broke away, to form the Kingdom of Vientiane and, in the extreme south, the independent principality of Champassak. Even today, the dynastic rivalries between the ruling families of Luang Prabang, Vientiane, and Champassak are more important in Laotian politics than the pressures of great powers and rival ideologies – more important, that is, in the minds of the Laotian politicians.

Being weak and disunited, the Lao were an easy prey for their stronger neighbours, especially the Siamese, who grabbed the Vientiane kingdom in 1782. More than a century later the French drove them out, and ruled Laos, directly or indirectly,

N

from 1893 to 1954. The French period in Laos can accurately be described as one of affectionate neglect. French administrators posted to Laos tended to fall in love with it, and in particular with its fair-skinned, graceful women; but it never occurred to them to do very much for the country (although France did form a small educated *élite*). Communications remained practically non-existent and the riches of the soil (if any) stayed unexploited. On the whole, relations between the French and Laotians were amicable, and still are. A number of well-known Laotians have written about their own country with charm and insight, the most engaging and useful of these books being Sisouk na Champassak's *Storm over Laos* (Frederick Praeger, New York, 1961).

Although Laos did become independent, on paper, in July 1954, the local Communists* remained physically in control of two north-eastern provinces. The Geneva Agreements had laid down that these were to come back under the authority of the Royal Government, but it was not easy to enforce this provision. Northern Laos is a country of soaring, hump-backed mountains and impenetrable rain forests, which merges into North Vietnam without a clear dividing line. The country looks the same on both sides; so do the local tribes, who speak the same language. An army or a team of inspectors might search in vain for rival forces or a dissident administration, which, at times of their choosing, could slip across the border into North Vietnam.

To state these facts is to show how impossibly difficult was the job the Americans undertook in Laos. One major objective of US policy was to bring the north-eastern provinces firmly under the Royal government's control. Another was to keep the Communists out of the Royal government. Since the Communists were in possession of the two provinces, it was even more difficult to reach both these objectives than either separately, for the Communists refused to surrender control (even theoretically) to the King unless, in return, they were given portfolios in the Royal government.

* Their military arm was the Pathet Lao, and their political party, the Neo Lao Haksat.

There is no need to follow in detail the tortuous course of the negotiations between the Royal government and the Communists. What interests us is that the Communists got what they wanted, and American policy was frustrated. On 18 November 1957 it was agreed that the Communists would be given two posts in the cabinet. In return, the two north-eastern provinces were formally handed back to the Royal government. On paper, this bargain may have sounded fair, but in reality the Communists came off best, for their Ministers actually took office on 19 November, whereas royal control of the communist provinces remained purely theoretical. In 1959 a sub-committee of the US House of Representatives, which had gone to Laos to find out how far the American aid programme had been successful, devoted some attention to the agreement with the Communists. Its report, published in Washington in June of that year, under the title *US Aid Operations in Laos*, sought answers to the question whether the agreement was a victory for the Communists or for the Royal government and the American aid programme. The sub-committee found what the report called a 'particularly interesting' divergence of views between the two State Department officials most closely concerned with Laos: Mr Walter Robertson, the assistant Secretary of State in charge of Far Eastern affairs, and Mr J. Graham Parsons, the American ambassador to Laos (who later succeeded Mr Robertson as assistant Secretary of State). It is hard to imagine divergences between two men with such equally uncompromising attitudes towards communism, but the sub-committee's report made its point.

It quoted Mr Robertson as telling the Senate Foreign Relations Committee in March 1958 that the Communists had 'made use of the inability of the royal Laotian government to drive them out' of the two provinces to get themselves into the Cabinet. 'This,' said Mr Robertson, 'may extend communist influence dangerously in Laos.' Rather sourly, the report commented: 'i.e., the negotiated settlement was a communist victory.'

Mr Parsons, on the other hand, later gave the House Foreign Affairs Committee a very different appreciation of what had happened. Testifying in May 1958, he forecast that the Communists would lose their two cabinet seats and that the Royal government would gain full control of the north-eastern provinces without bloodshed and without making concessions. He went on:

> If this is the situation – and I hope I am not over-confident when I express some confident optimism – if this is the situation in Laos, it will be due, in part, to our aid and will, I hope, indicate, in part, what you gentlemen and the rest of us will have received in value for our aid money.

The sub-Committee, though it did not say so in so many words, left no doubt that it agreed with the pessimistic, not the optimistic, assessment of the Laotian situation, and confessed itself unable to understand how experienced senior officials, though in constant contact with each other and in receipt of the same reports, could express such diametrically opposed opinions.

To be fair to Mr Parsons, he did his best to make his own prophecies come true. Within the next few months, largely through American money and Mr Parsons's persuasiveness, the communist ministers were ousted from the government and placed under house arrest, Prince Souvanna Phouma (the Prime Minister who had negotiated with the Communists) was sent to Paris as Ambassador, and a group of Laotian army officers and civil servants formed an anti-communist party, called the Committee for the Defence of National Interests (or CDIN, from its initials in French). The American victory appeared to be complete, but it was disappointingly short-lived. Once again without going too deeply into the complexities of Laotian affairs (which readers may not find as fascinating as I do), one may extract two incidents that show, in my opinion conclusively, that the Americans never quite succeeded in turning Laos into a satellite. These make an interesting contrast, in that the first shows the United States unsuccessfully trying to keep Laotian anti-communists in power, and the second unsuccessfully trying to get the anti-communists to form a coalition government with the Communists.

Seven communist leaders, including the two who had been Ministers in Prince Souvanna Phouma's Government, had been arrested, and were to be brought to trial on treason charges. Two communist battalions had been surrounded, but one escaped to North Vietnam and later returned greatly strengthened. The anti-communist CDIN, whose leading member was General Phoumi Nosavan, was firmly in control. This was the situation in April 1960, when the Royal government called general elections. The Communists, their leaders still under arrest, were allowed to nominate nine candidates at the last minute. The elections, held on the 24th, were scandalously faked: bribes and threats, together with a purposeful counting of votes, ensured an overwhelming right-wing victory. America's success seemed complete when, in June, a determinedly anti-communist government was formed, with General Phoumi, the strong-man apparent, as Defence Minister.

A very young man named Captain Kong Lae (he was twenty-six at the time of his sudden rise to fame) deflated this euphoria only two months later, with a *coup d'état* that brought down the right-wing government and sent its ministers in flight. It is an illuminating comment on the winning of friends that the anti-American Kong Lae was trained by the Americans, whereas the pro-American Phoumi Nosavan was trained by the French (he did more brilliantly at St Cyr than his subsequent military inadequacy would have led one to suppose). It is said, perhaps apocryphally, that while Kong Lae was attending an American military training course he asked his instructor for a lecture on the proper places to seize when capturing a city, and that, in time, he put theory to the test of practice when capturing Vientiane. At all events, at the head of his parachute battalion, he made a quick, clean job of his *coup d'état* on 9 August 1960. Putting himself at the head of a Revolutionary Committee, he proclaimed a neutralist programme which called for the evacuation of foreign troops (mainly American and French advisers, on one side, and North Vietnamese, on the other), the liquidation of military bases, and the acceptance of aid from whatever quarter it came – that is, from the Communists as well as from the Americans and French.

Although the United States did not immediately accept the fact, Kong Lae's *coup* marked the beginning of the collapse of American policy in Laos. Certainly it brought out all the latent dynastic rivalries in the little kingdom. Kong Lae's choice of Prime Minister was Prince Souvanna Phouma (the neutralist, who belonged to the junior or Vientiane branch of the royal family) but the King, in his senior branch stronghold at Luang Prabang, was reluctant to give his assent. In the end, he did and on 29 August the Prince set about finding Ministers. On 10 September, however, General Phoumi (the right-wing 'strong man') turned up in Savannakhet, in the south, in the company of a member of the hereditary ruling family of the old princi- pality of Champassak, Prince Boun Oum, and proclaimed a rival Revolutionary Committee, committed to the victory of the anti-communist cause. Within barely a month, Laos had thus turned back the clock to the eighteenth century and was again divided into rival petty kingdoms. To add to the confusion, the arrested communist leaders had slipped away from their guards in circumstances that have never satisfactorily been explained, and found their way to the communist strongholds in the north. Laos was on the verge of civil war.

The United States made a desperate attempt to restore the situation. It turned out to be the last. In effect, the American Central Intelligence Agency (CIA) took over the conduct of policy from the State Department. A quaintly named body, the Programme Evaluations Office, had been set up in Vientiane under General Hentges, whose biography did not appear in official publications. Under him were a few hundred tough Americans, trained in guerrilla tactics and labelled 'advisers'. In mid-December 1960 General Phoumi's right-wing forces, with support from the Americans and Siamese, fought their way into Vientiane. It was a fierce engagement, lasting three days, which left about 500 dead, including many civilians. Kong Lae pulled out with his paratroops, and Souvanna Phouma fled to Cambodia. Once again, success had come to the Americans, but once again, it did not last long.

At this point our first example merges into our second and the whole character of American policy changes. The right-wing capture of Vientiane had taken place during the last days of the Eisenhower Administration, and indeed after President Kennedy's victory in the November elections. The new President, who did not take office until January, soon found that the Laotian situation he had inherited from his predecessors was untenable. Kong Lae and his neutralist troops had set up headquarters in the Plain of Jars, in north-central Laos, and had joined forces (though not actually merged) with the Communists. During his brief spell of office Prince Souvanna Phouma had invited the Russians to set up an embassy in Vientiane and to start an airlift of food and petrol to offset shortages arising from the closing of the frontier by Siam (which supported the right-wingers). Now the food and petrol airlift became an arms airlift. Soon the neutralists and their communist allies were formidably armed. Gradually, they extended their control over the Laotian countryside, leaving only Luang Prabang, Vientiane, and Savannakhet firmly in right-wing hands. As for General Phoumi, his success at Vientiane proved solitary. Whenever his troops ventured to give battle they were roundly trounced, both by the Communists and by Kong Lae's neutralists.

The time had come to negotiate a settlement, and the only formula that seemed likely to be acceptable to all the great powers was Prince Souvanna Phouma's idea of a coalition government, to consist of right-wingers, neutralists, and Communists under a neutralist Prime Minister – himself. I am not concerned here with the efficacy of such a formula which, as its composition implies, is a marriage of incompatibles. The point I have to make is that in 1961 the American Administration came to accept that some such solution was inevitable. Thus, whereas the Eisenhower Administration had worked consistently to prevent the participation of Communists in the Laotian Government, the Kennedy Administration began to work *in favour* of their participation. But there was a snag, which puts this policy switch into perspective. For the coalition idea to be workable – that is, acceptable to the US – the proposed government would have to include anti-communists as well as Communists. Now the anti-communists were Prince Boun Oum and General

Phoumi, the same men the Americans had supported, protected, and put in power. Were *they* going to accept the change of policy and consent to take part in a government that included Communists and was to be headed by a neutralist? There was the rub. When it came to the point the puppets turned out not to be puppets at all.

The right-wingers were, in fact, curiously well placed to resist American pressure. In May 1961 fourteen powers, great and small, assembled in Geneva to confer on the future of Laos. It was common ground that Laos should be neutralized and demilitarized. But throughout the conference, which lasted, with intervals, fourteen months, the elusive key of success was the formation of a coalition government. Until that happened there could be no agreement, for when the conference opened Laos was represented by three separate delegations: that of Prince Boun Oum's right-wing government, recognized by the western powers, that of Prince Souvanna Phouma, recognized by the communist powers, and that of the Laotian Communists themselves. The neutralists were, of course, willing and eager to form a government, and so were the Communists, for their own purposes. But the right-wingers saw no reason why they should step down. General Phoumi well knew that the Americans could not drop him entirely: without him, there could be no coalition. Moreover, if he held on long enough, he reckoned the conference would collapse and the United States would be forced to conquer Laos for him.

Hopes had been aroused on 22 June 1961, when the three Princes who represented the three streams of Laotian politics met in Zurich and agreed to form a government. We have met two of them: Boun Oum (right wing) and Souvanna Phouma (neutralist). The third was Souvanna Phouma's half-brother, Prince Souphannouvong, a flamboyant but mysterious figure who, for the past thirteen years, had been regarded as the leader of the Laotian Communists. Was Souphannouvong really a Communist? Certainly his story suggested that he was one. He had undergone a course of indoctrination in China, married a Vietnamese Communist, and set up headquarters in Hanoi, the capital of communist North Vietnam. Yet he firmly denied he was a Communist, and I was never able to form my own opinion by actual contact (he had refused to see me in Vientiane). On each of the three occasions when I met Prince Souvanna Phouma in private conversation (in Vientiane, London, and Paris) he indignantly denied his half-brother was a Communist and commented: 'He is a patriot.' This, however, was less than convincing, for he also assured me that another Laotian communist leader, who happened also to be a member of the North Vietnamese Communist Party (Lao Dong) was just a patriot.

The Americans (and their allies) had no doubt that Souphannouvong was a Communist. But they were prepared to accept him in the government, so long as Phoumi also joined. Although Phoumi, who had gone to Zurich in June 1961, had agreed to join a coalition government, he did not actually do so until June 1962, a whole year later. Meanwhile Phoumi had resisted every kind of American pressure, including the suspension on two occasions of the monthly US aid cheque of $4 million. When, in the end, he did join the coalition government, thereby making the Laotian settlement possible, it was because his forces had been routed by the Communists in the battle of Nam Tha, in northern Laos, on 6 May. After that, it was no longer possible to believe in a military victory; nor, for that matter, in American intervention, for though the US had landed marines and other forces in Siam a few days after Nam Tha, the Americans were clearly reluctant to let themselves be drawn into a war in Laos.

Laos, then, was never an American satellite in the same way as, say, Hungary or Rumania was a Soviet satellite. Nor, for that matter, were South Korea and South Vietnam, for all that the United States poured money and military supplies into both. True, the United States retained the negative power to prevent President Syngman Rhee of South Korea from invading the communist North, or – should he have so desired – President Ngo Dinh Diem of South Vietnam from invading *his* communist North. But at no stage did the United States manage to exert the slightest influence on the course of domestic politics in either country. Both Syngman Rhee and Ngo Dinh Diem stubbornly rejected American criticism of their autocratic methods. In November 1961, for example, Mr Diem's controlled Saigon Press broke out in a rash of anti-American headlines. One of these, in the newspaper *Thoi Bao*, read:

REPUBLIC OF VIETNAM IS NOT A GUINEA PIG FOR CAPITALIST IMPERIALISM – Is it not time to revise Vietnamese–American collaboration?

Editorials complained that the United States was interfering in South Vietnam's internal affairs. The interference the Vietnamese were complaining of was an illuminating example of the kind of relationship that can develop between a powerful democratic State and a weak but autocratic one. Since the beginning of the year South Vietnam had been under military attack from communist North Vietnam. Guerrilla fighters who had buried their arms in 1954, when their war against France ended, unearthed them again. Further supplies, together with trained organizers, were reaching them from the North, across the unpoliced jungles of Laos. Mr Diem's officials and policemen in the villages were being kidnapped and murdered at the rate of twenty a day. By November more than 20,000 guerrillas were in action and large regions of the countryside were in their hands.

Alarmed at this situation, President Kennedy sent a powerful mission, headed by General Maxwell Taylor, to South Vietnam to find out what was happening and recommend countermeasures. I happened to be in Washington when the mission returned, and though the President had strictly forbidden any of its members to see the Press, it was possible to reconstruct what General Taylor had recommended by talking to officials who had seen him. I am not concerned here with the military recommendations but with the political ones. In effect, what General Taylor wanted President Diem to do was to liberalize his régime and reorganize his administration. His report proposed greater freedom of expression, economic projects designed to raise living standards in the rural areas, and decentralization of the administration (which, in itself, would have reduced autocratic control from Saigon). This was the 'interference' resented by the controlled Saigon Press, and the point to be noted is that – unfortunately for his country – Mr Diem's resistance to American pressure was successful. The Press remained controlled; only minor administrative reforms were carried out; Mr Diem and his tight little circle of brothers and in-laws retained their absolute grip on power; and the opposition leaders, who had been jailed at the time of an abortive military *coup* against Mr Diem exactly a year before the Taylor mission went to Vietnam, remained in jail. This was still the situation in January 1963, when American officers 'advising' the Vietnamese forces started complaining that the local troops lacked fighting spirit. Yet in the meantime the United States had greatly increased its military aid to South Vietnam and had built up its team of military advisers from 5,000 to more than 12,000. Whatever impact this build-up may have had on the war (and the complaints of the American officers were hardly reassuring), it was clear that the American military presence had had no influence whatever on internal affairs. Utterly dependent though the Ngo Dinh Diem family were on American support, it could not be said that they were puppets; nor that South Vietnam was a satellite.

Much the same could be said of American relations with South Korea. Though the United States was able to restrain ex-President Rhee in his declared intention of conquering communist North Korea, it was unable to persuade him to improve relations with Japan, Korea's former colonial power. Despite the presence of a powerful American force (thinly disguised under a United Nations label), United States influence on Korean domestic politics remained negligible. This was true of the Syngman Rhee period and has been true of the military régime since it was set up in May 1961. For a brief and therefore exceptional period, however, the Americans did influence the course of events in South Korea. This was during and after the student disorders in the spring of 1960, which led to the overthrow of Dr Rhee. The able American ambassador in Seoul at that time, Mr Walter McConaughy, showed great energy and awareness during this confused period. It was largely due to his enlightened pressure that President Rhee resigned, that the caretaker administration which succeeded him was steered in a liberal direction, and that fresh general elections took place (governmental brutalities and fraudulent methods in the previous elections in March having sparked off the students' revolt). The mild but inefficient régime that followed was also amenable to American influence. The Premier, Dr John Myun Chang, who had been educated in the US and had spent many years there, was not averse from accepting American advice, as well as American money. He was, however, overthrown by a military junta less than a year after coming to power, and the tenuous nature of America's influence was never more clearly demonstrated than at that time.

Observers of the Korean scene had been claiming, erroneously, as it turned out, that the US military presence was a guarantee against a military take-over bid, in that it had the South Korean army under control through the United Nations Command. There seemed good grounds for this supposition. For one thing, American military advisers had been attached to the Korean army's Counter-Intelligence Corps, as a first step towards the 'total reorganization' of this body, which had been Rhee's spy within the armed forces. For another thing, the Americans appeared to have had a hand in forcing the resignation as martial-law commander and army chief of staff, of Lieutenant-General Song Yo-chan, who had been credited with the ambition of seizing power. This was in May 1960. A year later, however, a group of military conspirators did seize power, and the Americans were taken completely by surprise.

In the event, Korean duplicity exploited American trustfulness. Dr Chang had brought about his own downfall by trying to carry out an election pledge to cut down the swollen Korean army from 600,000 men to 400,000. The American UN Commander, General Magruder, had persuaded him to go slow, and a first cut of only 50,000 had been announced. Though this was later scaled down to 30,000, the military officers felt a halt had to be called, and began conspiring against the civilian government. A curious aspect of this conspiracy is that both the

Americans and the government had got wind of it. Dr Chang took the warning seriously, but General Magruder apparently did not, mainly because the Korean chief of staff, General Chang Do-yun, had assured him that there was no truth in it.

The story was true, however, and the full truth of it was disclosed on 5 June 1961, in an extraordinarily candid press conference given by the intelligence chief of the new military junta, Lieutenant-Colonel Kim Jong-pil. The more damaging passages of Colonel Kim's statement appeared only in the Korean Press, foreign correspondents present having been persuaded to omit them in their cables. The original plan, as Colonel Kim described it, was to spread rumours of an impending students' uprising and get Dr Chang to call large forces into Seoul. Once there, these would have seized power. The plan went astray because it became apparent that the students were not, in fact, going to riot. The officers had deployed a large concentration of troops on the outskirts in anticipation of Dr Chang's call, which did not materialize. It was this deployment that had given the game away, both to the students and to the government. Plans were then recast; Seoul was to be taken by surprise on 12 May – about three weeks after the date originally fixed. 'But,' said Kim, 'one of our colonels became too excited and gave the game away. We have evidence that advance information of our plot reached not only Dr Chang and his national police but also the United Nations command' (that is, the Americans). 'This moment was the worst in our lives. We went through agonies a hundred times worse than on 16 May, when we finally struck.'

As Colonel Kim unkindly put it, in conclusion: 'Inadequate and superficial intelligence by the US Eighth Army was of considerable help to the success of the military revolution.' Whatever the reason, one point was plain: when the crisis came, the American military presence did not save a régime supported by the United States.

Korea and Vietnam are divided countries, with a communist north and an anti-communist south. Both are therefore interesting case-studies of the effect of the cold war on national independence. As I have tried to show, neither South Korea nor South Vietnam could be considered fully independent. But, on the other hand, neither could be regarded as, in the full sense, a satellite of the United States. This was due as much to the cunning and determination of their native rulers as to the reluctance of Americans to intervene in domestic affairs. Indeed, both President Diem and President Rhee have demonstrated (as the weak governments of the French Fourth Republic did) that stubbornness and obstructiveness can be effective tools of national sovereignty.

It is tempting to anti-communists to point to North Korea and North Vietnam as examples of the total satellization that overtakes small communist countries. Such generalizations, however, are never very helpful. In fact, there are differences as well as similarities between the two, and North Vietnam, in particular, has managed to retain a certain freedom of manoeuvre. In contrast, the Korean People's Republic began life as a thoroughgoing satellite of the Soviet Union. The Russians had occupied northern Korea at the end of the Second World War. They brought in Korean Communists trained in the Soviet Union, who set up a provisional government under Soviet instructions in February 1946. This was seven years before Stalin's death, and during those seven years Soviet control over North Korea was total, even though the Russians did not involve themselves directly in the Korean war: somewhere in the secret archives of the Soviet government the historians of the future will find documentary evidence to show that Stalin ordered the Soviet-trained North Korean army to invade South Korea on 25 June 1950 – if by then the evidence has not been thoughtfully burnt.

North Korea remained completely under Soviet control even after Stalin's death, and even after the Chinese (not the Russians) had come to their rescue; but eventually, geography did dilute their satellite status. For if history had made Russia temporarily dominant in North Korea and North Vietnam (as was as in Outer Mongolia), geography had placed them in China's shadow. Thus, when the great ideological schism between Moscow and Peking developed in the late 1950s the smaller Asian communist countries were given opportunities to turn it to their own advantage, by playing one side off against the other. This is almost certainly truer of North Vietnam than of North Korea. Both countries had their Moscow and Peking wings, consisting of party men who had been trained in Russia and in China respectively. In North Korea the Prime Minister, Kim Il-sung, was always regarded as a Moscow man. Between 1958 and 1960 he purged the Korean Workers' (Communist) Party of its pro-Chinese faction with impressive thoroughness. Earlier, in 1956, he had had the Chinese 'people's volunteers' withdrawn by persuading the Russians to put pressure on them. Had he left it any later, he might have found the Chinese unwilling to respond to Soviet pressure. Having got rid of his Chinese-trained men, Marshal Kim maintained a precarious neutrality between Peking and Moscow as the great schism developed. Some time in 1962, however, he seems to have remembered that if ever there came a day of reckoning, China, not Russia, would be the neighbour on the doorstep. In September of that year the North Korean Press began, at first cautiously, then with greater abandon, to defend the things China was defending and attack those the Chinese were attacking. Thus, the Jugoslavs were attacked and the 'Chinese line' on Cuba was adopted (this meant that Mr Khrushchev was left unpraised for bowing before American strength and the dangers of 'appeasing imperialism' were emphasized). Even more significantly, the North Korean Press took China's side during the Chinese invasion of India, whereas the Soviet Press had been neutral.

The North Korean example is perhaps inconclusive. It could mean that the North Koreans had learnt the delicate art of playing off one great power against another to make sure of continuing to receive economic aid from both. Alternatively, that the North Koreans, under pressure of circumstances, were merely exchanging one set of masters for another. The North Vietnamese example is more revealing and more interesting. Unlike the North Koreans, the North Vietnamese Communists had come to power largely by their own military exertions (though admittedly with massive aid from the Chinese in the final stages of their war against the French). In addition, Communists or not, the Vietnamese had unfading memories of a thousand years of Chinese occupation. Their leader, Ho Chi Minh, was a patriotic leader who had turned to communism in the 1920s when no other creed or organization seemed to offer a way to independence. As a patriotic leader, he was well aware that no Vietnamese who appeared to be a Chinese puppet could hope to win the lasting allegiance of his people. These circumstances explain why, broadly speaking, Ho tended to take Soviet advice, not Chinese, in his conduct of affairs. But he, too, had his 'Chinese' wing, which was identified with the fiercely anti-western party leader Truong Chinh. There was thus a fascinating duality about the Vietnamese Workers' (Communist) Party, long before the schism between Moscow and Peking first appeared.

There were complicating factors, too. Ho Chi Minh is a very senior personage in the communist world, much more senior than Khrushchev and indeed second only to Mao tse-tung in the hierarchy of revolutionary prowess and prestige. He had his own ambitions, which were independent of Soviet or Chinese plans, and perhaps even in conflict with them. In 1930 he had founded the Communist Party of Indochina – admittedly on behalf of the Comintern. The name was important: it was to be a communist party for the *whole* of what was then French Indochina, that is for Laos and Cambodia as well as for Vietnam. But the control was to remain firmly in the hands of the Vietnamese Communists, led by Ho himself. Indeed, Ho's clear ambition from those distant days has been to unite the successor States of the French Indochinese empire under Vietnamese communist control.

This is more than just a theory, for the evidence is plentiful. It was in pursuance of this plan that Vietnamese communist regulars invaded Laos in April 1953. Ostensibly they came to support a Laotian 'liberation army' – but this army, the so-called 'patriotic fighters' of the Pathet Lao, had been set up by the Vietnamese Communists. Any doubt there might have been was removed on 13 April 1963, when a Vietnamese communist broadcast declared:

The (Vietnamese) Workers' Party and the people of Vietnam have the mission to make revolution in Cambodia and
Laos. We, the Vietminh (Communist-controlled Independence League), have been sent to serve this revolution and
to build the union of Vietnam, Cambodia and Laos.

It was the Vietnamese Communist invaders who set up the
Communist Pathet Lao administration in two north-eastern
provinces of Laos, which served as a base from which Laos was
supposed, in course of time, to be taken over by the Communists (as we have seen earlier in this chapter). When Major
Kavinh Koenakorn, the former secretary of the Pathet Lao
delegation in Vientiane, asked the Royal government for
asylum, in September 1955, he gave full details of Vietnamese
control over the movement. Indeed, the Vietnamese trained,
armed, and indoctrinated Pathet Lao 'fighers', provided them
with funds and printed their newspaper, *Lao Haksat*. In Cambodia, too, but with conspicuously less success, the Communists
tried to capture the anti-French liberation movement (Khmer
Issarak) and set up a 'liberated zone'. The activities of the
Vietnamese Communists since Cambodia became independent
have frequently been denounced by the Cambodian leader,
Prince Sihanouk.

It must not be assumed that the Russians, or even the
Chinese, approved unreservedly of such Vietnamese initiatives.
The Russians, in particular, seemed anxious to avoid trouble
that might lead to a major war in Indochina. On more than one
occasion they showed themselves ready to override Vietnamese
communist desires in the interest of peace. Thus, during the
Geneva conference of 1954, which ended the Indochina war,
Mr Molotov, the then Soviet Foreign Minister, forced the
Vietnamese Communists to accept a settlement that fell far
short of their wishes, as part of a complicated deal with M.
Mendès-France, under which the French Premier agreed to let
the project for a European Defence Community die a natural
death. Those who are interested in the details can find them
in Donald Lancaster's *The Emancipation of French Indochina*
(Oxford for Chatham House, 1961) and *La Fin d'une Guerre*,

o

by Philippe Devillers and Jean Lacouture (Editions du Seuil, 1960).

It is not unreasonable once more, to suppose that neither Moscow nor Peking looks with wholehearted enthusiasm on the guerrilla war which Ho Chi Minh launched in South Vietnam in January 1961. The evidence is, in fact, inconclusive. But the Russians clearly had an interest in avoiding American counter-intervention on such a scale that the Chinese, and perhaps they themselves, might be drawn in. The Chinese, on their side, doubtless approved North Vietnam's display of revolutionary violence (which Peking had been advocating, in contrast to Moscow's advocacy of 'peaceful co-existence'). But they could hardly look with favour on the prospect that Ho Chi Minh might be within sight of his old dream of reconstituting the old French empire in Indochina under Vietnamese control. For in that event north Vietnam would look and behave a good deal less like a satellite. Whether the Russians or even the Chinese could stop the Vietnamese communist guerrillas in their tracks if they decided to try is an open question. Probably neither Moscow nor Peking – short of invading North Vietnam – could do it, even if both countries threatened to cut off their economic aid to Ho Chi Minh's régime. Thus, on his chosen battleground the tough old warrior probably retained some independence, in much the same way as his rival, Ngo Dinh Diem, did in the South.

PART III

Happy
though Independent?

Chapter 1

TOWARDS VIABILITY

Those who have stayed with me so far may well accuse me of sourness. I have argued that the newly independent countries are not really independent, or at any rate not as independent as they say they are. I have pointed out that in many cases sovereignty has brought a decline in living standards, and I have deplored the pointless acts of defiance with which the new governments have attempted to prove that they are indeed independent. I do not think I have exaggerated the gloom of the present, that is, of the immediate past. Nor could anyone reasonably have expected things to be any better. Revolutions, whether communist or not, are made by intellectuals armed with grievances and ideas. It should have been obvious to the western countries that disgrunted colonial intellectuals armed with western ideas of freedom and independence would demand such things for their own countries. (The Belgians indeed were aware enough; and were highly successful in keeping the Congolese happy with their material lot – an enviable one in some respects – for many years, until the invasion of ideas from elsewhere proved fatally contagious.) Nevertheless, and paradoxically, the western nations opposed demands for independence with greater or lesser persistence until forced to concede it. During the struggle for independence most of the nationalist leaders turned to anti-capitalist and anti-imperialist doctrines – all variants of Marxism – to further their struggle. The result was unfortunate, though predictable.

They came to power in their nominally sovereign countries with a mixed bag of intellectual equipment, including incompatible ideas, such as 'freedom', 'democracy', and 'independence', on the one hand, and 'socialism' and 'democratic centralism', on the other. Moreover, the illiteracy of their populations and the gap between promise and fulfilment encouraged dictatorship and demagogy.

The inevitability of such circumstances – with one or two shining exceptions – does not make them less sad. It is possible, however, to be less sour about the future, if only because the worst has not yet happened and may never happen. To be sure, the outlook is gloomy enough. Populations are rising faster than the ability of the countries concerned to feed them. The rising generation of nationalists seems, if anything, to be even less wise than their elders in all matters concerned with the real welfare of their peoples, as distinct from the short-lived comforts of slogans and promises. Experience could, however, teach them or their successors, just possibly before it is too late, that is, before mass starvation overtakes vast areas of the earth. In cold, objective fact, the possibility is slight; but it is worth exploring.

Left to their own devices, many of the newly independent countries would rapidly revert to traditional ways of living, or would stagnate in more or less picturesque fashion. This, after all, is roughly what happened to Haiti and to Liberia, which achieved independence in 1844 and 1847 respectively – that is, long before present-day notions of economic growth or the attributes of sovereignty became fashionable. The idea that the richer nations owe the poorer ones a living is indeed a fairly novel one; so is the notion that economic development is in itself a good thing. Both need to be examined critically.

Enlightened self-interest is probably the highest ethical motive to be expected of nation-States. If it really is enlightened it is probably a good enough motive – good enough, that is, to bring side benefits to other countries. In international economic terms the concept of enlightened self-interest means that a country does not necessarily serve its own best long-term interests by practising the law of the jungle. It can indeed improve its long-term prospects by parting, here and now, with some of its material wealth, just as the small man who sacrifices the immediate satisfaction of want or greed in favour of saving will in time be able to invest his money and get a return on it for his old age.

In individual countries a dramatic gap between rich and poor is a factor of instability and an incipient cause of revolution. So, too, in international terms, is the gap between rich nations and poor ones. It is therefore in the national interest of the richer countries to reduce this gap.

The other notion – that economic development is an absolute good in itself – should also be looked at closely for flaws in the texture. There is a closer correlation between poverty and misery than between wealth and happiness. Lack of material possessions is no bar to felicity so long as certain elementary wants are satisfied: food, clothing, a roof, and sexual fulfilment. Broadly speaking, the Cambodians and the Laotians had these things before independence, and they must have been among the happiest people on earth, certainly far happier than the American who is wondering whether his personal budget will stand the strain of a second or a third family car, a stereo tape-recorder, or a television set in each bedroom as well as in the living-room. The gentle charm of Buddhism, the traditional festivities, the joy of dancing and personal adornment: these things were worth more to the Cambodians and Laotians than the index of personal consumption to the highly developed Occidental. True, their company included mosquitoes, disease and early death. But the tropics, which forced such things on them, also gave them freedom from cold and a bountiful food supply. The Khmer peasant had only to bend down and scoop up fishes from the Great Lake, or plant the paddy stems and eat the rice when it was ripe.

These things are true and need to be repeated, because they are so easily forgotten. But it must be admitted that the bountiful regions are few. Burma and Thailand, Cambodia and Laos have plenty of land, but others have too little. The day medical science starts retarding death and ensuring the survival of more babies is the day when poverty and misery are ushered in hand in hand. The proper justification for economic development is therefore to anticipate and prevent the consequences of over-population: to prevent misery rather than attempt to promote happiness; to make sure the new bodies do not starve, not to provide prestige for national leaders. In Thailand I learned from

Prince Chula Chakrabongse, a man could still, in 1962, find a plot of land and own it by merely claiming possession. This will not, I fear, be possible for much longer. The day the United Nations World Health Organization teams eradicated malaria from Thailand they promoted longer life and enhanced sexual potency. In other words, they guaranteed that the population explosion will come to Thailand; and therefore poverty and misery. Unless, of course, something is done in time about economic development.

For good reasons that are rarely stated, then, the richer countries should help the poorer, and the poorer ones should help themselves. The key question is : What kind of help in each case? Never has so fundamental a question been so be-devilled by irrelevant considerations. The great bulk of the aid dispensed by the two super-powers – the USSR and the United States – has been economically irrelevant. To the greatest pos-sible extent this disastrous fact has been a consequence, though partly an avoidable consequence, of the cold war. The whole concept of American aid is bound up with military security and wrapped up in such labels as 'defence support' and 'mutual security'. The primary reason for this is that unless the Adminis-tration can persuade the ever-watchful legislators that its aid programme is essential to the security of the United States, it will never get it past Congress. As a result, purely economic aid has always been a fraction of the whole, the bulk consisting of various kinds of military assistance. Indeed, in practice, the bulk of American aid, whether military or economic, has been allocated for the purpose of keeping its allies happy, as anybody can see by examining the astronomical allocations to such régimes as those of South Korea, Formosa, and South Vietnam, each of which maintains much larger armies than its own secu-rity can possibly justify. Moreover, even the purely economic part of America's foreign-aid programme has been of limited value because of stringently imposed conditions which, in practice, have made much of it valueless in terms of promoting the viability of the recipient. One of these conditions is that at least 50 per cent of the export–import traffic handled under the American aid scheme must be carried in American ships.

Another, under President Kennedy's predecessors, was that allocations were made on a yearly basis. The effect of the first of these conditions is severely to restrict the scope of the 'shopping' done under the aid programme by recipient governments, and to increase substantially the cost of transporting what they do buy. The effect of the second was even more serious. Few governments will commit themselves to long-term economic plans on the basis of yearly allocations, not knowing whether the following year's allocation will enable them to pay their bills. One exception has been Formosa (Nationalist China), which has carried out impressive long-term development schemes, such as roads, power-stations, and factory building – perhaps because Generalissimo Chiang Kai-shek's Government was confident that the imperatives of American strategy would keep the money flowing in. To give President Eisenhower his due, he did ask Congress for authority to allocate aid on a three-yearly basis, but was turned down by his short-sighted legislators. President Kennedy obtained authority to make loans on a five-yearly basis, but remained ham-strung by yearly Congressional scrutinies of actual appropriations.

The built-in limitations on America's aid programme have produced further anomalies. In the early days of the aid programme countries receiving certain forms of assistance had to create and build up 'counterpart funds', that is reserves in local currency equivalent in terms of the official exchange rate (which in many cases bears no relation to national purchasing power) to the amount of dollar aid actually received. Consumer goods were then imported to mop up surplus currency and 'avoid inflation'. This sounds crazy and was. In China, in the years of the civil war and before the great post-war American aid programmes were launched, comparable methods encouraged a terrifying inflation and corruption on an unprecedented scale. While ordinary Chinese died of starvation, officials and business men made fortunes out of racketeering in medical and other relief supplies. Much the same thing happened in some other countries that receive United States aid on a very large scale.

The most notable examples have been South Korea and Laos, and even in countries where corruption, though evident, has not got out of hand, such as South Vietnam, the imports of consumer goods – especially in the early days – have given the towns a deceptive appearance of prosperity. The Laotian and South Korean cases, however, are worth looking at as extreme examples of what can happen to an underdeveloped country when enormous sums are injected into its rudimentary economy. In Laos, where the economy is even more primitive than the word 'rudimentary' implies, much of the trouble arose from the polite fiction that the US dollar was worth only 35 kips, the local unit of currency. Enterprising Laotians only had to buy dollars at 35 kips each and resell them for their true (that is, black market) price of anything up to 110, to make quick fortunes. And many did. In 1957, when the country's rackets were at their most flourishing, an American magazine drew attention to what sounded like a particularly profitable one. American aid money, it appears, was being used to import television sets, which were then re-exported to Bangkok and sold at a profit. Laos had no television service; Siam had. Laotian spokesmen denied this story, for what the denial was worth, but another story could not be denied. Enormous quantities of fountain pens and toothpaste had been ordered, on the American aid programme. The order was cancelled when the Laotian government got wind of the fact that the American government was wondering what was happening to its money. Had it gone through, there would have been enough fountain pens and toothpaste for the whole population, had it been literate or ever heard of the toothbrush.

Shortly afterwards the committee on government operations of the US House of Representatives sent a mission to Laos to see things for itself. It found that American officials and business men, as well as Laotians, had allowed themselves to be tempted by the prospect of a quick kip. One official had accepted bribes totalling at least $13,000 from an American company, in return for lucrative contracts and for overlooking deficiencies in their execution. Another official accepted a well-paid post in the same company, with the title of 'project manager' as his reward for sanctioning a contract. Yet another official sold his ten-year-old Cadillac to the head of an American company at an inflated price. The Cadillac, it happened, was unusable and 'shortly thereafter', said the committee's report, 'it was cut up and the pieces dropped down an abandoned well'. The report, headed 'United States Aid Operations in Laos', was published in Washington in June 1959 and caused something of a scandal.

It is only fair to add that in 1958 after a Laotian government mission had been called to Washington and made to feel the weight of official disapproval, the kip was devalued to the more realistic level of 80 to the dollar. Thereafter, racketeering became less profitable. One of the most important conclusions of the House committee's report, however, went ignored. This was that the main reason why the aid programme went wrong in Laos was because it was tied to the excessive size of the Laotian Army. The Laotians themselves (who did well out of having a large army) and the State Department (which wanted to keep the Laotians happy) insisted on having an army of 25,000 men, whereas the American Chiefs of Staff thought that a more efficient army of 12,000–15,000 would be more viable. Financially, as well as militarily, the Chiefs of Staff were right.

Anything that might be said about corruption in Laos, and about the size of its army, would be true of South Korea, if multiplied many times in each case. With a population of less than 25 million, the anti-communist greater half of Korea maintains armed forces of 700,000 men, the second largest in Asia (after China's), or possibly the third largest if Russia's Far Eastern forces are included in the reckoning. There are several excuses for the vastness of this force. One is the fear that North Korea or China or both will attack again if the size of South Korea's army is reduced. There seems little sense in this argument, for South Korea's only real guarantee against further aggression is the presence of an American force and the willingness of the United States to step in again, as it did on behalf of of the United Nations in 1950, should the Korean war begin again. Another argument is that unemployment, which is chronically high in South Korea, will become much worse if the soldiers are sent back to civilian life. This is true, though it would be cheaper to keep them on unemployment relief than in the Army (on the other hand, the American Congress, which tends to find the dole immoral in the US, itself would certainly refuse to vote funds to keep men in civilian idleness, whereas they approve, without too much fuss, funds to keep them in military idleness). The real reasons for the size of the South Korean Army, however, are political. Ex-President Syngman Rhee did not trouble to disguise his intention to conquer North Korea if ever the Americans' backs were turned. (The Americans, who were aware of this, kept the South Korean Army on short petrol rations.) Mr Huh Chung, who headed the caretaker government that took over after President Rhee had been deposed by the student revolt of April 1960, forced the retirement of eleven generals. Dr John M. Chang, who succeeded him, asked army officers who considered themselves guilty of such misdeeds as accepting bribes or helping themselves to military supplies to retire voluntarily. For his pains, he was deposed by an army junta.

The Army, then, has stayed large, and its size is the main factor in the astronomical 'aid' which the Americans have poured into Korea since 1945: about $6,000,000,000 (till June 1963) in cold zeros. Although South Korea, unlike Laos, has a number of light industries that might, in healthier economic conditions, be flourishing, the effect of this injection of dollars has been much the same: corruption and graft, inflation, and economic stagnation. It was like that under Syngman Rhee, it continued without change under Dr Chang, and it has not improved under the military dictatorship of General Park, despite the junta's pledge to stamp out corruption. Thus, in September 1962 the General Accounting office for the US Congress sharply criticized the aid programme for Korea in a major report which found, among other things, that the level of aid which, between 1957 and 1961, was running at more than $200 million a year, was 'beyond the capacity of the Korean economy to absorb productively or of its government to administer efficiently'. The report concluded indeed that the aid programme had aggravated the basic problems of the Korean economy, had weakened the 'moral fabric of business practice', and stultified economic growth. More important, because more specific, charges in the report, were that commodities that could have been produced economically in Korea, such as cotton and soya beans, had been imported in large quantities under the aid programme; that Korean officials who knew little about the country's requirements for fertilizers were running the fertilizer programme; that best-quality nylon yarns and other luxury items were being imported under the aid programme, despite the generally low living standards; and that industrial development was lopsided because of the way development funds were distributed. To be fair, the report conceded that the American aid programme in Korea had improved in 1962 because it had been substantially reduced.

The American aid programme is not, of course, all bad. I have already mentioned its accomplishments in Formosa, and I shall come back to the Formosan example, and more importantly, to the Japanese one. The point I am making for the present is that the Laotian and Korean cases are excellent examples of the kind of economic 'aid' that is considerably worse than useless.

Have the Russians and their friends done any better? The answer is complex, and in some respects unexpected. Like everybody else, the Russians are in the aid business to make friends and improve their influence. They are fast discovering that gratitude is the enemy of friendship. There was a time – during the Dulles era – when countries accepting Soviet aid were immediately suspected of incipent communism and when the thought of Soviet assistance sent nervous shivers down orthodox official spines in Washington, and even in London. Since then, reactions have become more sophisticated, and indeed it is hard to disprove the argument that Soviet competition in economic aid ought to be welcomed on two grounds by Russia's selected enemies in the cold war: that it puts an additional strain on the Soviet economy and contributes to make the Soviet Union unpopular.

Lacking the West's surplus wealth, the Russians tend to concentrate on spectacular key projects in selected countries. Soviet aid offers certain undeniable advantages to recipient countries. Much of it is aimed at promoting economic growth: the Soviet-built steel mill at Bhilai in India, the high dam at

Aswan in Egypt, and the extending of Conakry airport in Guinea come under this category. The interest rates on Soviet loans are invariably much lower than any 'capitalist' bank – including the International Bank for Reconstruction and Development – would consider viable; 2·5 per cent is a normal charge. Moreover, the Soviet system does produce one important surplus – engineers and other trained technicians – and Soviet assistance in this field is large and growing fast. In 1959 there were about 4,000 Soviet bloc technicians in 17 countries; by the end of 1960 there were nearly 7,900 in 23 countries.

These are all advantages that should not be underrated. They are largely offset, however, by equally serious disadvantages. One is that Soviet loans, though cheap in terms of interest, are usually for quite short terms – twelve years is a fairly normal period – and recipients therefore have to start repayments inconveniently early. Western loans are often for much longer periods. Moreover, the Soviet Union, unlike the United States, France, and Britain, has made hardly any *grants*. Now the value of a grant, to a struggling economy, is incomparably greater than that of a loan, which has to be repaid with interest. And there are other disadvantages. One is that the Communists, by the nature of their special delusions, confuse industrialization with viability. However, viability is the first need of a newly sovereign country, if it is to become economically independent; but industrialization before the time is ripe is not the only road to viability, nor in many cases the best. In all overpopulated countries certainly, and perhaps in all underdeveloped countries, agriculture ought to be given top priority. As Professor Maurice Allais, the distinguished French economist, observes in his indispensable work *Le Tiers Monde au Carrefour* (Les Cahiers Africains, Paris, 1962), the steel works President Nasser has had built, with East German help, in Egypt fulfils no useful economic purpose, in that the cost of the steel it produces is much higher than the cost of corresponding steel imports at world prices would have been. It thus constitutes an arbitrary diversion of Egypt's limited capital resources.

This, however, is the psychological core of the problem. To have a steel works is to possess a glamorous symbol of modern statehood, even if it is economically unjustifiable; it makes a new country feel like a great power. Since the Russians take approximately the same view of the value of steel works and of such symbols, they do not discourage requests for aid that will be devoted to building steel works, so long as these come from countries that seem likely at some stage in the future to turn to communism. (Whether they are right or wrong in this supposition is beside the point.) However, in their search for amenable friends, they have gone a good deal farther than the Americans in underwriting frivolous or extravagant prestige projects of no discernible economic value. The most spectacular example is probably the stadium constructed under Soviet direction at Djakarta in Indonesia for the Asian Games that were held there in 1962. The cost of this public amenity in a city that badly needs, for instance, a drainage system or a better telephone service, was estimated at £40 million; and it is hard to find any justification for it except as a sop to President Sukarno's love of mass oratory and preference for circuses over bread.

I have already mentioned some of Burma's early difficulties with Soviet trading methods (in Part I, Chapter 3), but these were not the whole story. Soviet aid to Burma has been no more successful than American aid. Indeed, with nice impartiality, the Burmans expelled the American aid mission in 1953, encouraged it to return in 1959, and four months later cancelled five Soviet aid projects; in 1962, to round off the story, they sent an American Foundation mission packing. The Russian projects were cancelled during General Ne Win's first period in power, on the grounds that they were either unnecessary or too expensive for an underdeveloped country. They included a sports stadium, an exhibition hall, and a theatre. Three other projects – all under the same aid agreement concluded in 1957 – had been completed: a hospital, a technological institute, and a hotel. But the Burmans were not too pleased with them, for they had proved expensive in local materials and labour costs; moreover, they complained that an unnecessarily large number of Soviet technicians had been employed on them. (There was a political reason as well as economic reasons for the cancellation of the Soviet projects, arising out of the forced repatriation of a member of the Soviet Embassy in Rangoon, after he had tried, first to defect, then to commit suicide. But this is irrelevant to the present argument.)

Probably the worst examples of communist failure in the field of economic assistance is Guinea. The opportunity had been as total, and so was the failure. As we saw in earlier chapters, all French officials had been pulled out of Guinea and all French assistance had been cancelled. Neither Britain nor the United States wished to offend France by offering immediate assistance (though both did offer aid, on a fairly modest scale, later on), and the Guineans naturally turned to the communist bloc. By October 1959 – a year after Guinea's break with France – the Czechs had sent arms and military instructors, radio specialists and powerful transmitting equipment; permanent Czech and East German trade missions had been set up, and Polish and Hungarians were to follow shortly; two trade agreements had been signed with the Soviet Union, the second of which provided a long-term Soviet loan of £12,700,000, covering the cost of materials and technical assistance for the building of factories and roads and for the development of Guinean agriculture; further trade agreements had been signed with East Germany, Czechoslovakia, and Hungary; China had donated 5,000 tons of rice; and specialists of many kinds, including agriculturalists, engineers, and doctors, had swarmed in from the communist countries.

How did this massive combined operation fare? When I visited Guinea a year later – in November 1960 – there was little to show for it. Retail trade was at a standstill and the shops were open only at certain hours. Unemployment was growing and the first shoots of a prolific crop of anti-communist stories were sprouting. At first I paid little attention to these, as they were being told in western embassies with an interest in running down communist aid efforts. Later, however, I took them more seriously. In the meantime, I had found the most articulate taxi-driver I came across in Africa. He was running a brand-new Czech car, and I congratulated him on it. He responded with his story. He had been a government clerk in the Conakry port authority and happy enough at his job, when Czech specialists were brought in to work beside him at three times his salary. His discovery of this injustice coincided with his winning the State lottery. His prize was the car he was now driving, and he was doing better out of taxi-driving than he had out of clerking for the Government.

I asked him how communist aid was working out, and he told me about the Russian sugar. Great quantities of lump sugar had been sent to Conakry, and the drawback of it was that it would not melt, however hot the tea or coffee. The current joke was that the Russians would have to use this sugar for concrete when they started extending the runway at Conakry airport to take jet aircraft. Then, less amusingly, there was the impressive yardage of Czech textiles that had piled up. Even African housewives who could afford the cloth would not buy it, because no attempt had been made to provide them with the splashes of primary colours to which they were accustomed. (While I was in Conakry, energetic young salesmen from Lancashire were taking brisk orders for textiles adorned with Sékou Touré's portrait.) There were complaints, too, said my taxi-driver, about the Czech tractors that were breaking down in the jungles and could not be started again for lack of spare parts.

Later visitors have added their quota to these stories. All agreed that there was one item the shops were not short of: red ink. Thousands of bottles had been imported from Russia, to remain obstinate non-sellers on the shelves of Conakry's shops. But the most attractive of Guinea's imports from the Soviet bloc must have been the Russian snow-plough, which some inspired functionary had thoughtfully included in a consignment of other State-aided trade. The average temperature in Guinea is over 80° Fahrenheit, with humidity to match.

More seriously, in the spring and summer of 1962 Sékou Touré was letting it be known that he would be happy to let bygones be bygones if the French would do the same and re-sume economic and technical assistance.* The observable fact was that communist economic assistance had been largely irrelevant to Guinea's current needs. To build a road or a factory might be an interesting experiment in the provision of

* This was finally resumed in May 1963.

P

an infrastructure or of long-term productive capacity, but did
nothing to breathe life, here and now, into a stagnant economy.
Barter trade in red ink was not the answer; nor was American
aid (though it had become a good deal more practical since the
advent of President Kennedy's Administration). Only the
French could bring Guinea's economy to life again, and Sékou
Touré was aware of it. In any case, the Communists had been
leaving in large numbers. Since the discovery of the communist
plot and the expulsion of the Soviet Ambassador (see Part II,
Chapter 2). There was, however, a notable exception to this
outward scramble. The Chinese Communists, hardy and adapt-
able, were doing much better than their co-religionaries from
eastern Europe. These were handicapped by white skins and
affluent appearances (by African standards). The Chinese,
their 4,000 years of history carefully tucked out of sight, made a
more convincing show of mixing with Africans at an African
level. Perhaps that was why, when all other communist aid projects had come to a standstill, in the spring of 1962 the Chinese
went on with theirs, which included a cigarette factory and
some rather effective advice on how best to grow rice.

In Cuba, too, the Chinese – at about the same time – were
doing markedly better than the east Europeans. True, their
effort was on a much smaller scale than the European one, but
they were going to some trouble to send nothing but the best
they had to Cuba. On one occasion they declined a Cuban
request for machinery because they knew they had only inferior machines of the type required. In contrast, the clumsier
Russians had made the elementary mistake of overlooking the
fact that the Cubans, through their long contact with the
United States, were used to higher standards than Soviet citizens. They were used, for instance, to machines that did not
break down irritatingly early and to electrical gadgets that did
the job they were supposed to do. When the full force of communist standards of quality hit them they expressed their disappointment with native volatility. Moreover, a breakdown
now tended to be permanent. In the old days of American
'capitalist domination' a telephone call to Miami would bring
spares or fresh supplies within a day or two. Now everything

needed had to make its precarious way along 5,000 miles of cir-
cuitous sea routes. Unused to tropical conditions, the first few
batches of Soviet specialists found the Cubans more skilled than
they were, and therefore unwilling to take their advice. Thereafter, the Cubans started looking Russian gift technicians in the
mouth; this the Russians resented. On their side, the Russians
felt, doubtless with justification, that their bureaucracy was more
skilled than the Cubans', and began to complain of Cuban incompetence. Besides these specific causes of friction, there was a
more general one which the Burmans and Guineans had learnt
in their time and which the Cubans were now learning: when
the Russians trade for political purposes, that is, with an underdeveloped country,* the resulting barter deals distort natural
economic needs and produce painful anomalies. When the
Russians and Czechs took Egyptian cotton in exchange for arms
in 1955 they started unloading it at low prices on the Western
European cotton exchanges. When the Chinese took Burmese
rice about the same time in exchange for electrical gadgets that
did not fit Burmese fixtures they sent the rice to Ceylon in exchange for rubber, undercutting Burma in one of its traditional
markets. Now the Cubans were incensed to find the Russians
reselling their sugar (which the Russians did not need in the first
place) in competition with Cuba's other sales. There were other
distortions, too: by the spring of 1962 the Cubans were seriously
short of shoes and fruit. Yet they were producing as many shoes
and growing as much fruit as ever. The cause of the shortages
was simple: Cuban shoes and fruit were being shipped to Russia
in return for Russia's inefficient machinery. To console themselves, however, they had large quantities of inferior Soviet
wine.

One could multiply such examples almost *ad infinitum*, but I
hope I have written enough to make the point that *most* of the
economic aid allocated for cold-war purposes, by either side,
has been worse than useless. The capitalist Americans have
smothered weak economies with irrelevant abundance; and the

---

* When the Soviet Union trades with a developed country, e.g. Britain, in
contrast, it does so to obtain such things as specialized equipment for which it has
a genuine economic need.

communist Russians have ruined the trade of several small countries and left a memento of irrelevant constructions.

What, then, is left? Is all economic aid useless? Clearly not. But there is hardly an economic aid scheme, group, or body at present in existence that is not open to criticism on one ground or another. The specific projects made possible by World Bank loans are almost invariably worth while, but the 'commercial' (that is, high) interest rates charged nullify a good deal of the value of the loans. The United Nations Special Fund and Technical Assistance Board do excellent work and have the great advantage that their advice, which is not that of a great power, is seen to be disinterested and is therefore often acceptable where a great power's advice would not be; but both are provided with derisory financial resources. The same criticism is applicable to the otherwise admirable Colombo Plan which, from a psychological point of view, is probably the most successful scheme devised, in that it is co-operative in inspiration, puts givers and receivers on an equal footing, and completely avoids the national resentments inseparable from cold-war aid. These examples, again, could be multiplied. Those interested in the whole subject of economic aid, and the agencies that distribute aid, cannot do better than read Andrew Shonfield's *The Attack on World Poverty* (Chatto & Windus, 1960).

I shall return to the theme of the proper use of aid in economic development. For now, let us just note that although aid can be a help (or a hindrance, as the case may be), it ought never to be treated as a substitute for indigenous growth. A nation's economy will grow if it gets its economic priorities right; and that means, primarily, if it sees to it that available resources are invested in sectors for whose products or produce there is a real demand, either nationally or internationally. In other words, the proper role of the State, in economic planning, is to make sure the economy gets the fullest possible benefits of a free market. This, I recognize, is a dogmatic statement which flatly contradicts the principles of socialist planning, for whether under communist or social democratic governments, the consumer comes last: it is left to bureaucrats to determine where the investment goes. Since the bureaucrat is the least representative of consumers, the average consumer tends to remain unsatisfied. A rising standard of living is, however, the only kind of economic growth which the consumer – you or I – recognizes; and a rising standard of living means a rising personal consumption and nothing else. It means a fuller or more appetizing plate or bowl at meal-times, another change of clothes, a bicycle or a car or a radio set. It does not mean another million tons of steel or a rising production of machine tools, except to the extent that such capital goods are actually used to improve living standards (as they are in western but not in communist countries).

The best way to understand such fundamental truths and to learn to distinguish between good planning (the encouragement of resources in the right direction in the interests of the consumer) and bad or socialist planning is to look at a few examples, starting with two that are in fierce competition with one another: those of India and China.

Chapter 2

RIVAL EXAMPLES

Most of the newly independent countries are traditional societies, agrarian and pre-industrial. In many cases their leaders are inexperienced, and in any event, the problems they face are largely unprecedented. Economic growth, their dominant preoccupation, was not, in general, a major concern of colonial powers, though in many cases the foundations of development were in fact laid by these powers. Once independent, however, the political leaders of the emerging countries had to face up to the problem of growth, if only because the subsidies paid by the former metropolitan powers could not be expected to continue indefinitely. Hence they could not fail to take an interest in the rival theories of growth advanced on all sides. Nor could they fail to watch, with a kind of anxious fascination, the race apparently taking place before their eyes between the two largest and most populous nations of Asia: India and China.

Besides their vast populations and sub-continental dimensions, the two countries had a common problem: that of raising depressingly low annual average incomes in the face of an exploding birth-rate. Both peoples, indeed, have to work very hard merely to prevent their already low standards from falling still further. Each, however, had set itself a goal – which was that of nearly all underdeveloped countries – of self-sustaining economic growth; and the drama of the competition between them lies in the fact that their approach to the same problem is startlingly different.

The Indians are committed to parliamentary democracy, the rule of law and individual freedom, the Chinese to one-party rule, arbitrary justice, and coercion by pressures of many kinds. The competition between these two great nations is thus one of ideas and minds, as well as of plans and statistics. What the Chinese are trying to do has been done before, up to a point: the use of State authority to squeeze an investable surplus out of a predominantly agricultural population. Japan and Soviet Russia did it, and both had authoritarian governments in the years of capital accumulation.

What the Indians are trying to do, on the other hand, is quite unprecedented: to raise an investable surplus without coercion and indeed while preserving the basic freedoms. Now clearly, to people living at the subsistence level, democratic freedoms are of less interest than the availability of better meals, clothing, and shelter. The great mass of populations at that level neither know nor care about the competition between the two Asian giants, but their rulers do, and they are interested, above all, in success. If the Indian experiment succeeds, and especially if it succeeds faster than the Chinese way, then the preservation of freedom will be seen in its true light, as a thing of value in itself. Moreover, if it can be shown that freedom actually contributed to success, then the Indian example will seem all the more worthy of emulation.

When prize-fighters are about to exchange blows it is customary to strip them, weigh them, and measure them, to see how evenly matched they are. If one applies this slightly distasteful image to China and India one notices that the contestants are not, in fact, as evenly matched as the fairest rules would have them be. There are physical and social, as well as ideological, differences between them. For one thing, huge though India is in size and population, China is very much larger in both – roughly half as large again. India had emerged from colonial rule with a heritage of law and peace, a first-class civil service, and twice China's railway mileage. The Chinese had emerged from a century of decadence and humiliation, banditry, war, and civil war. Colonial rule, on the other hand, though it had left certain lasting benefits, had done nothing to set India on the road to economic growth – indeed, the idea of economic growth is itself a recent development, which had made little headway, despite Russia's five-year plans, by the time India became independent in 1947. Moreover, India started its conscious drive for economic

betterment under heavy social handicaps, such as the caste
system, landlordism, and a proliferation of uneconomic small-
holdings. China under the Communists had, in contrast, made
a complete break with the past, executing landlords and other
'reactionaries' by the hundred thousand and surrending total
power to a group of men to whom the objections of the individual could not be allowed to interfere with the advancement of
the masses along lines which they – the rulers – had determined
in advance.

Both Pandit Nehru's Republic of India and Chairman Mao
Tse-tung's Chinese People's Republic, however, call themselves
'socialist'. But their interpretations of 'socialism' are so different
that each calls for definition. Indian socialism, as defined by
Pandit Nehru in many speeches, and by the Indian Planning
Commission, aims at reducing social and economic inequalities
(which owing to a caste system based on a line of descent and
not on wealth, do not always coincide). But – and this is
fundamental – these inequalities are to be reduced while safe-
guarding the dignity of the individual. The march towards
social co-operation is to be aided and guided by the State, but
the State's powers of intervention are strictly defined and
limited; the private sector has its rights and knows how to fight
for them.

The Chinese Communists' definition of socialism, in contrast,
does not envisage private enterprise of any kind, although one-
man businesses of various kinds are in fact still tolerated, as are
private plots of land. Indeed, neither China nor Russia could do
without the private farmer, who, working in his spare time on
tiny holdings, continues to make a contribution to national food
supplies out of all proportion to his numbers and the acreage at
his disposal. The power of the State – meaning the Communist
Party – is limitless. And it is enforced by an all-pervasive chain
of command stretching down from the Central Committee to
street committees or village committees throughout the vast
land. There is no question of opting out of this all-embracing
system; and neither taxes nor social responsibilities – constantly
enforced by relentless group persuasion – can be evaded.
The price of non-conformity, and even of doubt, is brain-

Laotians prefer
festivals
to fighting

WAR COMES TO A LAND OF PEACE

Neutralist Premier
Prince Souvanna
Phouma and his
deputy, 'red' Prince
Souphannouvong, vow
friendship while their
factions fight it out

PRINCES DOMINATE POLITICS

↑ INDIA'S LEGACY OF THE PAST:
Hinduism and sacred cows

CHINA'S 'LEAP' INTO THE FUTURE:
The backyard furnaces that fell flat →

THE SEARCH FOR MATURITY:
African summit, Addis Ababa

NEW LEADERS MEET:
President Radhakrishnan of India (*right*) greets Prince Sihanouk
of Cambodia

washing and forced labour; and in extreme cases physical
liquidation.

2. THE MEN AT THE TOP

The leaders, as well as their countries, need to be compared.
Both China's violent revolution and India's relatively peaceful
one have thrown up a handful of exceptional men, whose personalities have imprinted themselves on the countries they
govern. Since India is a free society, it has always been relatively easy to discover the biographies of its leading figures; in
China, a closed society discouraging to the inquisitive, it is hard
work. Facts have to be gleaned patiently, by noting attend-
ances at meetings of Communist Party or State organs, by
records of speeches, journeys, or resolutions. What emerges
from these painstaking investigations is not always a rounded
image of a human being, complete with emotions and prejudices. Rather is it a depersonalized entry in a hypothetical work
of reference. But then, this kind of image is consistent with the
kind of man that seems to be produced by communist indoctrination and practice.

By far the best-known Chinese Communist, in the sense of
familiarity with a physical presence, is Mr Chou En-lai, who
has been Chairman of the State Council, or 'Premier', since the
inception of the Chinese People's Republic in 1949. This
familiarity with Mr Chou's handsome, rather humorous face,
with its heavy eyebrows and ready smile, has been due to the
fact that he is one of the few Chinese leaders who have travelled
abroad outside communist countries. Mr Chou, however, has
had relatively little to do with China's economic planning.
Although, like the rest of the leadership, he has been a Communist from student days, Mr Chou is less doctrinaire than some of
his colleagues, and places greater reliance on common sense.
He is said to have disapproved of some of the more extreme
economic and social experiments of the régime, and specifically
of the breakneck pace of industrialization and of the creation of
People's Communes. In communist countries, however, the head
of government is not the chief executive, unless – as in the Soviet
Union under Stalin and Khrushchev – he happens to be

concurrently boss of the party. Mr Chou was thus never in a position to veto the experiments which he criticized.

The most powerful figures in communist China are Mao Tse-tung, who was Chairman (or President) of the Republic until 1959 and who remains Chairman of the Communist Party; and Liu Shao-ch'i, who replaced Mao as Chairman of the Republic and is also first vice-chairman (under Mao) of the Party's Central Committee. The extent to which Mao remained in control after 1959 is hard to assess. There has never been any hint or evidence of disloyalty on Liu's part, and though he has increasingly been responsible for giving day-to-day orders, it is probable that he has never, at any stage, deviated sensibly from policies approved, if not actually initiated, by Mao himself. Paradoxically, however, the policies which Mao did unquestionably initiate have been discredited by practical experience – by 'life itself', as Mr Khrushchev would put it – and tacitly abandoned. But officially, the policies themselves – the 'great leap forward' and the 'people's communes' – have never been explicitly disavowed, and indeed were reaffirmed as recently as October 1962 on the thirteenth anniversary of the Chinese People's Republic.

Western journalists have long labelled Liu Shao-ch'i 'the principal theoretician' of the Chinese Communist Party, perhaps because he is the author of various pamphlets that are required reading for Communist Party members. The best known of these is *How to Be a Good Communist*, written in 1939 and recently reprinted in Peking. The label of 'theoretician' has never been quite right, however; the great theoretician, in the sense of an innovator of ideas, has always been Mao himself. It was Mao who evolved a successful theory of revolutionary war, who departed from Marxist–Leninist theory by basing China's revolution on the peasants instead of the urban workers, and who, in recent years, has tried – with signal unsuccess – to master nature by regimenting the masses. Certainly this chubby peasant intellectual, at once practical warrior and deluded mystic, bears the main responsibility for policies that have gone dangerously awry in the late 'fifties and early 'sixties.

Liu Shao-ch'i, in comparison, important though his pamphlet

may have been in pouring Marxist concepts into specifically Chinese moulds, is above all the great organizer of the Communist Party's machinery of power. Lean, grey, and austere, he is the supreme organization man. In Communist Party terms, this means complete identification with the party, whose 'line' is always right even when demonstrably wrong by objective criteria. When Liu was elected Chairman of the Republic in April 1959 China was faced with economic collapse as an outcome of the hysterical irrelevancies of Mao's 'great leap forward'. It might have been supposed that Liu and the other six members of the powerful Standing Committee of the Political Bureau (including Mao himself) would abandon the policies that had caused such strain and confusion. Instead, Liu went on applying them with renewed vigour until the piti-less facts forced an (unadmitted) change of course late in 1961. Liu's fanaticism is, however, different in kind from Mao's. What moved Mao was a mystical belief in the limitless power of 'the people'; what impelled Liu was a cold conviction that the party (which was the vanguard of the people) could do no wrong.

The men chiefly associated with China's economic successes and disasters, but as the executants not the initiators of policy, are Li Fu-chun, Chairman of the State Planning Commission, and Po I-po, Chairman of the State Economic Commission. Since the party can do no wrong, it is the executant rather than the initiator of policy who is likely to suffer if something does, in fact, go wrong. Things have indeed gone seriously wrong in China in recent years, as we shall see, and next to the inner party circle the Planning Commission rather than the Economic Commission has been to blame. But the indications are that Po, the economist, instead of Li, the planner, is the agreed scape-goat for policies which certainly neither of them originated. At all events, Po I-po was absent from the secret session of the Chinese National People's Congress in April 1962, and has not been heard of since. To compound the irony of his apparent disgrace, he is generally believed to have been among the group, to which Chou En-lai also belonged, which had been advocat-ing a more gradual approach to economic development than that favoured by Mao and Liu. The fact that a man was probably right, however, does not necessarily count in his favour under a communist system.

What saved Li Fu-chun, on the other hand, was probably the fact that he is a boyhood friend of Mao's, whom he is said to have met during a game of soccer when Li was eleven and Mao nineteen. Li, now lean and grey, is sixty-one, a year younger than Liu Shao-ch'i. A veteran of the famous 'long march', Li thus belongs to the senior generation of China's Communist Party, whereas Po I-po, at fifty-five, is comparatively junior. Po, however, also has a long history of militancy behind him, for he joined the party when in Moscow in 1928 and was jailed in Peking under Chiang Kai-shek's Kuomintang régime from 1932 to 1935. In 1939, during the Sino-Japanese war, he organized two Communist-controlled 'patriotic' organizations, the 'Sacrifice for the Nation League' and the 'Dare to Die Corps'.

To turn from China's leadership to India's is to leave a vast but closed and ingrowing fortress for a rambling but airy mansion, open to the breezes and persuasions of other civilizations. Diversity replaces conformity and humanity takes the place of infallible theory. While these characteristics are inherent in the Indian people and their way of life, they do also, to an extraordinary degree, reflect the personality of Mr Jawaharlal Nehru, India's Prime Minister and guide since independence. On paper, Mr Nehru's powers are limited, and nobody would accuse him of being a dictator. But the force and charm of his personality, and his tenacity of purpose, have enabled him, in practice, to dominate the Indian political scene even more completely perhaps than Mao has the Chinese. Indeed, his fame is so universal that I feel I need do no more than draw attention to Mr Nehru's impact on India's economic development. One thinks of Nehru as a statesman and politician, not as an economist, and indeed he is not an economist in any formal sense. Nevertheless, he has been Chairman of the Planning Commission – in effect, a Chou En-lai and a Li Fu-chun in one – ever since it was set up a few weeks after India had adopted its republican Constitution in January 1950.

Though Mr Nehru comes of a prosperous family and constantly refers to his 'bourgeois' origins in his *Autobiography* (John Lane, 1936), he is a socialist by natural inclination. Indeed, certain aspects of Marxism have evidently had a profound influence on his political thought, although as a humanitarian and a liberal, he could not surrender to its violence or dogmatism. The following passage in his *Autobiography* should not be neglected by those who want to understand independent India:

> As between fascism and communism my sympathies are entirely with communism. As these pages will show, I am very far from being a communist. My roots are still perhaps partly in the nineteenth century, and I have been too much influenced by the humanist liberal tradition to get out of it completely. This *bourgeois* background follows me about and is naturally a source of irritation to many communists. I dislike dogmatism, and the treatment of Karl Marx's writings or any other books as revealed scripture which cannot be challenged, and the regimentation and heresy hunts which seem to be a feature of modern communism. I dislike also much that has happened in Russia, and especially the excessive use of violence in normal times. But still I incline more and more towards a communist philosophy.

It should be remembered that these lines were written in prison in India under British rule in 1936, when fascism was on the rise in Europe. They are the kind of lines Mr John Strachey, that elder sage of the British Labour Party, might have written in those days. Since Mr Nehru has been in power he has often denounced India's Communist Party in terms of scathing contempt; but he is not alone in having accepted certain aspects of a philosophy which, in its entirety, he utterly rejects.

On the whole, and understandably, Mr Nehru has taken advice from men who share his general socialist approach to India's problems: such men as Mr Krishna Menon, India's Defence Minister from 1957 to 1962, whose attachment to Marxism goes far deeper than his own; or Dr P. C. Mahalanobis, a physicist by training but Director of the Indian Statistical Institute in Calcutta, who is a convinced believer in 'physical' (as distinct from financial) methods of economic planning; and Mr T. T. Krishnamachari, who, as Finance Minister, got India's second five-year plan (1956–61) off the ground. 'T.T.K.', as Mr Krishnamachari is usually known in India, is a convinced socialist who has a useful facility for getting on with India's business men. A first-class administrator, he would probably have continued to guide India's financial affairs through the third plan, had he not been removed from the scene by the so-called Mundhra affair some years ago. Nearly £1 million had been invested by the State-owned Life Insurance Corporation in worthless shares floated by Haridas Mundhra, a financier. A one-man commission of inquiry, constituted by the present Indian High Commissioner in London, Mr M. C. Chagla, found that these shares had been bought to help Mundhra out of his private difficulties and held that T.T.K. had to accept constitutional responsibility for the actions of his principal Finance Secretary. He thereupon resigned, in February 1958, greatly to the relief of the Communist Party, which feared his ability to take the wind out of its sails. Mr Krishnamachari, who has never wavered from his advocacy of socialism by 'Indian' methods, rejoined the Government in June 1962 as Minister without Portfolio, with a special responsibility for economic planning.

Mr Krishnamachari's successor as Finance Minister, Mr Morarji Desai, is the least socialist of Mr Nehru's associates, though he has publicly declared that socialism is inevitable in India. His closest friend in the long years of civil disobedience in India was, however, the late Vallabhai Patel, always a firm believer in free enterprise. It is perhaps typical of India's un-doctrinaire approach to socialism that Mr Nehru should have appointed this non-socialist as his Finance Minister. Not un-naturally, this efficient, austere, and incorruptible personality has often been compared to the late Sir Stafford Cripps, Labour's Chancellor of the Exchequer, who, like him, was a vegetarian and a man of high principles. But this devout Hindu, who strictly enforced prohibition in Bombay State when he was its Governor, is also perhaps the man who best embodies the essential difference between the Indian and Chinese roads to socialism. 'I would rather remain poor for a hundred years,' he once said, 'than give up democracy. People may say democracy is slower to give results, but the people are working for themselves, whereas in the totalitarian system they stop working as soon as the pressure is taken off.' There could be no better definition of that essential difference.

3. CONTRASTS IN PLANNING

The fable of the tortoise and the hare may turn out to be the best way of describing the economic race between India and China. The Indians, like the tortoise, began slowly and were soon left behind; the Chinese began faster and, like the hare, soon leaped ahead. But this leap – the 'great leap forward', as the Chinese called it – was followed by a crash of terrifying dimensions, and the Indians, still creeping ahead steadily, may well in the end, like the tortoise in the fable, come in first. Indeed, if any single factor should prevent an Indian victory it would probably be the extra financial and economic strain thrown on the Indian economy by the Chinese invasion in 1962, which I shall discuss later on.

Apart from the term 'socialism', the only thing the Indian and Chinese systems have in common is economic planning. India launched its first five-year plan in 1951, and China followed suit two years later. India completed its second plan in 1960, and is now (in 1963) in the third year of its third plan. China's second plan still has a year to run, but at the time of writing not even a tentative draft of a third plan has been published. The application of the fable of the tortoise and the hare lies in the comparison between the two countries at this stage. India's industrial expansion is satisfactory without being spectacular; the people, though still undernourished, are beginning to eat more. In contrast, the Chinese, who probably produced more than three times as much steel as India in 1958, were painfully emerging from grave economic problems in 1963. Agriculture had been given priority over industrial expansion, and many factories were idle. Worse still, the average Chinese was eating several hundred calories less every day than before the Second World War. At that stage, even allowing for the cloud of China's military challenge, India's outlook seemed brighter than China's.

Promise and fulfilment in both countries make a fascinating study in contrast A democratic State like India, which deliberately restricts its own power of intervention in the economy, starts off with a built-in handicap. But because it has a free Parliament and a free Press, and a mixed economy with an active private sector, it is less likely to go off the rails than a totalitarian State. Debate is free and criticism is offered and accepted or rejected with some consideration for pragmatic possibilities. Moreover, if State planning goes wrong, as it did in India in certain important directions, all is not lost, for the private sector, obeying its own laws and creating its own impetus, provides an effective safety valve.

Totalitarian China, lacking these advantages, went almost unbelievably wrong in 1958, mainly for the simple reason that discussion of objectives and methods was never free but was predetermined by ideology. The damage caused was profound, and indeed perhaps – though it is still too early to say with certainty – irreparable. Whether or not the damage proves irreparable, the price of fanaticism at the top has certainly been high.

Until then, China had appeared to be easily outstripping India in the race towards self-sustaining growth. By 1952 the landlords had been liquidated as a class and so had the capitalists, though these, unlike the landlords, had in most cases kept their lives and even been modestly compensated for their losses. In 1955 and 1956 the land that had been given to China's 500 million peasants was being taken away again as collective farms were created all over the country. The Chinese had, with great difficulty, persuaded the Russians to evacuate Manchuria – the country's main industrial area – and re-equip the steelworks and factories they had stripped in the wake of the departing Japanese. Russian technicians had come in their thousands, and the Chinese were learning fast. Technical education was being accelerated. Disease was retreating and the fragile muscle power of the peasants, mobilized in their millions, was being harnessed to the building of massive dykes against flooding. Flies, sparrows, and other pests were wiped out by mass action. China was a cleaner place, and the Chinese were even said to have stopped swearing and jostling for places in the queues. The currency had been stabilized. China was on the move and a new hope was in the air. By 1957 collectivization of the farms had been completed. China was breaking into the export markets of South-East Asia with its light manufactures, such as bicycles and fountain pens, and its steel production – at that time about three times India's – was pointing towards early great power status.

This was the time chosen by Mao Tse-tung to launch the 'great leap forward'. All China's vast population, by that time well in excess of 600 million people, was to be mobilized in a tremendous, unified effort which, at one bound, would carry the People's Republic forward over the threshold of 'communism' (which even Soviet Russia, the original home of the communist faith, did not aim to reach for many years). All targets were raised, and continued to be raised, ever higher, at intervals throughout 1958. 'Communism' was to be achieved, both by this gigantic effort and by the creation of 'People's Communes' all over China. The operation had been planned with the greatest care, and almost overnight, the 750,000 collective farms were merged into vast communes – 26,000 of them – in which the individual was to be sunk, virtually without trace. From now on, meals were served in communal messes, and the peasants had to sleep in communal dormitories, with one room reserved for husbands and wives to be together at predetermined times for their matrimonial duties. In the cities and towns, too, communes were being created around the factories; though these urban communes were a failure virtually from the start.

Although Communists, including Chinese ones, claim to be scientific materialists, mysticism and hysteria were characteristic of the great leap forward. Mao Tse-tung's proclaimed belief that there were no limits to what the 'people' could achieve was pure mysticism. The slogans used to support this view were pure hysteria. Suddenly the people became a collective genius, capable of miracles of production, inventors and scientists by virtue of some unexplained mass alchemy, able to double, treble, or quadruple agricultural yields or make steel as the

Q

collective will decided. What did it matter that there was no fertilizer? Every human stomach was a fertilizer factory, and human waste products, combined with whatever rotting vegetation could be found in the slime of stagnant ponds, were equal to a chemical industry. As for the technicians and intellectuals – traditionally the focus of respect in Confucian China – their services were no longer needed, since the people, collectively, was demonstrating its inventive genius and infinite ingenuity. So the intellectuals, who, in any case, had been too free with their criticism during Mao's earlier experiment with free speech known as the 'hundred flowers', could be put to work in the fields, alongside their equals or superiors, the peasants; and if they thought tilling the fields was beneath their dignity they could always be made to collect the human fertilizer from the latrines.

The lyricism of slogans and newspaper exhortations matched the grandeur of China's unleashed ambitions and energies. The first signs of hysteria appeared in December 1957, when new long-term steel targets were announced by the All-China Trade Union Congress. By 1972, the last year of the fourth five-year plan, 40 million tons of steel – double Britain's annual production – would be produced each year. Indeed, the key slogan launched in the same month was: 'Overtake Britain in fifteen years.' Countless speeches, radio talks, and newspaper articles drummed home this exhortation. Posters went up all over China, showing a squat John Bull wheezing as he clambered over a stile, while an athletic Chinese Stakhanovite worker leaped ahead in the production race. By March 1958 the drive was beginning to acquire almost poetical overtones, and on the 15th the Peking *People's Daily* told its readers:

> A spring of great leaping progress is now at hand. All rotten and decayed things will inevitably die and fade away. The new buds will most assuredly be able to grow and prosper.

This clear allusion to the 'hundred flowers', and to the repressive 'rectification' campaign that had followed, was presumably not lost on Chinese readers. Indeed, behind the artificial enthusiasm of mass endeavour, the mailed fist was clearly visible.

Mao, however, really did seem to believe that the masses could do for China what electronics or atomic energy were doing for more advanced countries, for the following day, 16 March, he said in a speech in Peking: 'The great liberation of the productive force of the labouring people has the same effect as the smashing of the nucleus of an atom.'

The logical culmination of Mao's unprecedented theory was the 'backyard furnace' experiment of 1958. The weather had been good and the harvest had surpassed all hopes. Now was the time, in the last four months of the year, to turn all the national energies to the making of steel, the status symbol of greatness. Twice already, during the year, the steel target had been raised upward: from the original annual target of 6·24 million tons to 7 millions in March, and in May to between 8 and 8·5 millions. Now in August the target was raised again to the final and spectacular figure of 10·7 million tons – that is, more than double the actual 1957 figure of 5·2 millions. To this end, virtually the entire population was to be mobilized. It did not matter that the giant steel complexes at Anshan, Wuhan, and elsewhere could not produce much more than 50 per cent of the target figure, for steelworks in miniature could be built everywhere by the genius of the people.

The 'battle for steel' had to be won in the last four months of the year, and party committees were ordered to divert local efforts from agriculture to steel for the remainder of the year. Students were told to close their books and housewives to drop their chores; officials were taken away from their desks; journalists were to learn the art of steel-making after dashing off their stories; doctors and nurses were told they would be more useful building steel furnaces than fussing over patients; and actors learned that culture must give way to industry. All were directed to build or operate backyard furnaces. In October, only a few weeks after the 'battle for steel' had started, the Government announced that 40 per cent of current steel production was coming from the backyard furnaces; already, it was claimed, a million of them had been built. There was no limit to the people's ingenuity: in Shanghai shipyard workers converted old oil drums into small blast furnaces with fire bricks.

A *New China* news agency reporter felt inspired to write a description that reflects the frenzied exertions of this period:

> Over 6,000 small converters and other furnaces . . . have been built in Peking in the past few weeks. Cadres from government departments and factory workers, schoolteachers, students, housewives, peasants from communes on the outskirts have all taken part in this work. . . . In the busiest centre of Peking . . . after the neon lights go out, molten steel begins to flow from furnaces operated by workers in barbers' shops, photo studios, the children's store. . . . At the People's University, over 2,000 teachers, students and staff are among the volunteer army of steel makers.

By mid-November even the party zealots were beginning to realize that the pressure of such unremitting toil, even on a traditionally hard-working and long-suffering population, had become intolerable. The delirium of the great leap had raised the national temperature dangerously high, but its momentum was expending itself. Somebody in the Central Committee must have raised the undemocratic notion of quality, for party cadres – those who had been whipping up the population to ever greater exertions – started sending out reminders that workers must remember to take their proper rest. Otherwise, said those who had been exhorting the people to forget about sleep, quality would suffer. Raw materials, said another set of party instructions, must not be wasted; specifically, they must not be diverted from the large combines which, as the *People's Daily* pointed out, produce 'all the high-quality steel for China's basic industries'.

Belatedly, a return to sanity was setting in. But the awakening was as dreadful as the nightmare had been. From Shanghai, Canton, Hankow, and other cities came complaints that food supplies had become uncertain. A dangerous chaos had overtaken China's inadequate railway system. Goods wagons were shunting back and forth on the single-track rails, taking scrap iron and home-made 'steel' from place to place. From western Europe, too, came complaints and cancelled orders, as more and more goods failed to get shipped by stated times.

In December 1958, in circumstances that have never been fully elucidated, Mao Tse-tung stepped down from the Chairmanship of the Republic, to be replaced, four months later, by Liu Shao-ch'i. On 24 February 1959 the *People's Daily* rounded on those who had responded to the previous year's call for homemade steel. Now they were accused of 'dispersionism and organizational egoism'. The party had decreed the great leap forward and the battle for steel, and it was right. Economic chaos had set in, and the home-made steel, it turned out, was not steel at all; but the party was still right. Those who had obeyed its orders were wrong, even though they could be counted in millions. The Chinese economy, said the *People's Daily*, must be rationalized, and the 1958 slogan of 'balance – imbalance – new balance' (a Chinese Communist variant of Hegel's 'thesis – antithesis – synthesis') must go.

From all sides the cruel truth was coming in. Not only had the economy been disrupted by the great leap forward but the staggering production figures that had been held to justify the exertions of 1958 were patently false. All over the country, the party cadres, afraid to miss targets that were constantly being raised, had simply put down on paper whatever figures were required. When Peking originally announced a grain harvest of 375 million tons, western agricultural experts had raised sceptical bourgeois eyebrows. Now – in August 1959 – they were proved right. Peking officially admitted that the 1958 harvest did not exceed 250 million tons – and even this revised claim may have been higher than reality. The figure for cotton was cut by a third. As for steel, 11 million tons had been claimed, but now only 8 million tons were said to be 'usable in industry'.

Why had Mao and his colleagues launched the great leap forward in the first place? In so doing, they had ignored both the experience of the Soviet Communists and the evidence of science, or even of plain common sense. The Russians had advised against the communes, pointing out that the Soviet Union had tried them in its early days and given up the experiment. Their advice was brushed aside – an early sign of the great Sino-Soviet rift. Statistics and common sense alike showed the economic dangers inherent in an exploding population

(China's was expanding at anything between 12 millions and 15 millions a year). These, too, were brushed aside.

Before the great leap forward China had launched a half-hearted birth-control campaign – half-hearted because Malthusianism (the theory that population growth tends to outstrip food resources) was regarded as un-Marxist. Professor Ma Yin-chu, head of Peking University, had publicly pointed out that China's exploding population was the greatest obstacle in the way of economic progress. He was silenced and disgraced in 1957, when the great leap forward was being planned.

It is hard to avoid the conclusion that in defying the experience of others and the facts of demography, Mao Tse-tung was displaying a form of megalomania. It is difficult to say to what extent this was due to personal factors, to a historical sense of China's uniqueness and greatness, or to the ignorance and isolation of the small group of Communists at the top; probably to a combination of all three. Mao was aware that the Chinese Communist Party, under his leadership, in violation of Marxist–Leninist principles and in the face of Stalin's disapproval, had conquered China. This alone was potential material for a sense of infallibility; and the belief that he could do no wrong must have been boosted by a personality cult which was in no way less intensive than Stalin's had been. The attribution of almost divine powers by slogans of extravagant praise had turned Mao into a legendary figure, emperor and mythical hero in one. The historical factor was also of importance. The very notion of foreign affairs had remained alien to imperial China until the western incursions and pressures of the nineteenth century. China, the Middle Kingdom, was the centre of the world, self-sufficient and fringed by barbarians; the Chinese needed no lessons from other peoples. This is not the place to discuss the causes of China's present isolation, which are many and complex. But that isolation is a fact, and it has been reinforced by the self-deluding ignorance which is inseparable from totalitarian control of the means of communication and information. To give one example: the New China news agency (Hsin Hua) is a huge, complex, and on the whole efficiently run organization, with an army of correspondents in parts of the world which tolerate their presence; its reports are often deceptively factual and accurate; yet their entire purport is to discredit western values and performance and to present those of the communist countries in a favourable light. Inevitably, then, the picture of the outside world that reaches the isolated and ageing group of men in Peking is distorted beyond recognition. Megalomania flourishes more readily in such conditions than under those of free discussion.

In retrospect, it is easy enough to see what went wrong in 1958: *the precarious balance of China's economy was upset.* To some extent, such upsets are inherent in the peculiarities of Marxist planning. One such peculiarity is that Marxist planning has resulted everywhere in lopsided development, in which impressive overall increases in Gross National Product have not been matched in the consumption side. The other peculiarity is that communist performance usually outstrips planning in some sectors and lags behind in others, thus causing further imbalance. I have already quoted the 1958 slogan, 'balance – imbalance – new balance', which illustrates the point that communist planners make a virtue of passing through recurring phases of imbalance. Indeed, they rejoice when a plan is 'overfulfilled' in one sector or other of the economy – for instance, in coal or steel – though in fact if planning is to mean anything, overfulfilment is just as unsatisfactory as underfulfilment.

In the case of an underdeveloped country like China, this kind of lopsidedness is not merely bad, it is dangerous. With a soaring population and a 'stop–start–stop' policy on birth control, China's population is perenially and precariously poised on the brink of starvation. So delicate is the balance that it takes very little to disturb it; and the peril is increased by China's dependence on agricultural exports. If bills are incurred – for instance, for heavy machinery from the Soviet Union – and these have to be paid for, then the Chinese leadership faces what, in a democratic country, would be an agonizing choice between meeting its financial obligations and reducing the average food ration. During the years of bad weather and poor harvest (1959–62), however, the Chinese continued to export foodstuffs, principally to the Soviet Union, to pay for

earlier imports, and to Albania, presumably because the
Albanians were China's only European allies in the great Sino-
Soviet rift.

The built-in imbalance of China's economic growth was
further distorted, this time monstrously, as we have seen, by the
great leap forward. And in the frenzy of industrialization, the
autumn sowing was neglected. In 1959 nature added a tragic
burden to the already heavy consequences of the previous year's
follies. It was the beginning of a deathly cycle of drought and
heavy rains, of premature frosts and uncontrollable pests.
Gradually, belts were having to be tightened, and by 1960 the
ominous slogan, 'It is patriotic to eat less than your food ration',
began to appear on the walls of the communal messes.

Chinese agriculture was collapsing, if one may so term a fall
from subsistence level to actual undernourishment. Inclement
weather was only one of the causes of this tragic collapse; mismanagement was equally to blame. There was 'ordinary' mismanagement and there was 'extraordinary' mismanagement;
the kind that was inherent in communist planning, and the kind
that Mao inflicted on his people during the great leap forward
which, in turn, appears to be an inescapable risk of communist
systems of government. In both kinds, as we shall see, psycho-
logy – the feelings of the peasantry – played an important part.

It was typical of communist economic planning that only
8·2 per cent of total investment under the first five-year plan
went to agriculture, forestry, and water conservancy, compared with 56 per cent to industry. By 1958 gross agricultural output had indeed risen by 26 per cent (from the launching of the
first five-year plan in 1953), but this increase, which might have
been satisfactory in a static population, was only marginal in
real terms; in the same period gross industrial output had risen
by no less than 123 per cent. In the first place, then, agriculture
was deliberately starved of capital.

In the second place, there was the psychological factor I have
mentioned, which needs to be explained because it throws
further light on mismanagement at the top. Land reform in
Communist China was achieved on the basis of an artificially
stimulated class struggle. 'Struggle meetings' were held in the

villages, in which landlords were named, accused of various crimes and often summarily executed. The villagers then had to be reclassified. The poor (that is, landless) peasants and the labourers were to become – at least temporarily – the new, privileged class. Since those classified as rich peasants faced death or various degrees of humiliation, and those labelled middle peasants would not qualify for redistributed land, the jostling for the privilege of being downgraded must have been acute. In the end, some 50 million of the poorest peasants were given land, on an average 2½ acres each. The atmosphere of hate in which this enrichment had taken place could hardly have encouraged peace of mind among the new landowners; still less the fear that should they work hard and become richer than their neighbours, they, too, might be upgraded and face execution. They soon learned, however, that there was no security of tenure under communism. Between 1955 and 1957 they were forced, by pressures of various kinds, to join collective farms. This was bad enough, but within a few months the communes followed, and the last shreds of individual initiative were strangled. It is not difficult to imagine the feeling of hopelessness that these massive changes must have produced in the minds of the Chinese peasants. Mao, alone among communist leaders, had come to power as a peasant leader; no sooner was he in power than he set about, in effect, to create an urban proletariat; then he gave land to many peasants, who were made to participate in the brutalities that brought them land; now even this was taken away.

In the early stages of the communes the peasants may nevertheless have felt that they were participating in a gigantic joint effort from which all, eventually, would benefit. But the great leap forward diverted them from their purpose and sapped their energies by turning them into beasts of burden. Then came the cycle of bad weather which ruined crops in many areas, although not long before the Communist Party had boasted that floods and drought and other natural calamities no longer held terrors for China.

Against this background, it would have been surprising had the productivity of the individual peasant not declined, even

without assistance from the weather. The communes held together, more or less, however, in 1959 and 1960, the first of the
bitter years. Then in 1961, the third consecutive year of natural
calamities, the communes began to break up as their disadvantages became more visible: their unwieldiness, for instance, and the limited returns of what was, in effect, forced
labour. Instead, smaller production brigades of some seventy
party men each took over the leadership of the collective farms.
Private farming – on tiny and uneconomic plots – again became
tolerated and, at least in Shanghai, private trading and manufactures reappeared.

These misfortunes and failures clearly foreshadowed far-
reaching policy changes. But expectations had been raised so
high in 1958, and boasts had been so ambitious that it was not
easy to draw the inevitable conclusions from the reverses of the
ensuing years. The National People's Congress – Communist
China's 'Parliament' – was supposed to meet every year, but it
did not meet as scheduled in 1961. Instead, it was twice post-
poned, and finally met in March and April 1962, in the deepest
secrecy. The report that emerged from this secret meeting did
indeed produce a sensation in that it reversed the hitherto
sacred order of economic priorities. From now on, agriculture
was to come first instead of last, and heavy industry was placed
last, after light industry. From a Marxist standpoint, this was
like turning the world upside down.

A few weeks later the usual trickle of refugees knocking at the
gates – or rather the barbed wire – of that durable British
colony, Hong Kong, suddenly and unaccountably turned into a
flood. The tens of thousands who demanded admission within a
few weeks were not starving, but they *were* undernourished, and
it was a fair assumption that many others had stayed behind in
the villages because they were too weak to travel. The flood of
refugees died down as suddenly as it had started, after British
representations to the communist authorities, and the full story
of these few weeks has never, of course, been told from the
Chinese communist end.

By cross-checking the stories of the refugees and from a reading of the controlled Chinese Press, a picture of China's

economy in 1962 emerges. It was a dismal picture. The steel mills of Manchuria, and of Wuhan, in the centre, were working at a fraction of their capacity, and many factories were idle in Shanghai, China's greatest manufacturing city, in Canton in the deep south, and in other cities. In September 1962 the Central Committee's theoretical journal, *Hung Chi* ('Red Flag'), discussed this situation if not in detail, at least with unusual frankness. Rapid industrialization, it found, was out of the question. Progress would have to be gradual and productivity would have to be raised; to this end, both workers and managers would have to undergo iron discipline. There could be no large volume of investment in industry in the near future, so it would have to improve its output with the existing labour force and machinery.

Even by the autumn of 1962, no plan for the year had been published, let alone a draft of the fifth five-year plan, which had been due to begin in 1963. This alone was an admission of failure. So, too, in a more tacit way, was the return to birth control. Once again, dogma interfered with serious discussion. The Communists did not abandon their view that Malthus was wrong; nor did they officially rehabilitate Dr Ma Yin-chu, the disgraced advocate of population control. Instead, contraceptives were made available again after a long interval, and articles in the Press advised couples to marry late (23–27 for women and 25–29 for men) and have smaller families. On all fronts doctrine and performance had failed.

The Indians, unlike the Chinese Communists, never set themselves meaningless targets, nor did they allow hysteria to mar their calculations. This does not mean that they made no mistakes in their economic planning. What it does mean is these were honest errors of judgement and that their consequences could be contained within reasonable limits. Compared with China, India has made quiet, unspectacular progress towards its goals; on the other hand, it has not yet suffered the massive collapse of economic hopes that followed China's 'great leap forward'. This does not mean that India's problems have been solved, or even that India has avoided crises, especially in the financial field. To say either of these things would be to ignore the size of India's problems and its continuing inability to earn enough money by its exports to finance its own development. But the Indian system has shown itself free and flexible enough to prevent things going too far wrong; and India's friends abroad are both better able and more willing to help than China's are.

Two five-year plans had been completed and a third one launched. For reasons that were only partly within the control of the official planners, the first one was relatively more success-ful than the second. Between 1951 and 1956 – the period of the first plan – real national income rose by more than 18 per cent, and real *per capita* income by nearly 11 per cent. The rate of investment rose from about 4·9 per cent of the national income – the average percentage in static economies – to more than 7 per cent. To some extent, this satisfactory little leap forward was the work of favourable monsoons and excellent harvests in 1953–54 and 1954–55. But there was much more to it than that: irriga-tion had made great strides, and the Community Development Programme had set rural life in motion towards the goal of self-sufficiency in food.

These were no mean achievements, and they had been won without coercion or even excessive State intervention with private industry (indeed, at that stage the share of investment allotted to the private sector was about the same as that for the public sector). For the second plan, however, the planners, with their eyes firmly fixed on India's socialist ideas, greatly in-creased the role of the State. The public sector was to get £2,850 million in fresh investment, and the private sector only £1,800 million; together, these figures represented almost exactly twice the investment total under the first five-year plan. This preoccupation with the public sector was understandable on two grounds. One was the need – to which the planners rightly gave priority – to build up India's infrastructure: its roads and railways, its power stations, its schools, and its train-ing schemes. Without these essentials, development is an academic exercise, and India, despite its legacy from the colonial past, was woefully short of them, with the notable ex-ception of railways. Another consideration was that the planners knew agriculture could not absorb the army of youths coming on to the labour market. Their calculations showed that some 10 million new workers would be looking for jobs between 1956 and 1961. Since agriculture could not absorb them, industry, and especially heavy industry, had to be developed fast. The planners would not have been planners had they not thought it would be risky to leave the development of industry to private enterprise and the law of supply and demand; and time may prove they were right.

Though the planners were right in their general approach, they did, as I have mentioned, make several serious mistakes. Moreover, they allowed themselves a luxury no honest director of a private enterprise could afford: that of making certain perilously optimistic assumptions about where the money to meet the bills would be coming from. One mistake was the calculation that the population would rise by only 1·25 per cent a year; in fact, the rise was about 2 per cent. This meant a difference of 17 million in actual terms, for India's population probably reached 425 million in 1960–61, instead of the 408 million assumed by the planners. Another major mistake was to assume that the encouraging food crops of the first plan would be repeated during the second. When the monsoon failed in 1957 something of a disaster overtook India's economic progress. Grain output dropped by 6·7 million tons and food prices soared by 10 per cent in one year. The planners had thought India would not need to import more than 6 million tons of food over the five-year period; instead, food imports rose once more to more than 3 million tons a year.

The most optimistic assumption of the second five-year plan, however, had been that somehow enough foreign exchange would be forthcoming to meet purchases abroad. 'Resources to be raised externally', as the planner blandly put it, were estimated at £600 million for the governmental sector alone, and these were additional to India's own sterling balances, which were expected to provide £150 million. Even this highly optimistic assumption was, in turn, based on another assumption, itself optimistic: that the terms of trade – which determine the real value of a country's exports – would remain as favourable as they had been in 1954–55. In fact, they fell back to the 1952–54 level. The trade gap, which had been a manageable £47 million, widened alarmingly to £218 million, and India had to dip heavily into its dwindling foreign-exchange reserves to restore the balance.

At this critical stage, however, a forgotten but important factor intervened. India discovered it had friends. Whereas China, under communist rule, had isolated itself from the West and was even alienating the Soviet Union, India, by simply sticking – on the whole with dignity – to its chosen, uncommitted course, had not only kept its old friends but made new ones. (The underlying assumptions of non-alignment were, of course, severely shaken by the Chinese invasion of 8 September 1962, but this does not affect the point.) Moreover, India's friends, unlike China's, had money to spare and were willing to part with it. Although the United States had understandably never approved of non-alignment and was in alliance with Pakistan, the Eisenhower Administration grasped the importance of the competition between India and China. Most of India's food gap was met from American surpluses, under US Public Law 480, and cost India nothing in foreign exchange. But there were other friends among the affluent countries of the non-communist world, and three of them – Britain, West Germany, and Japan – combined with the United States in 1958 to form what has become known as the 'aid India club'. To tide India over into 1959, they raised £125 million in economic assistance. Since then the 'aid India club' has been enlarged, and has continued to come to the rescue, at intervals, though not with unfailing regularity. The planners, indeed, have been proved right in one respect, though not perhaps in the way they had thought.

How did India stand at the threshold of the third five-year plan (1961–66)? In ten years industrial production has risen by 110–120 per cent. Massive investments have been made in communications and electrification, in irrigation and fertilizers, in oil and machine-tools, and in many other ways. The private sector has been, in its own fields, even more successful than the public one. The output of the private enterprises has soared by anything between 350 and 1,000 per cent. Since independence,

India has become an important manufacturing nation, and its products for export or for home consumption range from bicycles to diesel-electric motors, and from sewing machines to refrigerators.

These things are true and encouraging, but they cannot be seen in perspective unless they are accompanied by a reminder of the vastness of India's problems and by some comments on the continuing gap between endeavour and fulfilment. When Mr Nehru and his planners launched India's second plan they termed it their 'grand strategy in the war against poverty' and announced eight basic decisions that were supposed to govern all India's development. These are worth recalling:

1. The second plan must be big – big enough and powerful enough to begin to lift the Indian economy across the 'threshold' to a developed nation.

2. India will develop first and above all its agriculture and its rural people.

3. India will develop its industries – but with a careful balancing of large and small industry, of the heavy industries basic to economic growth, and the traditional small and hand industries essential to employment and social stability.

4. India will increase living standards and consumption at the same time that it builds its industries.

5. India will take advantage of every possible way of growth consistent with democracy to develop the nation and its people.

6. India will seek the development of all groups and classes among its people, and of all regions of the nation, so that there may be a growing equality of income and opportunity.

7. India will at every step of its progress associate the people in the villages and districts with planning and development, so that their initiative, energies and co-operation are awakened and assured, and may serve as the constructive and creative instrument of development itself.

8. India will, in all its plans and policies, set as its highest single purpose the development of the individual, and his advancement in human freedom.

Neither I nor any other western liberal could quarrel with the principles that underlie the fourth, fifth, and eighth decisions; indeed, respect for the individual and refusal to sacrifice present welfare entirely to a future millennium are fundamentals that distinguish Indian planning from Chinese Communist. But principles alone do not promote economic growth, and while these principles have been rigorously observed, it cannot be said that the stated aims have been pursued – or if pursued, followed through – with adequate vigour or consistency. If the second point meant anything it implied a high investment priority for agriculture. In fact, however, only 11 per cent of the budget of the second plan went to agriculture; this was more than the Chinese Communists were ready to spare, but dismally less than the more than 50 per cent that went to India's industry. Under the third plan agriculture does get 14 per cent, but that is still insufficient, given the size and nature of the problem.

The core of the problem, as the publications of the Indian Planning Commission concede, is land reform; and the core of land reform is always the distribution of land to those who till it. In Formosa (nationalist China) this has been very largely achieved by expropriation with compensation in the form of industrial bonds (thus turning the landlords into industrial capitalists) and by a system of easy repayments for the new landlords; in communist China, as we have seen, it was achieved, while it lasted, by class hatred and judicial murder. India rightly rules out violence; and rather less understandably it eschews even the degree of compulsion that was used in Formosa. Perhaps as a result, it cannot really be said that India has done more than scratch the surface of the land-reform problem. By this, I mean that while many necessary but minor measures have been taken – such as cutting out *zamindars*, rent-collectors, and other intermediaries, passing anti-eviction laws, and fixing ceilings on land holdings – only a tiny proportion of former tenants have actually become owners. One result is that incentives are still largely non-existent, and productivity has hardly risen at all since independence. Nor has Vinoba Bhave's land gift (*bhoodan*) movement been of more than marginal value.

Other aspects of the basic decisions have been stultified by the crushing weight of India's religious and social heritage. The sixth decision, for instance, called for the development of 'all groups and classes among its people'. This was consistent with the Constitution, which forbids discrimination against the 'untouchables'. But most observers agree that this admirable provision remains largely unobserved, especially in the 570,000 villages. Some 80 million Indians remain condemned to perform only the most menial jobs and are unlikely, in their lifetimes, to improve their pitifully low living standards.

The sacred cow is, of course, another vigorous survival of the Hindu past. The Planning Commission has several times expressed concern over the rise in the cattle population. In 1958 it already stood at about 200 million, and by 1962 it was probably approaching a quarter of a million, several States having prohibited the slaughter of cows. Probably 70–80 millions of India's cattle are 'surplus' in the sense of not performing any economically valuable task, such as helping with the ploughing or the milk supply. Diseased but sacrosanct, they are competing with the people for India's scarce food resources.

The third of the basic decisions, dealing with the balancing of large and small industry, made a Gandhian gesture in the direction of India's cottage industries. By and large, India's planners, from the Prime Minister down, have accepted Gandhi's view that the rural hand weavers and other village craftsmen must be protected against the advent of industry. In a country with India's high proportion of unemployed or under-employed this concern is understandable enough, and in this instance the performance has lived up to the promise. The £198 million allocated to the cottage industries under the third five-year plan represents about 2·6 per cent of the total investment programme of £7,500 million, and stringent measures have been taken to prevent the factory made product from competing with the local one. In economic terms, as many western economists have pointed out, this makes no sense and is indeed a regressive policy. But in human terms, and in the Indian context – which includes a tendency to political extremism in areas

R

of maximum unemployment, such as Kerala – the policy can
be defended.

A more valid criticism concerns the seventh basic decision,
which proposed to associate the village people with every stage
of planning and development. There is no doubt that the intentions of the planners are beyond reproach and their personal
qualities of the highest; but many competent observers have
remarked on the reluctance of the city bureaucrat to go to the
villages, and – if he is once persuaded or ordered to go – to get
down to the work of meeting the village people and making sure
plans are executed. Too often, it seems, the flood of ideas unleashed from the centre peters out in a trickle of human inadequacy at the receiving end.

4. TODAY AND TOMORROW

Like China, India ran into serious economic difficulties in
1962 (though the Indian crisis did not compare in magnitude
with China's generalized disaster). Once again, the planners
had 'built' a prodigious foreign-exchange gap into their calculations – in this instance, of the order of £2,250 million. This
figure needs to be explained. India's total foreign-exchange
requirements for the period of the plan were estimated to be
about twice that sum – £4,500 million. Only £1,800 million of
this was for imports of capital goods, and the rest would consist
of imports outside the plan and about £400 million for capital
repayments. It seemed unlikely, however, that Indian exports
would pay for more than half the total gap, leaving the rest to be
filled somehow, either by inflationary budgetary devices or by
foreign aid.

India's exports unfortunately remained stagnant in 1961,
largely owing to a disappointing fall in jute production. When
Mr Morarji Desai, the Finance Minister, presented the Budget
in May 1962 he revealed that India's sterling reserves had
fallen to the dangerously low level of £83 million, compared
with £560 million in 1956 and £150 million in 1960. On 8 June
he announced drastic import cuts and restrictions on foreign
travel. In the meantime Mr Desai had met the 'aid India club'
in May, but for once his urgent plea for assistance had gone

without response, for the 'club' adjourned without taking a decision. In July, however, it met again, in Washington, and this time sanctioned allocations to India totalling $1,070 million. This was some $80 million less than India had asked for at that stage, but it was enough to reduce the immediate pressure on India's dwindling reserves.

The Chinese, too, have been having their payments difficulties. It is known that towards the end of 1961 the Russians called on them to repay their Korean war debts. This demand aroused considerable resentment within the Chinese Communist Party, for the Chinese were still repaying previous debts for Soviet 'aid' to China in earlier years. The best estimate of China's outstanding ordinary commercial debt to the Soviet Union in the autumn of 1962 was somewhere between $450 million and $500 million, which was expected to be repaid by 1965; the amount of the Korean war debt is not known. In addition, however, the Chinese had incurred fairly heavy debts to western countries, principally Canada, Australia, Western Germany, and France, for grain purchases. In 1961 China paid out £65 million for western grain, leaving £45 million to be paid in 1962. This amount was for the purchases made in 1961, but it has since been swollen by further purchases. Since the collapse of hopes in 1959, the capacity of the Chinese People's Republic to shoulder such burdens has been seriously impaired by a catastrophic fall in its exports. In three years China's foreign trade fell by 65 per cent – from $5,300 million in 1958 to $2,399 million in 1961.

Such was the situation of the two countries, in general terms, in September 1962 when China began its invasion of contested territory in the Himalayas. This is not the place to analyse China's motives for this determined attack. These were certainly of some complexity, but one of the main reasons may well have been a desire to throw India's economic planning out of gear. Mr Nehru's policy of non-alignment had imposed on the Indian government a self-denying ordinance about armaments. Military assistance of any kind was ruled out, and such arms as were purchased abroad were treated as commercial transactions. Clearly the Chinese attack faced India with a delicate decision. Officially, the policy of non-alignment was reaffirmed (much as China kept on paying lip service to 'the great leap forward' long after the leaping had stopped). Russia, however, showed itself reluctant to honour an order for MiG jet fighters which Mr Krishna Menon, the then Defence Minister, had placed in Moscow, and India turned to Britain and the United States for arms. The dilemma before the Indian government was how to pay for western arms without upsetting the already precarious balance of the third five-year plan. The alternative seemed to be either to abandon the plan or drastically reduce its targets (which was unthinkable); or to accept military assistance and abandon the policy of non-alignment (which was distasteful).

In the long term, however, India's prospects continued to be better than China's. Its planning had not gone so seriously awry as China's, and its system had shown itself better able to pursue its goals while keeping the people reasonably contented. Moreover, as I have said, its friends were wealthier than China's; and a face-saving formula for arms purchases did not seem to be beyond human ingenuity. China, too, had its dilemmas, but these seemed harder to solve than India's. The events of 1958 and after seemed to show that China could not hope both to feed its population and make rapid strides towards an economic take-off. Progress was liable to be slow and not very sure. True, the new emphasis on agriculture pointed the way towards economic recovery, and certainly towards the recovery of China's export trade. But this merely emphasized China's inability to build up its industry as fast as its leaders would have liked. Meanwhile, by setting up as a rival source of communist doctrine, Mao Tse-tung had alienated Moscow and deprived China of Soviet help.

His dilemma, then, was how to persuade the Russians to resume assistance (even on the unsatisfactory earlier basis, on which China paid for help received) without eating ideological humble pie. The trouble was that the Soviet Union, though it had a surplus of certain types of machinery and of other capital goods, had little else – and certainly no grain – to spare. All things considered, the outlook seemed brighter for India than for China; and the leaders of the underdeveloped countries watching the economic race between Asia's giants could have found more to attract them in India's example than in China's.

Chapter 3

THE PITFALLS OF PLANNING

I have, of course, been too kind by half to the Indian planners. But that was because I was comparing bad with worst: half-baked socialism with communism at its most fanatical. I use the term 'half-baked' deliberately, because that is just what Indian socialism is. Indeed, that it is half-baked is its saving grace and the main reason why there is still hope – though a diminishing hope – for the Indian economy.

Let us follow this line of argument through. Time and again, as we have seen, the Indian planners are unable to accomplish their objectives because they so admirably refuse to use coercion or offend against tradition. So land reform remains largely a project, sacred cows multiply unhindered, and the crushing heritage of India's caste system goes on much as before, stultifying individual initiative and social advancement. In fact, the Indians are constantly pursuing *incompatible* objectives: centralized planning and individual liberty, tolerance of private enterprise and priority of investment for the State, creation of large-scale industries and stimulation of the cottage crafts.

As I have pointed out, despite the priority given to the public sector, private industry has progressed much faster; and it would presumably have progressed faster still under a different State policy and with a lighter burden of taxation. In effect, private industry, which has to be efficient if it wishes to survive, has been penalized for the benefit of public industry, which survives whether efficient or not in any system that gives excessive power to the planning bureaucracy. In fact, virtually limitless power has been vested in the Planning Commission in that, from the start, it was under Mr Nehru's chairmanship. Starting from a preconceived socialist theory, instead of adapting the economic lessons of history to India's special problems, the Indian planners made the mistakes that seem, alas, to be inseparable from centralized *dirigiste* planning. In economic terms their fundamental error was to give priority to industry over agriculture. In political and philosophical terms it was to overlook the clear correlation between economic and political liberty. True centralized planning can be followed through in practice only when the State has total power, that is, power to direct or conscript labour as well as to requisition materials and consequently to suppress all the opposition that will inevitably manifest itself. In this respect, the Chinese (and the Russians) are right and the Indians wrong. That the Indians have been spared the worst consequences of State planning has been only *because* their socialism is half-baked. The uncontrolled State is by nature totalitarian. Its decisions are arbitrary and its people are denied the advantages of both freedom to criticize and free economic competition. India has been saved by its attachment to democracy, not its belief in socialism. In the end, however, the Indians will have to choose between democracy and social-ism, for they cannot have both (let nobody say the Scandinavian examples prove the contrary, for the socialist parties of Scandi-navia are socialist in name only). They will also have to choose between socialism and economic development, for these, too, are incompatible objectives. They do not, however, have to choose between democracy and economic development, for there is nothing incompatible between *those* objectives. Indeed, there is an intimate and demonstrable connexion between the two.

True, there was no democracy to speak of in Japan during its first period of economic expansion from the 1850s to the Second World War, and little enough in Britain during the early stages of the industrial revolution. But the rapid growth promoted by the free play of market forces, together with the parallel de-velopment of education, was creating the conditions for de-mocracy. The phenomenal economic expansion of Japan since the Second World War has been accomplished under a parlia-mentary democracy which, defective though it is in certain respects, has allowed the Japanese people to exercise the fundamental freedoms, including that of speech and of the Press, and of choosing one's place and form of employment. True again, this last freedom has been circumscribed by paternalist traditions among Japanese employers, but the Japanese worker is infinitely freer than the Chinese worker under communism.

Our main concern at this stage, however, is the race towards economic viability, and beyond that, affluence. It is astonishing, in the face of all the examples that can be freely studied, that there are still people who put their faith in the supposed economic benefits of 'socialism'. As far as the leaders of the new countries are concerned, I can find two reasons to account for an attitude of mind which the facts cannot justify. One is the mental and emotional association of 'imperialism' with 'capitalism', carefully fostered by communist propaganda. In fighting against imperialism the nationalists have come to believe that they should also fight against capitalism because the 'imperialists' were also 'capitalists'. The belief in the efficacy of socialism or communism has been further encouraged by the deplorable fact that during the years of the struggle for independence the nationalists found almost their only western friends among socialists and communists, the former mainly for idealistic reasons, the latter mainly for interested ones. The other reason for the persistent faith in socialism is the efficiency of the communist propaganda machine in fostering the myth of economic growth in the communist countries, in which they are helped by the totalitarian secrecy with which they prevent outside observers from finding out the truth.

The first of these reasons is absurd, because it rests on a fallacy. Though Lenin argued that imperialism is the ultimate stage of capitalism, it is nothing of the sort. There were great empires long before capitalism was heard of, and the advent of communism in Russia and China has not prevented the extension of the Soviet and Chinese empires. True, the European merchant-adventurers of the eighteenth and nineteenth centuries sought trade in far-off lands and, on their insistence, their home governments created the colonial empires that are now almost completely dissolved. To that extent, there is a connexion between capitalism and imperialism, but it is a fortuitous one. Nor is there much substance in the further myth that the colonial powers grew rich at the expense of the colonies, especially in its pure Leninist form, which argues that capitalist countries need colonies to prevent depressions; for the colonial powers have continued to increase their wealth since they started shedding their colonies. (The Marxists attribute this awkward fact to 'neo-colonialism', but anybody who compares, say, the prosperous 'neo-colonialist' economy of the Ivory Coast with the depressed 'independent' economy of Guinea will see at a glance which system bestows the greater benefits on the local population.)

The myth of higher rates of economic growth under communism needs to be critically examined. It has had an extraordinary run of success owing to the secrecy of the system, the Communist party's monopoly of all means of information, and the efficiency of communist presentation of long-term target figures as though they were accomplished facts. In 1959 Herr Ulbricht, the East German party boss, boasted that East Germans would be buying more, on the average, than West Germans by 1961 – in other words, that their standard of living would be higher. In March 1961 the régime's chief planner, Herr Leuschner, had to admit that this was one target that was not going to be hit. Mr Khrushchev had made a similar but more modest boast. Russians, he said, were going to produce more meat, butter, and milk than Americans by 1961. Mr Khrushchev's boast fared no better than Herr Ulbricht's, and the Soviet Prime Minister spent a good deal of his energy in 1961 and 1962 bewailing the inadequacies of Soviet agriculture and exhorting the collective farmers to do better. The Poles and Jugoslavs could have told him how to get the farmers to produce more: in both their countries agriculture has been flourishing since collective farming was virtually abandoned a few years ago. Otherwise, agriculture has been an almost total failure under communist methods, with the possible exception of Bulgaria which had a strong co-operative farming tradition before the Communists took over. The American farmer produces *seven or eight times* as much as his Soviet counterpart. Some of the most efficient farming in the world is done on the privately owned farms of Japan and Formosa.

The need for efficiency in agriculture is indeed so fundamental in the underdeveloped countries, especially in the overpopulated ones, that any appeal socialized agriculture might have for them would be beyond comprehension. Nearly all the leaders of the new countries, however, have been lured by the more spectacular attractions of industrialization, and the Communists have been extraordinarily successful in 'selling' the Soviet Union as the great example of the underdeveloped country that became a great industrial power by communist methods in thirty or forty years. It is true that the Soviet Union has become a great industrial power (though it is still far from producing an abundance of consumer goods); but it is not true that it has done it in forty years. Russia's industrialization began in Tsarist days, and was making rapid progress by the time the Bolsheviks took over.

> By 1914 [writes Professor W. W. Rostow, in *The Stages of Economic Growth*, Cambridge U.P., 1960] Russia was producing something like five million tons of pig-iron, four million tons of iron and steel, forty million tons of coal, ten million tons of petroleum and a food-grain export surplus of about twelve million tons.

It took Lenin, Trotsky, and Stalin ten years to get back to the 1914 level, before the five-year plans were launched; it is debatable whether, even today, agriculture has reached the Tsarist level. If one compares the graphs of Russian and American industrial growth between 1870 and 1955, as the American economist Warren Nutter has done, one notices that Russia's rate of growth was comparable with America's (at a lower level of total production) until the Communists came to power, and that Russia's growth under communism has never, at any time, been faster than under the Tsars. Colin Clark, Maurice Allais, and Nutter himself, each through independent research, have found that in 1957 each Soviet worker produced in one hour on an average only one-fifth the amount of his American counterpart. Output per man-hour – or productivity

– is indeed the only true indicator of industrial performance. Between 1913 and 1955 industrial productivity rose 118 per cent in the Soviet Union and 223 per cent in the United States. As Maurice Allais points out (in *Le Tiers Monde au Carrefour*), real wages (that is, wages in terms of actual purchasing power, allowing for price changes) rose only 1·2 per cent in the Soviet Union in that same period, whereas in the United States they rose 3·1 per cent. As American real wages were already 2½ times as high as Russian in 1913, this meant that at the end of the period an American worker could buy 5·6 times as much with his wages as a Russian worker. One should add that just as productivity is the real indicator of efficiency, so real wages are the only true indicator of the economic benefits a society is bringing to its citizens.

Even if one considers gross industrial output, including heavy industry – the apple of the Soviet planner's eye – the picture is not unfavourable to the United States. In economics, as in other things, one should compare like with like. Russia has remained fairly consistently thirty or forty years behind the United States in economic growth. To get a true picture, that is, one of interest to developing societies, one should compare comparable periods. If, for instance, one takes the period 1913–58 in the Soviet Union one ought to compare it with the period, say, 1850–75 in the United States. During these periods, production of energy from all sources rose by 7 per cent in Russia and by 18 per cent in the United States. If one takes a later period, say, 1948–58 in the Soviet Union and 1875–1910 in the United States, the growth rates are closer, but only slightly in Russia's favour, the Russian yearly percentage being 8, and the American 7·2.

Professor Allais, who quotes these figures, points out, as does Rostow, that the United States paid for its own development at this prodigious rate by its exports of agricultural produce and raw materials, which in turn financed imports of machinery and other capital equipment. In the mid-nineteenth century the United States was an underdeveloped country; by the early twentieth it was a rising great power. This rate of growth was achieved under a liberal economic system in which, admittedly, some of the weaker members of the community got hurt; but the United States, unlike Stalin's Russia, did not starve 5 million peasants, execute people in tens of thousands, and deport others in millions; nor did it use an army of between 10 and 15 million expendable slave labourers, as Russia did until well after Stalin's death.

One should never forget, of course, that communist statistics are suspect. I have recalled, in the preceding chapter, the gross statistical distortions that occurred in China during the 'great leap forward'. Though the Soviet Union's recent statistics are obviously more reliable than China's, if only because the Russians are now less ashamed of their own performance than they used to be, their statistical history is studded with fanciful claims. As Professor Allais has pointed out, if one adds all the percentage increases claimed year by year by Soviet statisticians since the Bolsheviks seized power, one reaches the observably false conclusion that in 1959 each Soviet citizen's real wages were twice as high as each American's. Indeed, whereas in western liberal societies there is a tendency for industrial and other returns to be kept as low as possible for taxation purposes, in communist societies all the pressures are in favour of exaggeration. Each Soviet factory manager is under constant pressure to fulfil and 'overfulfil' stated targets, and the temptation to cook the books when things go wrong must be strong (China's statistical 'errors' were, of course, the result of wholesale cooking of books by local officials who wanted to say they had reached the ever-rising targets named by the party as the year 1958 went on).

Allowing for such errors, and taking into account the work of Soviet as well as western economists, one reaches the view that the Soviet Union's industrial output was about three-fifths of the United States's in 1962 (when American industry was working well below capacity). Industrial production was certainly rising faster in Russia than in America. Russia's economy continued, however, to be lopsided: the total value of goods and services in the Soviet Union (gross national product) was certainly no more than one-third the American level. The Russians, however, had been promised the millennium – communist abundance for all – by 1980 under the new Programme of the Soviet Communist Party issued for the party's 22nd Congress in October 1961. Were they going to get it? This seemed highly unlikely, especially if world tensions remained high, for whereas the giant American economy seemed able to support an astronomical defence budget *plus* an abundance of the good things of a material life for most citizens, the Soviet economy seemed unable to do both at once. Steel, factory building, and electricity were lagging far behind plans in 1962; agriculture, as usual, was unsatisfactory; and Mr Khrushchev, addressing the Soviet Party's central committee in November, called on communist planners to study American methods and borrow from them where necessary.

In sum, then, there is nothing much of value for the under-developed countries to learn in the communist experience. And one suspects that the Russians, for their part, are uneasily aware of this. Mr Khrushchev, in effect, gave the game away in two important speeches in May 1962. On the 19th he attacked the leaders of the 'national bourgeoisie' in the uncommitted countries – that is, men like Presidents Nkrumah and Nasser, or Mr Nehru – for not tackling their problems in a Marxist way; and added a scarcely veiled threat that if they persisted in going their own way they would have to be overthrown (presumably by the Communists). On the 30th, speaking in Moscow in the presence of President Modibo Keita of Mali, he switched his attack to the European Common Market, which he accused of neo-colonialism and of pursuing policies designed to prevent underdeveloped countries from industrializing. He called on their leaders to look to the Soviet bloc for a solution of their economic difficulties.

Now the leaders of the underdeveloped countries, though they often say foolish things, are not actually as foolish as Mr Khrushchev seemed to believe. They well know that the Soviet bloc, with its standards and expectations of consumption, simply cannot provide substitute markets for the tropical produce of, for instance, the African countries, should they decide to switch their trade from the western markets. And their experience of Soviet aid has already shown at least some of them its limitations. It was therefore distressing to read some of Dr Nkrumah's speeches in 1962, with their references to the 'neo-colonialism' of the Common Market. Probably the Ghanaian President had his private pan-African reasons for using this term, but the Nigerian Prime Minister, Sir Abubakar Tafawa Balewa, who is not a pan-Africanist in President Nkrumah's sense and is in most respects a sensible and moderate man, took up the same attitude of non-co-operation with the Common Market when he came to London for the Commonwealth Prime Minister's conference in September 1962. Since Nigeria, Ghana, and the other African members of the Commonwealth were being offered the same terms of association with the Common Market as the French-speaking associates (that is, free entry and high prices), Sir Abubakar's attitude was as incomprehensible, in economic terms, as Dr Nkrumah's.

If communist methods don't offer a solution to the problem of development that is worth while either in results or in terms of human cost, what models *should* one offer to the economists of the new countries? The American example is apposite enough, but it is evidently very difficult for many people to imagine the United States of today as the underdeveloped country it was just over a hundred years ago. Nor, because of anti-capitalist prejudices, can one expect a President Sukarno or a Mr Nehru to look at western European examples with unbiased eyes (though one cannot forbear to mention that the astonishing economic recovery of West Germany from the devastation of the Second World War was accomplished by economic liberalism; and until the Communists built their wall across Berlin in 1961 East Germans showed what they thought of communism by crossing into West Berlin and West Germany in vast numbers). There are, however, examples that are closer to the experience of the underdeveloped countries. The thriving economies of Lebanon, Hong Kong, Formosa, and, above all, Japan – all owing their prosperity to free competition – are the models that ought to stir the expectations of Indians or Indonesians, Nigerians or Egyptians, Cubans or Chileans.

In 1961 Formosa's industrial production rose by more than

12 per cent, a higher rate of growth than any yet achieved by a communist country. Japan's economic 'miracle' since the Second World War has been, if anything, more astonishing still than West Germany's. It has been achieved by free competition and by such non-Marxist devices as a highly efficient and flexible banking system, offering continuous credit and attracting foreign capital by high profit rates. (The 'secrets' of Japan's economic growth were described in detail, for those who would like to study them, in two Supplements of *The Economist*, on 1 and 8 September 1962.*) Between 1953 and 1960 Japan's gross national product doubled in value, and so did income *per capita*. And this was achieved in the face of a 10 per cent population increase in an exiguous country, only one-third of which is arable, and which lacks raw materials. Just one more figure: Japan's industrial production rose by no less than 20 per cent in 1961. No communist country comes within sight of such achievements.

In Japan's case, as in that of the western countries, there is a legacy of imperialism to be fought. On the one hand, the Japanese are Asians, and their experience of economic growth ought to be of greater interest to the leaders of the under-developed countries than, say, Russia's. On the other hand, the Japanese conquered most of South-East Asia during the Second World War and behaved with memorable arrogance. For years not one of the countries that had been occupied by Japan would allow the post-war Japanese governments even to send an economic mission to their countries. In the 'fifties, however, this understandable prejudice was gradually broken down. The Japanese, in a masterly display of enlightened self-interest, concluded reparations agreements with the countries they had conquered, thus boosting their economies *and* providing long-term outlets for Japanese goods and skills. There persists, however, a curious lack of interest in Japan's economic growth, which can be attributed only to the socialist bias of the generation of leaders conditioned to associate imperialism with capitalism and to find their friends among western socialists or communists.

* Now available in book form, under the title *Consider Japan* (Duckworth, 1963).

If, however, the new leaders refuse to face the facts of American, West European, or Japanese success they might profitably study the example of two Latin American countries that have made giant strides towards affluence in the past decade: Mexico and Brazil. One should, perhaps, state one's obvious reservations at the outset. In both countries corruption on a grand scale has, at times, diverted large slices of the national cake into more or less unworthy pockets; and both can show only oases – though rapidly growing oases – of affluence – in the midst of desperate poverty. Again Brazil, in particular, is developing at the cost of a frightening inflation. Both, moreover, are in the middle of population explosions ($2\frac{1}{2}$ per cent per annum in Brazil and 3 per cent in Mexico), so that real wages at the lowest level are rising much more slowly than one would like. Having made these points, however, it remains true that both, under the impulse of freedom for local capitalists, have drawn dramatically nearer the stage of self-sustaining economic growth which could lead them to European and even North American living standards in the foreseeable future. Brazil's industrial production, for instance, doubled in the five years between 1955 and 1960, the expansion in steel, heavy engineering, and electricity being especially spectacular.

On all counts, as the verifiable facts clearly show, liberal economic methods offer advantages that socialist or communist ones cannot match. If economic advance were all that the new countries wanted there could, in objective fact, be no doubt about the models they should choose. But of course, most of them want more than just economic growth: they also want what they call social justice, meaning a reasonably equitable distribution of income and social security. Affluence, plus the welfare state. It is time we turned to this facet of their aspirations.

I should, perhaps, correct a possible misunderstanding. It should not be assumed, because I have so roundly condemned socialist planning, that I am against planning of any kind; much less that I am against social justice. To the extent that 'socialism' means social justice, I am not anti-socialist. But there can, in the long run, be no social justice without the essential freedoms, and in the long run socialist planning is incompatible with freedom, for if it is to be effective it implies the coercion of labour. Social justice, on the other hand, is by no means incompatible with economic freedom, as the examples of France, Britain, and Sweden clearly show.

One of the most serious of the errors that come naturally to socialist planners is to confuse liberalism with chaos. Another is to assume that the period of the accumulation of capital under economic liberalism must necessarily approximate to British conditions during the Industrial Revolution. Liberalism is no more synonymous with disorder than dictatorship is with order (Iraq under the late General Kassim and Indonesia under President Sukarno's 'guided democracy' have been more chaotic than the United Kingdom under a Conservative government). Liberalism, indeed, gives of its best only under conditions of law and order, with a strong government and judiciary. Under a liberal system the State has certain essential functions to perform, which, in most countries, private initiative cannot tackle satisfactorily. It has to levy taxes (avoiding discriminatory, punitive, or confiscatory ones if growth is the objective); it has to instruct, educate, and train citizens in the technical skills necessary for a growing economy; it has to provide, or improve, an infrastructure of roads, railways, postal services, telecommunications, etc., and maintain it; and it has to pass laws defining working conditions and providing social security *within the means of each individual country* (as economies expand social benefits can thus expand accordingly). Finally, it has to legislate for a market economy. Specifically, this means determining monetary policy (bank and other interest rates) according to the demand for capital; and rigorously prohibiting all monopolistic practices, whether by companies or trade unions, or through official discrimination in favour of nationalized industries. In overpopulated countries, or countries like Thailand which are now threatened by a population explosion, there is an additional task of the utmost importance for the State to perform: to legislate for, then administer and promote with the utmost energy, a birth-control policy. These ideas are more fully discussed in Professor Maurice Allais's

S

book *Le Tiers Monde au Carrefour* – the indispensable handbook which I have already mentioned and which was not available in English when these lines were written.

In the field of planning the State and private enterprise both have roles to play, and if either plays its role in isolation the outcome will be inefficient planning. Under a free economy planning is mainly a matter of accurately assessing available resources, both physical and financial, determining the objectives that are both desirable and realistic, and seeing what can be done to stimulate demand in the right directions. Both for the State and for the private company, the main task is to see that what money there is is spent wisely; and in the execution of policy the main task is to make sure productivity is increased as fast as possible, especially, in the early stages, on the land. In the first few years of planning the task is *not* to fix meaningless quantitative production targets. That can wait until the economy has acquired some momentum.

Capital formation is, of course, of the first importance; indeed, a slow rate of saving is one of the characteristics of an underdeveloped economy. The socialist-minded new governments, such as India's, in their zeal for promoting equality, are often tempted to impose such high taxes that they put a brake on initiative and therefore slow down development to the general loss of the community. In traditional English this is cutting off the nose to spite the face. It is not by accident that the United States had no income tax during its maximum period of growth in the late nineteenth century; nor that Mexico's highly enterprising *entrepreneurs* were not taxed during the 'fifties, when their initiative was promoting rapid growth. There are many ways of raising revenue besides taxing incomes: by indirect taxes of various kinds, for instance, or by taxation on land and property transactions (excluding usefully employed capital equipment). The State that taxes private enterprise to the hilt for the purpose of raising money to be invested in public enterprises is, more often than not, penalizing the efficient producer on behalf of the inefficient one. In the end the community as a whole suffers more than the taxed capitalist.

A word is needed, at this point, about nationalized industries. The experience of nationalization varies so widely from country to country that it is very difficult to make universally applicable rules about the industries that must not, and those that can in certain circumstances, be nationalized. One general rule *can* be stated, however: no industry should be nationalized if public ownership will create a monopoly. By disregarding this principle, the British Labour government that came to power after the Second World War created a number of inefficient industries under its programme of wholesale nationalization. The widespread awareness that Britain's nationalized industries, by and large, provide a less-efficient service at a higher cost to the public than the private industries they replaced has provoked a good deal of soul-searching in the Labour Party. One of the causes of bafflement is the knowledge that certain nationalized industries in other countries have proved formidably efficient. An excellent example is the State-owned Renault concern in France, which makes profits, competes successfully in the international export markets, is never tired of searching for improved techniques and designs, and in general is run with energy and initiative. The reasons for this success are, of course, many, but the fundamental one can be stated very simply: Renault is not a monopoly. It has to compete with many privately owned car-manufacturing companies, such as Citroën, Simca, and Peugeot, and is no exception to the rule that competition promotes efficiency. Australia provides the interesting example of a nationalized airline competing with a private one. There can be no objection to nationalization under such conditions – so long as the State does not distort the conditions by discriminating against the private company, for instance by subsidizing the purchase of new equipment by the publicly owned company.

The peril of nationalization is a double one in an under-developed country: first, because of the danger of substituting an inefficient or non-productive enterprise for a flourishing one, and secondly, because the company to be nationalized is likely to be a foreign one. Nationalism being the enemy of economics, the new leaders have even more trouble in grasping the second of these dangers than the first. The reason why it is economically dangerous to seize a foreign company is, however, simple enough. It is a matter of capital accumulation. A government that is not prepared to squeeze an investable surplus out of a regimented population, as the Communists do, must raise money by other means: by taxes, by loans or grants from other countries, and so on. But by their nature these sources are limited. Nor are they by any means the most efficient way of getting development moving. A far better way is to attract foreign investment. Investors from the richer nations will not, however, invest in the poorer ones unless they are given reasonable guarantees against xenophobic violence, expropriation, and confiscatory taxation. Any government that makes it difficult for foreign investors to start up new enterprises in its country, that threatens to nationalize existing enterprises, or that impedes the repatriation of profits is simply putting a brake on its own economic development. If it goes farther, listening to advice from Communists or its own misguided nationalists, and actually nationalizes a foreign company, it does one of two further self-destructive things. Either it saddles itself with a compensation burden (if it is an honest government) or it destroys its international credit (if it expropriates without compensation, as the Communists advocate). The English have a word for this, too: killing the goose that lays the golden eggs. When Dr Mossadegh of Persia nationalized the Anglo-Iranian Oil Company in 1951 he deprived the Persian people of the royalties paid by the company and of the employment and other benefits that flowed from the great refinery at Abadan. When President Sukarno of Indonesia seized many Dutch enterprises in 1957 he did not, as some Indonesian officials had naively hoped, usher in a wave of rival British investment; he merely destroyed much of what remained of his government's creditworthiness. President Nasser's nationalization of the Suez Company in 1956 was different, however, and ought to have been an example of the kind of nationalization that is not counterproductive. Despite carefully fostered myths to the contrary, here was a public utility which the Egyptians were well able to run for themselves; moreover, they offered compensation on what sounded like reasonable terms. The manner of the Egyptian leader's action was so deliberately an affront to the western countries, however, that it brought worse consequences than he had foreseen, and in the event the Canal was closed for several months, to the general loss.

Chapter 4

TOWARDS POLITICAL STABILITY

I believe with Kropotkin that all government is bad. I do not expect the institution of government to be abolished in my lifetime, however, and therefore concede a case for seeking forms of government that are less harmful than others. The least harmful of governments is undoubtedly the kind that grows out of a parliamentary democracy, if only because it can be changed every few years peacefully at the polls. For the converse reason, the most evil is that of a self-perpetuating ruling party.

A parliamentary democracy, however, is a luxury most underdeveloped countries cannot afford. For one thing, the ability of the people to decree a change of government presupposes that an alternative team is available to take office; undereducated countries are, however, hard put to it to provide one team of Ministers, let alone two. For another thing, an efficient parliamentary democracy presupposes an able and disinterested civil service. Most underdeveloped countries, though not all, lack such an amenity.

Though some of us hope that, for the sake of their peoples, most Asian, African, and Latin American countries will eventually have efficient and uncorrupt parliamentary democracies, most of us know that this is not likely to happen for many years, if at all. Nor is it as desirable as some people have supposed that the attempt should even, at this stage, be made. The British, through that ever-dwindling institution, the Colonial Office, have made consistent and well-meaning attempts to inculcate the Westminster habit in their dependencies. These, by and large, have failed, as they were bound to. In Ghana the Opposition has been stamped out in name, if not quite in fact. In Nigeria, where the form of government is federal, the parties unfortunately divide on regional lines, the western region's Action Group being in opposition; in 1962, only two years after independence, the Action Group was suspended and its leaders, including Chief Awolowo, the official Opposition leader, were placed under detention. Tanganyika, on the east coast, emerged into independence with a single mass party. In Burma and in Pakistan parliamentary democracy failed and the soldiers took over; in Ceylon it survives precariously. In India, the only country where it has worked pretty well, it may not survive the traumatic experience of Mr Nehru's failure to provide for the nation's security.

Such a record should make one ponder the desirability as well as the realism of proposing a model that resists export so vigorously. That it is unrealistic is clear enough; that it is also undesirable may be harder to admit. My reason for thinking so is that democracy as it is understood at Westminster rests on universal suffrage. Now universal suffrage is a monster that guarantees weak governments and chaos unless it is built on the foundation of a reasonably educated and mature electorate (though the experience of France under the Third and Fourth Republics suggests that even where the foundation exists, the results may be undesirable). The monster becomes grotesque as well as dangerous in any society where there is mass illiteracy. To be fair to Whitehall, the able officials who try to lead Africans gently by the hand in a parliamentary direction are well aware that the franchise must be limited. They remember Britain's history, even if the English-speaking Africans forget it. After all, this 'mother of parliaments' is of respectable antiquity, since its story can be traced, without too much strain, back to the *witenagemot* or 'court of wise men' of Anglo-Saxon times. Yet it was not until 1928, when women of twenty-one were given the vote, that universal adult suffrage came to Britain.

In African eyes, however, those who resist the extension of the franchise in Britain's remaining dependencies, such as Northern Rhodesia and Nyasaland (and Southern Rhodesia, if it was a British dependency, as some seemed to doubt), are 'colonialists'. If, however, men like the amiable Mr Kenneth Kaunda of Northern Rhodesia and the defiant Mr Joshua Nkomo of

Southern Rhodesia do not readily concede the absurdity of 'one man one vote', they ought to see that any such concept carries dangers for themselves. If they gain the objective of universal suffrage they should, in logic, entrust their political future to the illiterate masses and the stability of their governments to the elected representatives of the voters. If they do, however, they will risk the kind of chaos that overtook Burma and Indonesia; and will therefore court the further risk of a military take-over. If, however, they more wisely decide to curtail the sovereign power of the people they will have to find devices to make such a decision acceptable to those they so lately enfranchised; and will thus be driven to rule by the arts of the demagogue.

These are hard facts (or probabilities), but they must be faced, and first of all by the new or emerging leaders. Facing the facts means, primarily, deciding what kind of country they want to build and giving it the kind of political framework most likely to produce the desired result. The first priority in any new country's programme is, or ought to be, economic viability. What kind of government, then, should such countries aim at having? Clearly the kind best calculated to provide stability *plus* rapid economic growth.

This is as difficult as it sounds, but it need not be impossible if the lessons of the post-war years are digested. The first and most fundamental lesson is that a free economy is the quickest passport to affluence. It is no more difficult for a dictator to grasp this fact than an elected Prime Minister responsible to a sovereign assembly. President Nkrumah is considered in some quarters to be a dictator, and he is fond of calling himself a socialist; so long, however, as he continues to implement the pledge he made in July 1957 when opening the Bank of Ghana (and repeated since at intervals) to protect foreign investors and encourage new ones, he is doing his bit to promote a rising standard of living for Ghana's people.

In the long run, it is far more important, for a country's political as well as economic future, that it should have a government, however authoritarian, that will guarantee a free economy than that it should have a democracy in name at the outset. To have a democracy without being prepared for it is to pave the way for chaos or military dictatorship. To have a government that encourages free enterprise, especially if it already has the beginnings of a native *entrepreneur* class (as Ghana and Nigeria both have), is to make it probable that an educated middle class will emerge which in time will insist on the democratic freedoms.

In our western capitals we are so accustomed to western concepts of democracy that we tend to assume that the most important of these freedoms is that of forming political parties. I find myself unable to support this view. Freedom of speech (which means the right to criticize) and freedom from arbitrary arrest (which means protection from the consequences of voicing criticism) are really far more important. The dictator who feels strong enough to tolerate criticism is providing himself with a barometer and a safety-valve. If he feels stronger still and admits the need for an independent judiciary the people he rules will be the less likely to rebel against him.

The past few years have provided interesting, though not entirely conclusive, examples of the survival or rebirth of freedoms under more or less authoritarian governments. Poland's revolution of October 1956 brought the Poles freedom of speech and even, for a while, freedom of the Press, even though the country remained under communist rule, that is, under a party that had a monopoly of political power. General de Gaulle was tampering with the judiciary early in 1963, but the fearless satirists of *Le Canard Enchaîné* were left free to lampoon him mercilessly. But these examples, although they show that freedom need not be quite as indivisible as we might think, are inconclusive in that they leave unanswered a great and anguished question: How long can it last? In the long run everything depends on the personality of the dictator and his resistance to the corruption of power, just as, in the long run, the proper functioning of a democracy depends upon habits of tolerance built up over generations.

It is idle to expect such habits to be forged under colonial rule (which is, by definition, arbitrary) no matter what trouble is taken by the colonial authorities to train local leaders in externals of democratic practice. And it must be recognized that in most of the emerging countries, especially in Africa, there is an apparently irresistible tendency towards one-party rule and the single boss. In time, this tendency may be attenuated, but for the moment the best that the governed can hope for is probably that their dictator will prove liberal-minded. Since in most cases he will have had a western education, this is not as unlikely as it sounds. The more young Africans and Asians are brought into contact with the liberalizing influences of the West, the more likely it is that when the most prominent of them take over in their own countries they, too, will be liberal-minded.

The personality of the supreme ruler, which is an imponderable, is certainly far more important in actual practice than the theoretical soundness of institutions or the paper-promises of ingenious constitutions. Stalin's Constitution of 1936 was an admirably democratic document, but its noble sentiments did not save the Soviet people from the monstrous excesses of the dictator's remaining years. As institutions go, however, the Indonesian experiment in 'guided democracy' is one that deserves the attention of the newly independent peoples. Like Nasser's constitution, it owes a good deal to the inspiration of Mussolini's corporative State and to the adaptations of it in Dr Salazar's Portugal and General Franco's Spain. The horrid memories aroused by such fascist associations should not blind one to the merits of Mussolini's corporative idea, which was one of his few constructive legacies. To be sure, neither President Nasser nor President Sukarno has, as far as I am aware, acknowledged a debt to Mussolini, although Nasser is known to think highly of Dr Salazar.

President Sukarno launched his 'concept' (as he called it) of guided democracy in a speech on 22 April 1959. The Constitution, he said, should 'fit the soul, character, and personality of the Indonesian people'. The Assembly or Parliament should cease to be 'a place for endless and wasteful debates and a battlefield for political parties or leaders'. It should be a place for consultation and constructive opinions, but not for opposiiton. Political parties were to be 'simplified' (they had indeed been too numerous for efficiency). They would be represented in Parliament, which was to be known as the Council of People's Representatives, but they would have to share Parliamentary living space with representatives of 'functional groups' (in effect, Mussolini's corporations), such as professional people, the armed forces and farmers. From these 'functional' representatives would be created a 'National Front' which would have the right to present its own list of candidates for Parliament, though it would not itself be a political party. Apart from the People's Council, there were to be a People's Consultative Congress (apparently a borrowing from communist China, which deeply impressed President Sukarno on his visit in 1956) and a Supreme Advisory Council. A National Planning Board was also to be set up, for 'guided economy' was to supplement 'guided democracy'.

There was only one major snag in these complex but not unintelligent proposals: the clear understanding, later confirmed, that President Sukarno himself was to guide his guided democracy. No one who has studied Indonesian affairs during the past few years could honestly claim that guided democracy has been a success. But this does not prove that it was bound to fail; it merely confirms the general rule that institutions are less important than the men who run them.

Anything that contributes to the political stability of young nations and seems to offer some outlet for discussion and constructive criticism is to be welcomed, whether it is Indonesian-style guided democracy or President Ayub Khan's 'basic democracies' in Pakistan. But constitutions are no protection against demagogues. The man at the top in a new country is more likely to be there because he has gained control of an apparatus of power than because he enshrines the will of the people.

Chapter 5

TOWARDS
INTERDEPENDENCE

As Europeans know to their cost in the age of General de Gaulle, nationalism is not yet a spent force, despite the efforts of enlightened men like Jean Monnet to foster the idea of supra-nationalism. In struggling for their national sovereignty the new countries began to create nationalisms of their own, or to revive ancestral memories of greatness. Probably this was inevitable. But the destructive potential of a hundred and more competing nationalisms is alarming enough to justify a search for ways of attenuating the danger.

To do so, one must first look squarely at the facts. Nationalism has good points as well as bad. It can provide a dynamic, a spur to action and advancement that might otherwise be lacking; and it has proved, many times over, that it is the only idea that can resist and defeat communism in the new countries (though conversely, when communism and nationalism are in alliance, as for instance in China, the evils of both ideas are multiplied immeasurably). Nationalism begins to become a danger at the point where it becomes exclusive: at home when it is wedded to a totalitarian doctrine, abroad when it expresses itself in economic and political aggressiveness. The ultimate outcome of exclusive nationalism is war. We have seen many examples of this kind of nationalism in these pages.

The shrill anti-colonialism of the militants among the new leaders is a symptom of the dangerous kind of nationalism, which the emulative forum of the United Nations has made even shriller than it need have been. Doubtless 'colonialism' deserves many of the epithets that have been heaped upon it. But this does not alter the fact that the 'anti-colonialism' of countries that have ceased to be colonies is a negative and sterile passion. It is in the interests of both former colonies and ex-rulers to find a way of rising beyond it. This does not appear to me to be an impossible objective, but the nature of the exercise rules out short cuts or panaceas. In time, when there are no colonies left, the passion will expend itself. Already in Asia – with the vast and disquieting exception of Indonesia – there are welcome signs that sterile anti-imperialism is being replaced by a more mature relationship between the former colonies and those who once ruled over them.* This is true of India and Britain, and of the States that used to form French Indochina, on the one hand, and France, on the other.

In Africa there are still painful years ahead. The Europeans like to point to the number of colonies freed during the past few years; the Africans see only those that remain to be freed, among which they include the white man's independent South Africa, as well as the Portuguese colonies, Kenya, the Rhodesias, and Nyasaland. The last cases are also the hardest; that, indeed, is why they are the last. From Nairobi to Capetown the outlook is sombre. In Kenya the white man's days are numbered, and the departing British face the most painful of their dilemmas. A country lacking national awareness, rent by tribal dissensions, oppressed by memories of Mau Mau's atavistic horror, with capital in full flight, heading for independence in destitution and insecurity, Kenya reflects the insoluble dilemma: to stay is to invite violence, to leave is to invite chaos. But Britain's colonial vocation is spent, and the only question is how soon the British will leave. By 1965, at the latest, Kenya will be sovereign, and so will those more reassuring countries, Northern Rhodesia (which is blessed both by mineral wealth and by the sensible leadership of Mr Kenneth Kaunda) and Nyasaland (which is poor but better endowed than its neighbours with administrative talent). By that time, if the omens of early 1963 are fulfilled, Southern Rhodesia, like South Africa, will be an independent State under minority white rule. As far as Britain, France, and Belgium are concerned, colonialism in Africa will then be over, whatever word African nationalists

* And even Indonesia has resumed diplomatic and economic relations with Holland since these lines were written.

T

feel like using to describe Southern Rhodesia and South Africa.

As for Portuguese colonialism, which is both more ancient and different in kind from the imperialisms of the nineteenth century, it seems unlikely to survive the Salazar régime in metropolitan Portugal, if only because the country's hidden or exiled opposition has reconciled itself to the need for change. In the worst of cases Angola, Mozambique, and the smaller Portuguese territories will emerge into a Congo-type sovereign chaos. In the best of cases they will preserve a federal or confederal link with Lisbon.

There is no need, however, to wait on events. If a fruitful and co-operative future is to replace the bitterness of the past and the sterility of present recriminations there is no time to lose. Adjustments will have to be made on both sides, and indeed in many cases already have been made. Europeans, as individuals, have to learn not to expect any special privileges for the accident of their birth. As members of governments, they ought to accept the notion that duty should not end with the departure of colonial officials. Africans, too, must learn to shed the complexes of a humiliating past, to look beyond anticolonialism to co-operation and beyond independence to interdependence.

Fortunately there are good examples to guide us on the path of the possible. The French, whatever their shortcomings in Indochina and Algeria, have achieved a masterpiece of decolonization in black Africa. Year in, year out, they continue to pay out huge sums in aid to their former colonies (£251 million in 1960, for instance, or more than five times the sum Britain was prepared to spend in Africa). The budgets of the poorer French-speaking African States, such as Gabon or Niger, are virtually a 100 per cent charge on the French Treasury, that is on the French taxpayers. French teachers, administrators, and technicians are still working in large numbers in Africa. Moreover, French sponsorship has given the African States advantageous access to the European Common Market. On their side, the French-speaking Africans, except – at first – defiant Mali and Guinea, have had the sense to realize that interdependence on such generous terms is infinitely to be preferred to 'independence' in destitution. The only flaw in an admirable arrangement is its possible impermanence. On the French side, voices like that of the well-known journalist Raymond Cartier, have been raised to argue that France would do better to pull out of Africa altogether and invest its money at home. On the African side, the necessarily authoritarian governments of the men who were in power in 1963 may be under threat from younger and wilder Africans willing to exchange freedom from want for the parrot cries of African nationalism.

The British, if they were so minded, could learn a good deal from the French example, and even from the American example since President Kennedy came to power. From the French they could learn that financial generosity can be an instance of that peculiarly Anglo-Saxon concept, enlightened self-interest. From the Americans they could learn the value of an institution like the Peace Corps; indeed, the fund of men with experience in tropical and underdeveloped countries is clearly far greater in Britain than in the United States. A 'Service Overseas', staffed and trained in Britain, could bring enormous benefit to former colonies while providing a constructive outlet for youthful British energies.

Another American initiative that deserves study was taken in 1962 by the Agency for International Development or AID, the latest of many names by which the US foreign-aid administration has been known. It was decided to help American private investment in four countries – Nigeria, Pakistan, Colombia, and Siam – selected for their friendliness, potential for economic growth, and readiness to welcome American capital. Under the new system loans to cover investment projects are made to the government of the country concerned, for a term of forty years and at only $\frac{3}{4}$ of 1 per cent interest. Out of this money the recipient Government makes a further loan to the investing American company, on the more normal commercial conditions of fifteen to twenty years at $5\frac{3}{4}$ per cent. The company repays the loan to the receiving government, and the government repays its own loan to the United States. This ingenious and imaginative wedding of public and private enterprise seems bound to yield rapid dividends, both literally to the companies involved and figuratively, in terms of faster economic growth, to the selected governments.

There is yet another American initiative that will have to be copied fairly soon by the countries of western Europe. This is the disposal of agricultural surpluses as a form of economic aid. For many years the problem of America's bulging farm surpluses in a world of want seemed insoluble. But the passing of Public Law 480 under the Eisenhower Administration in 1954 was a giant step forward. India, Egypt, and, latterly, Algeria, are among the countries that have benefited from the efficiency of American agriculture and the generosity of the US government. Already western Europe is beginning to face the same problem, and a similar solution to it will have to be found. The field is unlimited, for the need is increasing fast in pace with exploding populations, and the communist world, whose failure in agriculture is total, has nothing to offer.

Other problems to be solved in a spirit of co-operation and interdependence are the stabilization of raw-material and tropical-food prices, and education for growth. It is a terrifying anomaly that falling raw-material prices, in a bad year, can wipe out the total value of *all* foreign aid to underdeveloped countries. The problem is fraught with difficulties, but none is more urgent. 'Education for growth' is perhaps more easily soluble. The phrase needs an explanation. It used to be thought that the only things that mattered in economic growth were land, labour, and capital. Now economists know better: a fourth factor, education, is at least as important as the other three. Mr Malcolm S. Adiseshiah, Assistant Director of Unesco (United Nations Educational, Social, and Cultural Organization), drove the point home with a few well-chosen illustrations in a lecture at a conference on the UN Development Decade at Christ's College, Cambridge, in April 1962 (since reproduced in a verbatim report of the entire conference under the title *War on Want*, published by the Pergammon Press). In Japan between 1950 and 1960 there was almost no increase in the labour and capital used in agriculture, and only 2 per cent more cultivable land came under the plough; yet rice production soared by 20 per cent. Israel, during the same period, stepped up its investment in land, labour, and capital by 10 per cent, but registered a 60 per cent increase in agricultural output. Mexico doubled its agricultural production, though it had increased its traditional investment by only 22 per cent. The missing factor, in all three cases, was education. The advanced countries, especially France, the United States, and Britain, are already doing much, both in providing experts for overseas and in training or educating Asians and Africans in western universities and technical colleges. But a good deal more could be done, and no money could be better spent.

Africans in the Union Africaine et Malgache, and Asians in the Colombo Plan, are showing the value of the co-operative and interdependent approach. Once the habit of international co-operation has been formed, it proves resistant even to the destructiveness of political nationalism. Thus, at times when Cambodia was at loggerheads with Siam and South Vietnam, it was encouraging to find the Cambodians, Siamese, and Vietnamese turning up at committee meetings under the Colombo Plan and concerting their efforts in such schemes as the Mekong River development plan, from which their countries, and Laos, stand to benefit. Other desirable habits among countries that aim at economic viability are those of honesty with, and fairness towards, foreign investors. The bad examples of, say, Ceylon or Indonesia inevitably get more publicity than more encouraging ones, such as India or Nigeria. With its socialist aspirations, India reserves a major share of its economy to the public sector and restricts foreign private capital to certain fields. Whatever one thinks of Indian planning, however, it must be said that the Indian government has never interfered with the remittance of the profits, dividends, or interest of foreign companies, or discriminated against foreign capital in favour of Indian entrepreneurs. And there is a general confidence that if ever private assets are nationalized, full compensation will be paid. Nigeria, which looks like avoiding the dead weight of State enterprise except in public utilities, is a more attractive country than India to the foreign investor, but offers a much smaller market. It has already established an excellent reputation for fairdealing and – unlike Ghana – does not play on the nerves of foreign investors with talk of socialism and hints of expropriation.

It is too early, then, to take a uniformly pessimistic view of the prospects before the newly independent world. Hardship may be inseparable from independence, but the worst excesses of nationalism are avoidable. The Franco-Algerian agreements of January 1963, so soon after the savageries of the Algerian war, showed how fast old antagonists can learn. If Mr Benbella, the militant admirer of Nasser and Fidel Castro, can adapt himself to economic realities, so can others. If the French can be generous, so can the British and even affluent non-imperialists like the Germans. The prosperous minority of mankind can no more afford to tolerate slum States than the enlightened nation can permit its cities to be disfigured by slums. The horrors of contemporary wars of independence will not have been in vain if this truth is absorbed and if sovereignty turns out to be only a stage on the road to interdependence.

Index

INDEX

ABUBAKAR Tafawa Balewa, Sir, 127, 270

Administration, 78, 81, 82, 87, 88, 89, 93, 112, 113, 127, 157

Adoula, 97, 101

Africa, 25, 38–40, 285, 286

Africa Looks to the Future (Potekhin), 178

Afro-Asian Conference, The (Kahin), 131

Afro-Asian Group, 100, 131, 133–6, 155

AFPFL (Anti-Fascist People's Freedom League), 72, 73, 80, 81, 83

Ah-Ba, *see* Ne Win

AID, 287

Alexander, General, 94–5

Algeria, 32–8, 51, 93, 101–13, 290
and Tunisia, 56–60, 145–51

L'Algérie d'Evian (Allais), 107

Allais, Professor Maurice, 107, 267, 273

ALN (Algerian Army of National Liberation), 61

Amman, Vice-Admiral, 148, 151

Anti-Colonialism, 114, 117, 121, 129, 138–69, 153, 162, 173, 175, 284

Arabs, 132, 133, 138

Asia, 86, 132, 133, 183, 285

Aswan High Dam, 139, 140

Attack on World Poverty, The (Shonfield), 228

Aung San, General, 69, 70, 79

Australia (*see also* New Guinea), 152, 157, 162, 275

Autobiography of Pandit Nehru, 237

Avon, Lord, *see* Eden, Sir Anthony

Awolowo, Chief, 127, 279

Ayub Khan, Field-Marshal, 63–9, 75, 283

Baghdad Pact, 132, 135

Banda, Dr, 99

Bandaranaike, Solomon, 90–2, 130

Bandung Conference, 131, 133–6, 138, 154

Belgium and the Belgian Congo, 92–101

Belkacem Krim, 33

Benbella, 33, 51, 106, 110, 111, 112, 290

van Bilsen, Professor A. A. J., 98

Bizerta, 59, 60, 128, 138

BNA (Burmese National Army), 69–70

Borneo, 121, 123

Boumendjel, Maître, 35–7

Boun Oum, Prince, 198–201

Bourguiba, President Habib, 56–60, 144–51

Bourguibisme, 59

Brazil, 272

Brazzaville Group, 24, 26, 50, 151

Britain, *see* United Kingdom

Brunei, 121, 123

Buddhism, 52, 73, 83, 85, 90–2, 193

Burma, 69–76, 77, 78–86

Cambodia, 29, 51–6, 124–5

Cameroun (French Cameroons), 186–7

Canard Enchaîné, Le, 281

Casablanca Group, 26, 42, 50

Castro, Fidel, 79, 138, 189, 190

Central Treaty Organization, 132

Ceylon, 86, 89–92, 130
Chang, Dr John Myun, 204
Chiang Kai-Shek, 175, 236
Childers, Erskine, 142, 143
China, Chinese, 31, 55, 119, 120–3, 125, 284, 133–4
Chinese Empire, 174–5, 177–91
and India, 230–61
Chinese Nationalist Government (Formosa), 133, 175
Chinese satellites, 206–10
Chou En-Lai, 134–5, 233–4, 235, 236
Cinq Hommes et la France (Lacouture), 34
Client states, 175, 192–3
Co-existence, 117, 134, 179
Cold War, 173–6, 205
Colombo Plan, 289
Colonialism, Colonial Powers, 23, 41, 77, 86, 89, 92, 119, 138, 154, 173–6, 180, 264, 265, 281, 284
Common Market, 270
Communism, Communist, 20, 23, 31, 41, 44, 48, 55, 80, 119, 122, 159, 163, 177–91
in Africa, 186–9
aid, 180, 190
in Asia, 183–6
in China, 230–61
Colonialism, 173–6
and economic growth, 265–70
and Laos, 194–201
Satellites, 206–10
subversion, 182
Congo, 75, 77, 92–101, 126
Congo, French, 98
Consider Japan, 271
Constitution:
of Burma, 72, 80
of the Congo, 99
federal, 84, 99
of India, 236, 257
of Indonesia, 282
of Malaya, 120
of Pakistan, 66, 68, 283
of Stalin, 282

Corruption:
in Brazil, 272
in Burma, 72, 82, 85
in Indonesia, 87
in Mexico, 272
in Pakistan, 65
Coups d'État, 61–2, 71, 74, 123, 197
Cuba, 62, 79, 176, 180

Dakar, 45
Democracy, Western, 83, 99, 116, 119, 179, 190, 263, 278–83
in India, 230–261
Dia, Corneille, 113–14
Djakarta, 87, 96
Djinn, Mr, 93, 97
Dulles, John Foster, 20, 55, 131, 132, 139
Dutch, see Netherlands
Duval, Raoul, 146, 147

Economic aid, 20, 21, 23, 24, 127, 192–210, 197, 199, 207, 287, 288, 289
Economic assets, 120, 126, 156
Economic infrastructure, 252, 273
Economic liberalism, 270, 272
Economic planning, 239, 262–7
Economic progress, 68, 81, 202, 265, 267, 272
of China and India, 230–61
golden rules for, 270
and independence, 23, 77, 79
and political stability, 21, 278–83
Economic viability, 264
Eden, Sir Anthony (Lord Avon), 28, 140–4
Education, 77, 78, 98, 112, 113, 115, 120, 125, 157, 288
Egypt, 27–9, 138–44
Eisenhower, President, 139, 162, 175, 199, 254
Emancipation of French Indochina, The (Lancaster), 209
Enlightened self-interest, 271
Evian Agreements, 103, 105–12, 149

Facing Mount Kenya (Kenyatta), 40
Federalism, 84, 85, 99, 121–3, 124, 126, 279
Ferhat Abbas, 33–5
Fin d'une Guerre, La (Devillers and Lacouture),
FLN (Front of National Liberation), 32–7, 58, 102–12
Foreign policy, 129–69, 178, 182
Formosa, 175, 270–1
France, French, 137, 180
  and Algeria, 32–8, 93, 102–13, 157
  and Cambodia, 52–3
  and economic aid, 23, 24, 192
  and ex-colonies, 24, 31, 39, 41, 153, 182, 285, 286
  and Guinea, 42–3, 115
  and Indochina, 132, 184, 193–4
  and Mali, 41, 113–17
  and Senegal, 45
  and Tunisia, 57–60, 144–51
  and Vietnam, 29–32
French community, 96, 116

De Gaulle, General Charles, 41, 42–3, 50, 98, 137, 281, 284
  and Algeria, 102–7, 111
  and Bizerta, 145–51
  and Mali, 115
Ghana, 93–4, 96, 174, 278
Glubb Pasha, 138
Goa, 130, 163, 165
GPRA (Provisional Government of the Algerian Republic), 37
The Great Leap Forward, 235, 241–6, 248, 268
Greater Malaysia Federation, 121–3
Guatemala, 175
Gueye, Lamine, 46
Guinea, 21, 41, 42–4, 180, 187–8, 265

Hanoi, 29–31
Hatta, Dr, 88
Ho Chi Minh, 29–32, 55, 185, 208–10
Holland, *see* Netherlands

Houphouët-Boigny, Felix, 50
How to Be a Good Communist (LIU), 234
Hungary, 174

Independence, 15–24, 25, 75, 97, 120
  and colonial powers, 20, 23, 42, 93
  and communism, 25, 173–6, 177–91
  and economic aid, 20
  and economic progress, 22, 23
  and foreign policy, 129–69
  meaning of, 16, 42
  and political viability, 21, 84
  and positive neutralism, 20
  and poverty, 77
  problems of, 19, 21, 26, 77–128
  symbols of, 117
India, 77, 78, 118–19, 130, 132, 274
  achievements of, 254
  and China, 230–61
  economy of, 262–3
  Socialism in, 238
Indochina, 29, 31, 53, 55, 132, 134, 153, 210
Indonesia, 19, 78, 84, 86–8, 92, 99, 128, 130, 282–3
  and Communism, 163, 184
  and Dutch New Guinea, 152–69
Indonesia and the Dutch (Palmier), 152, 156
Industrialization, 80, 248, 251, 266
Interdependence, 24, 284–90
Iraq, 132
Irian, West, *see* New Guinea, West
Israel, 141, 143, 288
Ivory Coast, The, 50, 116, 265

Jagirdars, 66
Japan, 78, 263–4, 271
Java (*see also* Indonesia), 87, 88
Jinnah, Mohammed Ali, 64, 68
Jordan, King Hussein of, 132, 138
Jouhaud, General, 105, 109
Joxe, Louis, 104

Kalat, Khan of, 65
Kashmir, 119, 132
Kassim, Brigadier, 62, 273
Katanga, 96, 99, 100, 126
Kaunda, Kenneth, 279, 285
Kennedy, President, 162, 163, 167, 199, 202
Kennedy, Robert, 167
Kenya, 285
Kenyatta, Jomo, 40
Khmer Issarak, 52
Kim Jong-Pil, Lt-Col, 205
Kong Lae, Captain, 197–9
Korea, 130, 137
Korea, North, 174, 206–9
Korea, South, 62, 201, 202, 203–5
Kotelawala, Sir John, 90, 130, 134
KPM (Dutch Packet Navigation Company), 158, 160
Krishna Menon, 119, 237, 260
Krishnamachari, T. T., 238
Krushchev, 23, 119, 178, 208, 265, 269
Kuwait, 22
Kyaw Nein, 83

Land reform, 180, 184
  in China, 248–50, 256
  in Formosa, 256
  in India, 256
  in Iraq, 62
  in North Vietnam, 31
  in Pakistan, 65, 66–7
Laos, 192–201, 208–9
Last Empire, The (Conquest), 174
Leaders, The, 25–76, 130, 133, 233–9, 282
  father-figures, 25–7
  inadequacy of, 92
  militants, 27–44
  military, 61–76
  moderates, 44–60
  uncommitted, 179
Lee Kuan-Yew, 122–3
Leopold II, 97
Leopoldville, 93–7

Letourneau, Jean, 52
Li Fu-chun, 235–6
Liu Shao-Ch'i, 234–5, 245
Lloyd, Selwyn, 140, 142
Loi Fundamentale, 97, 99
Lumumba, Patrice, 94–101
Luns, Dr Joseph, 155, 156, 157, 163, 165

Maghreb, 60, 146
Magruder, General, 204, 205
Makarios, Archbishop, 134
Malaya, 22, 119–23, 184
Mali, 41, 113–7
  Federation of, 41, 46, 49, 115
Mao Tse-Tung, 208, 234–6, 241–50, 260
Marxism, 48, 49, 80, 116
Ma Yinchu, Professor, 246, 251
Mers-el-Kebir, 144, 149, 150
Messali Hadj, 106
Mexico, 272, 288
Military assistance, 21, 130–2, 163, 259, 260
Military bases, 130, 144–51, 190, 197
Minorities, 84, 120, 124
Mirza, President Iskander, 64–5
MNA (Mouvement National Algérien), 35, 106, 107
Mobutu, Colonel, 75, 94, 95, 96
Modibo Keita, 40–2, 49, 50, 113–7
Mollet, Guy, 140, 141
Morarji Desai, 238, 258
Morocco, 130, 146
Moscow Declarations, 180
Moslems, 90, 102, 106–9, 112
Mossadegh, Dr, 276
Muslim League, 64, 65
My Chief (Mohammed Ahmed), 63

Nasser, Gamal Abdel, 27–9, 50, 60, 131, 135
  and Britain, 27
  Philosophy of the Revolution of, 27
  and 'positive neutrality', 20, 130

Nasser: (contd.)
  and Suez, 138–44, 276
Nationalism, 20, 49, 149, 275, 284
  African, 38–40, 49
  Arab, 140
Nationalization, 91, 112, 138–44, 158, 275, 276
Negritude, 46, 49
Nehru, Pandit, 119, 133, 236–7
  and co-existence, 134
  and uncommitted nations, 20, 128–9, 179
Néo-Destour Party, 145, 146, 147
Netherlands, The (Dutch, Holland), 89, 161
  and Indonesia, 88
  and New Guinea, 152–69
Netherlands New Guinea Oil Company, 156
Neutralism, 19, 41, 54, 55, 90, 117, 119, 129–30, 200
New Guinea, 152, 157, 162
New Guinea, East, 152
New Guinea, West (Dutch), (West Irian) (see also Indonesia), 89, 92, 152–69
New Imperialism, The (Seton Watson), 174
Ne Win, General (Shu Maung, Ah-Ba), 62, 69–76, 83, 86
Ngo Dinh Diem, 29, 31, 185, 201, 202–3
Nigeria, 126–8, 278–9
Nkomo, Joshua, 279
Nkrumah, President, 50, 93–5, 97, 270, 280
Non-alignment, 254, 259, 260
Norodom Sinahouk, King, see Sinahouk, Prince
NUF (National United Front), 83
Nuri es-Said, 132
Nyasaland, 100, 285

OAS (Organization of the Secret Army), 36, 103–112
O'Brian, Conor Cruise, 96

OCRS (Organisation Commune des Régions Sahariennes), 104
Official Language Act, 91
Oil, 143, 146, 156

Pagan, 84
Pakistan, 63–9, 119, 132
Pan-Africanism, 38–9, 96, 127, 270
Panchayats, 67
Papua, West, Papuan (see also New Guinea), 152, 154, 157, 162, 167, 169
Park Chunghee, General, 62
Parsons, J. Graham, 195–6
Pathet Lao, 194
Peace Corps, 287
People's Action Party, 122
Philippines, 132, 184
Phoumi Nosavan, General, 197–201
Philosophy of the Revolution (Nasser), 27, 138
Po-I-Po, 235–6
Poland, 174
Political stability, 83, 278–83
  and economic progress, 21
  lack of, 84, 85, 86, 90, 91
  and military dictatorships, 76, 83
Politics, Personality and Nation Building (Pye), 85
Population, increase in, 77, 88, 89, 118, 141, 247, 251, 253, 272
Portugal, 285–6
Potekhin, Professor I. I., 178
Poverty, 116, 118, 124, 127, 272
Prakrama Bahu, King, 90
Pye, Professor Lucian W., 85

Race, 46, 48, 84
  in Burma, 84, 85
  in Ceylon, 89–92
  in the Congo, 92
  in India, 119
  in Indonesia, 84, 153
  in Malaya, 119
Rebels, The (Crozier), 183
Republic of Indonesia, The (Woodman), 131

Road to Suez, The (Childers), 131
Rhodesian Federation, 100
Rhodesia, Northern, 279, 285
Rhodesia, Southern, 79, 80, 285
Rocher–Noir Agreements, 110, 111
Rostow, Professor W. W., 266
Russia, 31, 55, 62, 82, 84, 100, 137,
    173, 265–9
    and aid, 21, 23, 89, 163
    and China, 245, 260
    Russian empire, 177–91
    and satellites, 206–10

Sahara, 103–6, 146
Sakiet, 150
Salan, General, 105
Sangkum Reastr Niyum (People's
    Socialist Community), 124
Sardauna of Sokoto, The, 127
Sastroamidjojo, Dr Ali, 133
Satellites, 174, 192–210
SEATO, 132, 135
Sékou Touré, President, 21, 22, 23,
    40, 42–4, 50, 187–9, 191
Senegal (*see also* Mali), 41, 44–51,
    115
Senanakes, The, 90
Senghor, President Leopold Sédar,
    44–51
Short History of Africa, A (Oliver and
    Page), 116
Shu Maung, *see* Ne Win
Siam, 78, 132
Sinahouk, Prince (King Norodom
    Sinahouk), 51–6, 124–5, 133
Singapore, 121–3
Sinhala Maha Sabha, 90
Sinhalese, *see* Ceylon
Socialism, 80, 86, 117, 119, 122, 262
    African socialism, 181, 188
    Arab socialism, 188
    Indian socialism, 238
Soudan (*see also* Mali), 41, 115
Souphannouvong, Prince, 200–1
Souvanna Phouma, Prince, 196–201
Sri Lanka Freedom Party, 90
Stages of Economic Growth, The, 266

Stalin, 178, 206, 246, 282
Storm over Laos (Cham Passak),
    194
Suez, 27, 28, 138–44, 276–7
Sukarno, President, 88–9, 138, 155–
    69, 273, 276
    and 'guided democracy', 273,
    282–3
Sumatra (*see also* Indonesia), 88
Susini, Jean-Jacques, 109, 110
Syngman Rhee, 201, 202, 203–4

Tamil (*see also* Ceylon), 91–2
Tanganyika, 279
Taylor, General Maxwell, 202
Terrorism, 109
Thakins, 69, 70, 79
*Thirty-year Plan for the Politica
    Emancipation of Belgian Africa, A*
    (van Bilsen), 98
Tibet, 174, 178
Tiers Monde au Carrefour, Le (Allais),
    267, 274
Togo, 173
Trade, 81–2, 86, 269
    in Algeria, 112
    in Burma, 86
    in India, 253–4
    in Indonesia, 87
    in Malaya, 120
    in Mali, 117
Tripartite Declaration, 141
Truman, President, 175
Tshombe, Mr, 99
Tunisia, 19, 56–60, 144–61
Tunku Abdul Rahman, 119–23
Turkey, Turkish, 93, 134

U Ba Swe, 72, 81, 83
UNESCO, 288
Union Africaine et Malgache, 50
Union of Burma, The (Tinker), 80
Union Minière Company, 99
Union Soudanaise, 116, 117
United Kingdom, Britain, 84, 137,
    156, 180
    and Burma, 78, 83–4, 85–6

United Kingdom: (*contd.*)
  and Ceylon, 89
  colonial administration of, 89–90, 278–9
  and ex-colonies, 39, 68, 153, 182, 231, 252, 285, 287
  and Malaya, 120
  and military aid, 166
  and South-East Asia, 121
United Nations, 16, 18, 22, 23, 24, 25, 130, 135, 143, 165, 284
  and the Congo, 93–101, 137
  General Assembly of, 136–7
  and Korea, 203–5
U Nu, 71, 72, 80, 81, 83, 86
U.S.A., 62, 135, 173–76, 266–8, 274, 287, 288
  and client states, 192–206
  and economic aid, 23, 24, 112, 127, 131, 192–206, 254
  and military aid, 21, 31, 130, 204–5

U.S.A.: (*contd.*)
  and neutral states, 20, 21
U Thant, 166

Vietnam, 130, 185
Vietnam, North, 29–32, 134, 174, 196–201, 207–10
Vietnam, South, 29, 31, 32, 201–3
War on Want, 288
Welbeck, Nathaniel, 93–5
Welfare, 79, 80, 81, 87–8, 122, 125, 126, 157
West Indies Federation, 124
Wibaux, M., 115
World Bank, 139
World Order and New States (Calvo-coressi), 182

Yazid, Mohammed, 37
Yorubas, 126, 127

Zamindars, 64, 66, 67, 256